AMERICA'S MISTRESS

AMERICA'S MISTRESS

The Life and Times of Eartha Kitt

JOHN L. WILLIAMS

New York • London

Quercus
New York • London

Picture Credits:
p.i top left, © Bettmann/CORBIS; bottom, © FPG/Getty;
p.ii top left, © estate of Russell Westwood / National Portrait Gallery, London;
bottom left, © Bettmann/CORBIS; p.iii © FPG/Getty;
p.iv bottom left, © Bettmann/CORBIS; p.v top left © Bettmann/CORBIS;
bottom left, © ABC/Getty Images; bottom right, © PA; p.vi, top left © Mirrorpix;
bottom left © Anthony Wallace / Associated Newspapers /Rex Features;
p.vii, top left, © Bettmann/CORBIS; bottom left © Jan Persson/Getty

ISBN 978-1-62365-823-6

Library of Congress Control Number: 2014945192

Distributed in the United States and Canada by
Hachette Book Group
237 Park Avenue
New York, NY 10017

Manufactured in the United States

10 9 8 7 6 5 4 3 2 1

www.quercus.com

For Lee Tyler (1962–2011)
A kindred spirit.

CONTENTS

PART 3
THE END OF THE AFFAIR

EPILOGUE

INTRODUCTION

Here is why Eartha Kitt is extraordinary, why she's been written out of history, and why she should be remembered.

It all comes down to four songs in a movie, filmed half a century ago. The film in question, almost entirely forgotten now, was called *New Faces*. It was the Hollywood version of a Broadway revue, shot in full color CinemaScope and released by 20th Century Fox in 1954. The undisputed star of both the original revue and the subsequent movie was a young cabaret singer named Eartha Kitt. She had five featured songs in the film. Four of them are truly remarkable.

The first is the show's opening number. The simple stage set is a street scene at night. Leaning against one of the lampposts is a dark-skinned woman dressed in a demure long skirt and a racy strapless tiger-print top: Eartha Kitt. As the camera pans over to her she begins to sing, her attention apparently directed somewhere off screen. She sings in French, a perky modern chanson called "C'Est Si Bon." After a little while she focuses her attention on the viewer. There's a startling intensity about her that cuts against the cheeriness of the song. Then she starts dropping in asides in English, encouraging the object of her affections to show his appreciation by buying her a Cadillac. She appears to be a shameless gold digger, growing visibly excited as her thoughts turn to money. Finally, transported by the prospect of riches, she bares her teeth at the viewers and rips her skirt off. There is no question at all what is going on here: the girl by the streetlight is offering sex in exchange for money—lots of money.

But who is this girl meant to be? A Parisian streetwalker? On the face of it yes, but there's nothing in her performance of the real Parisian prostitutes of the postwar era, none of the poverty and desperation that would drive women to sell themselves for a packet of cigarettes or a pair of nylons. Instead, she projects an unnerving ferocity: she's throwing down a gauntlet—are you man enough, and rich enough, to take me on? But as to who she is, that's still a mystery. She's dark skinned, but with unusual features, and she speaks English, but with an odd, slightly European accent. Is she French, North African, Latin? Her age, as well as her nationality, is unknowable. One moment she looks like a teenage girl and the next like a woman who has already seen far too much. The only thing that's obvious about her is her sexuality, deployed confidently, even aggressively.

Her second appearance in the movie comes half an hour later, following some sketches, dance routines, and cabaret songs, and it makes things a little clearer. When the camera finds her, Eartha is pressed up against a frosty window. She appears to be stark naked apart from a white fur stole that just about keeps her modesty intact. This time she's singing in English but the subject matter is much the same: it's a song of seasonal seduction directed at her "Santa Baby," who she's exhorting to make her Christmas complete by buying her a yacht, or maybe just a duplex apartment—she doesn't want much. All the while she's toying with the stole, letting her potential lover get a very good idea of what's on offer if he would only hurry down the chimney with a '54 convertible in his sack. The whole thing is wildly sexy and flirtatious and brings the singer into clearer focus. Her domestic surroundings no longer suggest a streetwalker but a sophisticated woman looking for her ideal mate. Her Monroe-ish little-girl act only points up the obvious: that she's a grown woman in her midtwenties who knows her way around. And hearing her sing in English makes it clear that the singer isn't French or Latin but, shockingly, a black American.

Why shockingly? Because this was 1954, and at that time, if black American women appeared in mainstream movies at all, they were devoted domestics, simple souls full of homespun wisdom. Black women only got to play romantic leads if they appeared in all-black films, like *Stormy Weather* or *Carmen Jones,* whose stars, like Lena Horne and Dorothy Dandridge, were either stiff paragons or tragic victims. The films certainly never featured anyone like this woman, this Eartha Kitt, singing in French, flaunting her body, and parading her lust for worldly goods. Yet somehow, at a time in which it was still illegal for a black person and a white person to have sex together in twenty-eight out of fifty states, *New Faces* managed to bring to the screen a black woman who is quite evidently ready and willing to seduce Mr. Middle America.

Eartha's third appearance in the film is in a bizarre number called "Uska Dara," which sees her emerge from a silken tent and perform a belly dance routine while singing in Turkish. The song ends with her returning to the tent and revealing that she has a male companion waiting: her "secretary." She smirks at the camera and purrs "Oh, those Turks" before pulling the curtains closed. This time she's the one with the money, while the man in the tent is at her beck and call. The roles have been reversed and it's clear that, once Eartha has her material needs taken care of, she will take her pleasures as and when she pleases. It's another blatant affront to the declared morality of the time.

And then there's the show's grand finale, Eartha's pièce de résistance, a song called "Monotonous." The setting for this is a room full of chaise longues. As she sings Eartha drapes herself across a chaise longue, all the while bemoaning the fact that her life of unimaginably decadent hedonism is actually oh-so-boring, whether it's T. S. Eliot writing poems for her or Jacques Fath designing dresses for her. The refrain is the one word *monotonous*, which she uses to express the utter tedium of having men fall at her feet.

It's the strangest number yet. Eartha is portraying a character that's almost unimaginable in reality: a black American woman who's tasted all the world's most fabulous delicacies and found them lacking. Men have given her all the yachts and convertibles she craved and she feels nothing but ennui. It's an extraordinary song to sing at a time when, in the real world, black Americans were engaged in a long struggle for basic human rights, never mind couture and caviar. Once again we wonder, who on earth is this woman? And how can she appear to be so supremely indifferent to the laws and mores of her time?

The answer, at least in part, is simple. Eartha Kitt could act like that because she had already had a remarkable life and a range of experiences far outside the norm. She'd traveled the world: she knew men and she knew audiences. She'd learned that people loved this act of hers; that she scandalized them, but only in the way that people loved to be scandalized in the years after the war. Audiences adored Eartha Kitt because she was exotic—she seemed to come from everywhere and nowhere—and because she was undeniably sexy, and, perhaps above all, because she was funny. She understood the importance of the occasional knowing wink to diffuse the sexual heat. She knew she represented all the desires Middle America couldn't admit to, all the racial and sexual taboos, and she was able to exploit them brilliantly. She managed a balancing act that should not have been possible.

Around the time of *New Faces* Eartha Kitt was the biggest new recording star in America. Yet if you were born after 1965, say, you may not remember her. You may never have heard her string of fifties hits, from "I Want To be Evil" to "Just An Old Fashioned Girl," or seen any of her films: as well as *New Faces* she starred in movies like *St. Louis Blues* and *Anna Lucasta*. You may only have encountered her as Catwoman in the *Batman* TV series, or come across her seasonal standard, "Santa Baby," on some Christmas compilation. It doesn't matter. For, at heart, hers is not a story of long-gone hit records and movies. It's the tale of one of the most singular women of her age: a black American entertainer who would never allow herself to be reduced to a racial stereotype, who always insisted on her individuality.

Eartha Kitt was a woman who had spent her first eight or so years on a South Carolina cotton field, and the rest of her childhood in Harlem, yet by the time she reached her early twenties had rein-vented herself as the epitome of cosmopolitan glamour. Small, and with striking rather than conventionally beautiful features, she nev-ertheless carried herself with an apparent absolute certainty that she was, as Orson Welles famously called her, "the most exciting woman in the world." And this supreme confidence, which apparently came from nowhere, ensured that it wasn't just America that fell in love with Eartha Kitt. Britain, in particular, was bewitched by her appear-ance in *New Faces,* and invited her over to star in all the big TV variety shows from the *Royal Variety Performance* to *Sunday Night at the London Palladium.* From the mid-fifties right up until the early seventies, she was a fixture on the British entertainment scene.

She offered the British a much-needed shot of exoticism, a Tech-nicolor presence in a black-and-white world. After the war the Brit-ish looked to Europe and America for glamour, excitement, and sex, and Eartha Kitt provided all three in copious quantities. Her appeal crossed both social and cultural divides: Kenneth Tynan raved about her in the *Observer,* while the *Daily Express* featured pictures of Eartha showing off her fabulous outfits. She had all the sophisticated allure the war-weary British were seeking.

Looking back now, this seems very strange. How odd that one of the most popular postwar sex symbols should have been a black woman who sang in half a dozen languages, favoring French chan-sons and Mexican ballads over rhythm and blues or jazz. How odd that, in the supposedly hidebound fifties, a mainstream audience was ready to take such an unconventional singer on her own terms, while, in our own free-thinking times, artists are expected to stay in their boxes. Yet she made it all seem so natural.

As I wrote this book it continually struck me just how thoroughly remarkable Eartha Kitt's popularity was, how little she fit into any established category of what I thought I knew about music history, or even social history. If a black American singing in French and Spanish and Turkish, while purveying a frank if cartoonish sexuality, could be a transatlantic star in the early fifties, then clearly the attitudes of that period were rather more complicated than we like to imagine.

Not only that, but the story of her personal life was also something of a mystery. I researched a little, and it soon became clear to me that no one had ever really made the effort to trace the story behind the myth she created, so persuasive was her power of self-invention. There was no biography in existence. Eartha herself had written several contradictory, fanciful, autobiographies that generally preferred to tell a good story rather than reveal her true feelings. After reading them I had many more questions than answers.

So I started work on this book and soon discovered that not only was Eartha's actual story far more intriguing than her self-created myth, but also that, one-off though she was, she still had her antecedents, her influences. She was a link in an alternative history of black America, one that is not simply concerned with roots and authenticity and ghetto suffering, but with sophistication and vaulting artistic ambition, a tradition that goes back to the Harlem Renaissance of the 1920s. Seen in this light, Eartha Kitt stands alongside dancers like Alvin Ailey and Katherine Dunham, writers like Ishmael Reed and Langston Hughes, musicians like Billy Strayhorn and Nina Simone, all of them artists who wanted to redefine black America, not simply to reflect it.

Ironically, however, Eartha's singular personal style found favor more readily with white Americans than black. Perhaps this was hardly surprising, given that the overwhelming majority of black Americans were still struggling against explicitly racist Jim Crow laws forbidding them from sitting at the front of the bus, drinking from the same water fountains as whites, and so forth, rather than living the glamorous life, like Eartha. Yet that contradiction meant that her style would prove unsustainable as the civil rights struggle gained momentum. By the mid-sixties Eartha Kitt was suddenly both behind and ahead of her time.

And so for decades since, Eartha Kitt has been seen as an outlier. Her career, her role in the culture, her extraordinary popularity, make no sense according to the orthodox histories of her time, and as a result her achievements have been overlooked. As one looks more closely into what really happened in her life, one cannot escape the conclusion that much of what we think we know about race, about sex, about America, about Britain, about the 1950s, must actually be wrong, or at least grossly oversimplified.

Here, then, is the story of how a girl from a South Carolina cotton field grew up to become America's mistress, defying the racial stereotypes just at the time when those stereotypes were most powerfully in force. A woman who, rather than rage against white America and its values, decided instead to seduce it. And, extraordinarily enough, succeeded.

At least, she did for a while . . .

PART ONE

Learning the Game

ONE

At the White Man's Door, in the White Man's Dwelling

There is a road that leads between the small towns of North and St. Matthews in the South Carolina lowlands, where Eartha Kitt was born. It's a smooth blacktop these days, no longer a dirt track. On one side of the road there are cotton fields, on the other side woods and swampland. From time to time the road winds past small settlements: not shacks, these days, but trailer homes.

The fields are empty now, the harvest carried out by machines. Which is surely a blessing, for at midday here the sun is implacable overhead and the blue sky empty apart from the occasional buzzard and the fluttering of oversized butterflies. Even the cotton plants themselves seem hostile: three feet high, tough, and spiky. To pick the burrs of fluffy cotton from the plants, you have to stick your hand right in and twist hard, even if you do you risk tearing the skin from your fingers.

Halfway along the road there's a church, St. Peter's AME Church. The AME stands for African Methodist Episcopal. It was, and remains, the church for the black people that worked this land.

There's a graveyard next to the church, little used now. The old headstones are sinking back into the soil, but if you look carefully you can still read the names of the dead.

Their names are curious—Amaker, Dantzler, Inabit. They sound German. To be specific they sound Swiss German. There's a reason for that. The people who owned this land were mostly Swiss German; they came over at the end of the eighteenth century and they settled this land. And like every landowner in the South, they used black slaves. These unfortunates came from Africa, shipped to the nearby port city of Charleston, where they were bought and sold in the slave market. Over to one side of the graveyard there's a collection of tumbledown headstones, dating back to the early years of the last century. The inscriptions on some are unreadable but on others you can make out another Germanic family name, that of Keitt. One of them bears the name of Fannie Keitt, another that of Hilliard Keitt. These are Eartha Kitt's forgotten kinfolk.

In her lifetime Eartha Kitt knew very little about her family background. She had only dim memories of her mother and knew nothing at all about her father, not even his name. She knew her mother's name was Annie Mae Keitt and that she had died young. She suspected her father to have been a local white man, perhaps the plantation owner's son. In her various unreliable memoirs, she also mentioned having two half sisters, Pearl and Almeda. She also claimed that her mother abandoned her at a young age, leaving her in the care of an older woman called Aunt Rosa.

Curiously neither Eartha herself nor any of the journalists who wrote about her ever really expanded on these sketchy memories. So my first task was to establish whether these basic claims about Eartha Kitt's parentage were true.

Eartha Kitt's birth was registered on January 17, 1927, in the small town of St. Matthews, which lies a half-hour drive south from the state capital Columbia. The town straddles a road and rail junction, and even at midday there are few people around. However, there is a town museum, which as it turns out has an archive that helps to answer these questions as to who Eartha's family were and where exactly they lived.

An Annie Mae Keitt of the right age to have been Eartha's mother shows up in the census record. She is recorded as living close to Bull Swamp. By 1930 she had a young daughter identified as "Essie Mae," quite possibly a mishearing of "Eartha Mae." This "Essie Mae," however, appeared to be an only child. The records also suggest that Annie Mae Keitt herself had sisters called Pearl and Almeda—the names that Eartha gave her own sisters in her books. Furthermore they are all recorded as living with a "cousin," an older woman called Rosa Houser—presumably "Aunt Rosa."

Confirmation that these must be the right Keitts comes in the shape of a 1968 clipping from a local newspaper, in which a reporter went looking for Eartha's family. The one close relative the reporter found was called Almeda Keitt, but she was Eartha's aunt, not her sister.

So how to explain the discrepancy? The one plausible answer is that the confusions of Eartha's earliest memories come from the fact that they were a mixture of her mother's recollections and her own: thus it was her mother who had younger sisters called Pearl and Almeda, not Eartha herself.

Annie Mae Keitt, Eartha's mother, was the daughter of William and Fannie (née Riley) Keitt. William's parents, Delia and Hilliard Keitt, had grown up during the days of slavery. Hilliard had been in bondage to the white Keitt family before receiving his freedom at the end of the Civil War. In the absence of a surname of his own, he took that of his former masters, as freed slaves generally did. All these Keitts, Eartha's maternal family, were black people who lived and died around Bull Swamp, on the former plantations of Caw Caw and Limestone townships.

So far so good. But tracing Eartha's maternal lineage was always going to be the simpler task, given that Eartha did at least know her mother's name. The identity of her white father required rather more detective work. Common sense suggested that he would have lived close by.

Initially the most obvious candidates were the local white Keitt family, the former slave-owners. These white Keitts had been major players in the region. The most famous of them, Laurence Massillon Keitt, was a US congressman in the years before the Civil War. He was a passionate believer in the right of the white man to own slaves. He once took part in the savage beating of a fellow politician, an antislave Northerner named Charles Sumner, on the floor of the House of Representatives. Afterward, he was censured by the House of Representatives but still came home a hero. Keitt became one of the leaders of the "Fire-Eaters," the Southern politicians who wanted the South to secede from the Union as an independent slave-owning confederacy. He fought for this cause during the Civil War and died leading a vainglorious charge toward Yankee guns.

It would have been a lovely irony for such a man to have been one of Eartha's forebears. Unfortunately there's absolutely no evidence to back up this theory. By the time of Eartha's birth the white Keitts had moved away from Bull Swamp. Instead, combing the census records for white people living anywhere near Annie Mae Keitt, the only candidates appeared to be a family called Sturkie.

And, sure enough, an investigation into this Sturkie family produced a breakthrough, in the shape of an article written for a tiny local paper in Lexington County, South Carolina, by a woman called Claudette Holliday. She claimed to know the identity of Eartha's father. She believed he was her own grandmother's uncle, a Dr. Sturkie:

> I first learned about this secret in the 1950s in overheard conversations between my grandmother, mother, and her sisters. It's the kind of thing women talk about in hushed tones . . . My grandmother's uncles lived in North, South Carolina. One was a doctor and a lawyer and he served in the state legislature around the turn of the last century. He was also the state prison doctor for a while. His brother was also a medical doctor.[1]

This information turned out to be backed up by the census data. The Sturkie living close by the Keitts in Caw Caw Township was indeed a doctor called Daniel Sturkie. Following further inquiries

Ms. Holliday supplied the information that the liaison had probably come about when Eartha's mother worked for Dr. Kitt, after his wife died.

Once again, the local records of births and deaths confirmed that Daniel's wife had indeed died at that time. And so it seems very likely that Claudette Holliday's story is correct. It's an all-too-plausible tale: a doctor living close by to the Kitts, a teenage Annie Mae finding work as a domestic servant with the recently bereaved doctor, Annie Mae giving birth to the doctor's child. So this man, Dr. Daniel Sturkie, was most probably Eartha Kitt's father.

The Sturkies were Swiss originally, from Interlaken, arriving in the US in the 1750s. They were mostly less successful than their former neighbors the Keitts. The branch of the family that lived around Bull Swamp were simple farmers rather than plantation owners (they don't feature as slave owners in the registers of 1850 and 1860).

A further trawl through the archives produced a photograph of Daniel's father, a man called Calvin Sturkie. This offers perhaps the most compelling evidence that Claudette Holliday's story is correct: Calvin Sturkie is a dark-complected man, and his face does indeed have a striking resemblance to that of Eartha herself.

Eartha's mixed parentage was a matter of shame for all concerned, and would go on to blight her early life. However it was not unusual. This mixing of the races was the South's guilty secret. Historians differ over exactly how many female slaves bore their masters' children, but there's no question that it happened often. So much so that, extraordinarily enough, the oldest black university in the US—Wilberforce, in Ohio near its border with the slave states—was initially paid for by Southern white planters who wanted their mixed-race children to have an education.

But while white society had been prepared to turn a blind eye to what went on between masters and female slaves, it was horrified by the prospect of open sexual relations between the races following the collapse of slavery. In particular there was much hysteria over the prospect of black men taking white women as lovers. This fear, fueled by sexual paranoia, was the wellspring for many of the worst excesses of racism over the coming century.

Not as well documented is the concern felt by white Southerners that, post emancipation, black women would continue to have children by white men. A remarkable illustration of this is a book called *Dixie After the War*, written by a Southern gentlewoman called Myrta Lockett Avary. According to Avary's hysterical account, rather than female slaves being the victims of legitimized rape, they were temptresses, luring upstanding white men into sin:

> Because he was white, the crying sin was the white man's, but it is just to remember that the heaviest part of the white racial burden was the African woman, of strong sex instincts and devoid of a sexual Conscience, at the white man's door, in the white man's dwelling.

So horrified were white southerners by the prospect of sexual relations between the races that they invented a word for it: miscegenation. It appears to be a scientific term, but in fact it was a deliberately ugly new formulation, designed to alarm people and to pave the way for new laws forbidding interracial sex that were enacted as soon as white men regained control of the South, a decade or so after the end of the war.

The laws didn't work, of course, and such relationships have become one of the more inconvenient realities of American racial history. There's the founding father Thomas Jefferson, with his black mistress Sally Hemmings. And in South Carolina there's the remarkable skeleton in the closet of one of the arch-racist politicians of the twentieth century, Senator Strom Thurmond. Here was a man who championed the segregationist values of the Old South until he died in office at the ripe old age of one hundred, and yet was afterward revealed to have fathered a child with a sixteen-year-old black maid named Carrie Butler.

The daughter in question, Essie Mae Washington-Williams, was born in South Carolina in 1925. A year or so later, Eartha Mae Kitt was born. Essie Mae would eventually meet her father, and was acknowledged by him, if only in private. Eartha Mae was less fortunate: she grew up barely remembering her mother and never knowing her father at all.

TWO

We Come Up Tight

For Eartha Kitt, the South was an ambiguous place. The time she spent there was mostly unhappy, but she retained a love for the land itself. It was, after all, that land that inspired her distinctive first name. At the time of her birth, in January 1927, "Eartha" was actually quite a common girl's name among the rural black people of South Carolina. In Eartha's case it was highly appropriate: she may not have had much in the way of family, but throughout her life she retained a love of planting and gardening.

Eartha's family worked these fields like every other poor black family around them. The old plantations may have been broken up after the end of slavery in 1864, but the lives of the former slaves still revolved around the service of King Cotton. The families now had their own shacks or, often as not, rented them from the former plantation owners. The ex–slave owners still lived among them in their big old houses, but their former chattels now had the illusion, at least, of self-determination. If the families owned their own shack and field they could style themselves farmers; if not, they were sharecroppers. Sharecroppers rented everything they needed from the landowner: the land itself, mules or horses, and fertilizer. The

sharecroppers grew the cotton, and at the end of each year the profits, if any, would be shared between landowner and sharecropper.

And so the life of the sharecroppers of the South Carolina lowlands was lived year to year. At the start of each year they would
plant cotton to sell and grow food to eat, and pray for a decent
harvest and good enough cotton prices to pay off the loan. The
following year they might well move on to new land as the crude
fertilizers of the time rendered the land unusable. In the 1920s,
when Eartha was born, they were faced with more problems: the
boll weevil wrecked many crops and then the Great Depression
descended, and the price of cotton stayed low. The sharecroppers
got deeper and deeper in debt to the white landowners. What
money they had was spent at the white man's country store.

The Kitts, along with the rest of the black population, lived hard
lives. Their conditions were an improvement on slavery only inasmuch as they had the option of walking away. In the first years of the
century many of their neighbors did just that. One of Annie Mae's sisters left, made it out all the way to New York City. Annie Mae wasn't
so lucky. She had given birth to Eartha when she was sixteen, and had
to stay.

In 1930, when Annie Mae was twenty and Eartha was three, they
were living in Caw Caw township, a ramshackle arrangement of
backwoods shacks. The only amenities were a country store on the
main road and, just along the way, St. Peter's Church, with its one-
room school attached.

Annie Mae and her child lived with her sisters Pearl and Almeda, as well as an older woman known as Aunt Rosa and Rosa's
teenage son Willie. Before long Annie Mae found herself a new man
and moved in with him, but he didn't want to take on her child, so
Eartha was passed on to Aunt Rosa. A little while later Aunt Rosa
moved closer into the nearby small town of North, taking Eartha
with her.

Being given away by her mother was to haunt Eartha's early
years, and indeed her entire life. Over the years she tried to make
sense of it. She came to the conclusion that it was something to do

with her skin color, that her mother's new man didn't want her in the house because he was dark-skinned and she was relatively light. However, it was not her skin color that was really the problem, since in actual fact Eartha was not particularly light skinned.

The real problem lay with the identity of her father. All the black people around about must have known, or at least suspected, the story of how Eartha came into the world: how Dr. Sturkie's wife had died young, how he'd employed Annie Mae to cook and clean for him, and how Annie Mae had then conceived a child. That was why Annie Mae had been cast out of her parents' house. That was why Annie Mae's new man didn't want little Eartha around—her very existence was a shame and a scandal.

Aunt Rosa made it very clear to her new charge that she was only accepted on sufferance. As an adult, Eartha never forgot the beatings she got from Aunt Rosa, the domestic drudgery, the constant hunger, the long hours picking cotton. The memories she had of her childhood were so lurid that her New York friends would wonder if she'd exaggerated it all. In terms of the details, it's possible that she did; but in general, it seems clear that her childhood was, indeed, one of persistent abuse and neglect, both physical and emotional.

Many of the stories that Eartha tells of her early childhood are difficult either to confirm or contradict. There's a vivid account in her autobiography of walking through the woods and St. Peter's graveyard at night to get to the country store and buy some medicine for Aunt Rosa. There's a story about being given a banana for the first time and eating it skin and all. There's a lurid tale of being tied to a tree by Aunt Rosa's teenage son Willie, stripped naked and whipped on her bottom till the blood ran down her legs.

All of these stories clearly had emotional resonance for Eartha, but it seems that her memory of her early years was sometimes muddled. For instance, Aunt Rosa did have a son called Willie, but he was a lot older than the sadistic young teenager Eartha describes. It's perhaps best to treat her recollections as a mixture of dream and reality, often possessing a truth that may not always be literal.

This is particularly true of the climactic event of her early childhood: her mother's death when she was somewhere between six and
eight years old. At the time Annie Mae was living with her new man
and his children, some small distance away from Eartha and Aunt
Rosa. One evening, as Eartha later told the story, a neighbor came to
see Aunt Rosa with worrying news of Annie Mae. Rosa quickly headed
off into the night. On her return Eartha heard Rosa tell the lurid tale
of what had happened. Apparently Annie Mae had become very sick
after eating a dinner sprinkled with an unusual pepper. She'd taken to
her bed and the following morning the doctor had been called, but
said that Annie Mae had been poisoned and there was nothing he
could do for her. She had subsequently died. There was no mention of
who might have been responsible for the poisoning.

It's an extraordinary story, full of Deep South horror, but it's also
one remembered by a child and entirely based on hearsay. For what
it's worth there's no trace of a death certificate for anyone called
Annie Mae in this part of South Carolina, with even approximately
the right dates of birth or death. That said, records for African-
American births and deaths are far from complete, and if there was
some suggestion of foul play, then it's conceivable that her death
might not have been reported to the authorities at all.

Whatever the precise truth of the matter, there's no question that
by the age of eight Eartha was in effect motherless and living with
a woman who was far from maternal. These facts are corroborated
by her best friend of the time, another of Aunt Rosa's many nieces,
a girl with a name derived from her own forebears' Swiss German
owners: Mildred Amaker.

Today, Mildred is a spry woman with piercing dark eyes, wearing
gold earrings and a brightly patterned housecoat. She still lives in
North and she readily confirmed the basic truth of Eartha's childhood story:

> She was living with this old lady, who was real mean to her. She was
> called Rosa, she was my mama's sister. She used to beat her for nothing.

She wouldn't let her play in the house, she had to play out in the yard. Me and my mama would come over Sundays and Eartha and I'd play in the yard together. She said her mama gave her to Aunt Rosa and then her mama had died.[1]

On being asked about Eartha's contention that the real reason her mother had given her away was because she was light skinned, Mildred was frankly incredulous. Incredulous, as it turns out, for two reasons. First of all, there was no question in her mind that in South Carolina, back then, it was nothing but good to be light skinned. The paler your skin, the better your chance in life. It was as simple as that. Secondly, Mildred refutes the idea that Eartha was light skinned: "She wasn't light at all."

Mildred's daughter, who had been watching TV up until then, was moved to join in the conversation at this point. A lively debate with her mother on her relative "brightness" of skin established that Eartha as a child was a similar color to Mildred: that is to say not "dark" but "brown" rather than "light."

However, there are plenty of other aspects of Eartha's autobiography that Mildred was happy to confirm. She well remembers the two of them going to school at St. Peter's, out among the cotton fields, and she backs up Eartha's account of actually working in those fields. Sent out there by Aunt Rosa, Eartha later claimed to have picked one hundred pounds of cotton, all by herself, at a time when cotton fetched a cent a pound. "I was the happiest kid alive," she remembered, "to know I had earned a whole dollar."

Mildred laughed at the idea that anyone might not believe that a child could pick a hundred pounds of cotton in a day, age eight or less: "We had to pick cotton—a hundred pounds easy. At ten I picked two hundred pounds of cotton, price was fifty cents a hundred. Me and Eartha had to pick cotton together, and if you stopped and kneeled down for a second you got a switch across your back. We come up tight."

"We come up tight." With these four words it's clear that Mildred is distilling the essence of a ferociously tough struggle for survival that began in childhood and never let up; an entire life rooted in a communal experience of bitter hardship. It's a life that Eartha Kitt was narrowly spared, and one whose early imprint she carried with her always.

At the age of eight, some while after her mother's death, a miraculous event occurred in Eartha's life. According to her own account, she—or some unspecified "relatives"—received a trunk of clothes and a train ticket to New York, along with a letter explaining that on arrival in New York she would be met by her Aunt Mamie, who would have Eartha live with her.

Mildred Amaker's recollections add a gloss to Eartha's own account of what happened. She's clear that whoever these "relatives" were they didn't include Aunt Rosa. For Eartha's escape from the South was evidently conducted with some degree of subterfuge: "She just slipped off without telling me, I figured afterward she didn't want the old lady to know. Because after she went Aunt Rosa was looking around all over town trying to find her."

So who could have been behind this remarkable turn of events? One obvious possibility is Aunt Mamie in New York. But while she was clearly involved in the planning, it seems highly unlikely that she could have afforded to have paid for the whole operation. The other, more plausible, candidate is Eartha's father, Dr. Sturkie. He could easily have heard of Eartha's mistreatment and decided to intervene. Most likely one of Eartha's other aunts came to him with the plan to send Eartha up north. He could have afforded the new clothes and the train ticket, and he was well placed to make the arrangements needed to ensure she made the long journey in one piece. And of course if Eartha was in New York her existence would remain no more than a rumor to his friends and neighbors.

However the plan was put together, one thing is sure: it worked. Around eight years old, Eartha Kitt took the train from North to New York City. Once she got there, she rarely looked back to where she came from, and when she did it was with an understandable lack of affection.

Thus it was that Eartha Kitt escaped the cotton fields of South Carolina while her friend Mildred Amaker stayed put, raising a family and making it through to a hard-earned retirement. Unlike Eartha, she is still alive today, and seemingly in good health.

Eartha never got in touch with Mildred again once she became a star. On a rare visit to the South, years later, she appeared not to recognize her. "She seemed confused," commented Mildred. It's clear that Mildred, too, has difficulty imagining what Eartha Kitt's life might have been like. And from this vantage point, on a semi-paved street in a forgotten town, deep in the backwoods of South Carolina, it's not hard to see why. For Mildred, Eartha might as well have gone to the moon.

THREE

Cotton Comes to Harlem

The train ride changed everything. Eartha's life before that journey took place in dream-time: in an indistinct land of high cotton and dusty tracks, a world of sensation rather than memory. Now the world started to come into focus and Eartha's own recollections from here on are much clearer and more reliable.

Even at eight years old Eartha knew this train ride north was momentous, and afterward she would recall it in detail: how she stared out the window and ate her catfish sandwiches as the rural landscape of the South was replaced by the cityscapes of the North.

Eventually the train arrived in New York and her aunt was there to meet her. Mamie turned out to be "a tall, pretty, brown-skinned woman." She led Eartha through the hubbub of the station and out into the streets where she was, unsurprisingly, overwhelmed by the scale of the buildings and the number of people bustling about. They took the bus, heading north through Manhattan.

When they arrived at Mamie's lodgings, on 143rd Street and Lenox Avenue, at what would then have been the northern end of Harlem, just a block from the Harlem River, Eartha was relieved to find the neighborhood less crowded, less hectic, than midtown Manhattan.

Mamie was lodging with a family called the Waydes, who had two children including a girl named Joyce who was Eartha's age. Her first few days in the city were full of revelations as she discovered electric lights, gas cookers, indoor sanitation, and radios.

School was a challenge at first. Eartha went to a nearby elementary school, PS 136, in Harlem. At first she was put in with a younger class so she could catch up on learning to read and write, but she soon adapted and became popular. Her aunt took her to school each day at first, but soon Eartha was confident enough to make the journey herself. After the initial shock she began to enjoy her new life in Harlem.

Harlem in the mid-1930s was at something of a crossroads. Originally an upscale white suburb of Manhattan, it had been taken over first by new waves of white immigrants arriving from Europe and then, from around 1900 onwards, by African-Americans. And, as the flow of black Americans fleeing the South became a torrent in the years after the First World War, Harlem became universally recognized as the preeminent black community in the United States.

Its reputation flourished during the Prohibition years from 1920 to 1933. For the first time elements of white society started to take an interest in black culture: music particularly, but also art and literature. The advent of recorded music had made jazz the first great modern music craze. There was talk of the "jazz age" and the clubs of Harlem were its epicenter. In some ways its flowering was helped by Prohibition, as the new alcohol laws were imposed less stringently uptown. No one cared too much what went on in a place like Harlem, where respectable white people were few and far between.

The white people who did make it up to Harlem were the thrill-seekers and celebrities of the day—the likes of Tallulah Bankhead, Mae West, and Al Jolson. They and their friends would head uptown to hear the new music, as played by Duke Ellington or Cab Calloway, in the swanky Cotton Club, where the only black people allowed entry were the artists and the kitchen staff.

Thus, by the early 1930s, Harlem was both a fantasy town—a playground for hedonistic jazz fans and socialites—and a reality, a teeming black ghetto full of recent arrivals struggling to make their mark in a harsh and overwhelmingly racist world.[1] Throw in the effects of the Wall Street crash, on New York in particular, and the subsequent Great Depression, and Harlem, for all its fame, was a community struggling to survive: the quality of its nightlife was in many ways something of a fig leaf, distracting attention from the social issues.

But what a fig leaf! The Harlem Eartha Kitt arrived in was a mecca for black American music. The twenties had seen the rise of Louis Armstrong and Bessie Smith, Ma Rainey and Ethel Waters, and by the early thirties the great swing bands were holding sway: those of Ellington, Calloway, Jimmie Lunceford, and Fletcher Henderson. The high-toned white crowd came to seem them at venues such as the Cotton Club and Connie's Inn, while the really intrepid visitors would follow the black audiences and eventually find their way to the speakeasies of 133rd Street: places like the Nest, Basement Brownie's, and the Clam House, where the remarkable lesbian blues singer Gladys Bentley held court with her raucously pornographic takes on the hot tunes of the day. Pod's, another 133rd Street joint,[2] was the place where the great piano player Willie "The Lion" Smith could be found, often accompanying new vocal talent, such as a very young Billie Holiday.

This was a time when the matter of identity was very much up for grabs for black Americans. Should African roots be celebrated or repudiated? The Cubists were crazy for African artifacts, perhaps Harlemites should likewise be celebrating the primitive and the "barbaric"? Or perhaps not. Perhaps they should be following the advice of the leading black intellectual of the day, W.E.B. Du Bois, and forming what he called "the talented tenth"—an educated elite who would become teachers and lawyers and doctors and raise up the race by setting a good example.[3]

So, one way or another, Harlem occupied a special place in American society from the First World War until the mid-thirties.

It seemed for a while as if it could be the launching pad for a new, multicultural America. Certainly that's what the black intellectuals of the period hoped for. Whether the whites who frequented the Cotton Club, et al. ever saw Harlem as much more than a fashionable place to go to shock their conservative neighbors is rather less certain.

What is clear is that an outbreak of rioting in Harlem in 1935, no more than a year after Eartha's arrival, saw white New Yorkers' brief love affair with the neighborhood come quickly to an end. The Harlem riot began on the afternoon of March 19, when a dark-complected Puerto Rican boy was caught shoplifting in a Harlem store. A rumor went around that the shopkeeper had beaten the boy severely, later that the boy had died. The fact that this wasn't true didn't matter. It was easy enough to believe, and that night saw an outbreak of rioting and looting along Harlem's main drag, 125th Street, with white-owned stores being singled out for robbery and destruction.

The riot itself fizzled out the next day, once the supposedly dead boy had been produced alive and well. However, if whites had previously suspected Harlem to be dangerous, they were now convinced of it. The clubs that relied on white patronage, like the Cotton Club, moved operations to midtown, and the new home of jazz was proclaimed to be 52nd Street, never mind that it was merely a sanitized and, in every way, pale imitation of 133rd Street.

Eartha had arrived in Harlem just in time to see it begin its long, slow decline. Even so, it was still a place full of possibilities, and before long the overawed little girl from the South started to blossom. This wasn't Mamie's doing. She was a hard-working churchgoing woman, but she seemed to find Eartha more of a burden than anything else. Instead Eartha's real inspiration came from two particularly sympathetic teachers in her elementary school. The first of these was a Mrs. Beans. She soon noticed Eartha's remarkable talent for reading. Where other children stumbled their way through the stories selected for reading out loud, Eartha was fluent and, more than that, able to captivate an audience. Mrs. Beans encouraged and praised her, and soon saw to it that Eartha was moved up a couple of grades to a new class presided over by a Mrs. Bishop. Mrs. Bishop was the teacher who really saw Eartha's potential. She gave Eartha books and encouraged her to read out loud in school. She also took an interest in Eartha's general well-being. She raised concerns, for instance, around Eartha's domestic situation, which was far from ideal.

Mamie was always busy, either at work or with her boyfriend, Mr. Charles, and their landlady, Mrs. Wayde, was starting to resent this. To make matters much worse Mr. Wayde was starting to make inappropriate advances toward Eartha. Matters came to a head one day when Eartha was in the apartment, sick in bed suffering from whooping cough. Mrs. Wayde accused Mamie of neglect and, following a heated argument, Mamie picked Eartha up, wrapped her in a blanket, and headed out of the apartment, never to return.

They moved to a rooming house a few blocks away on 7th Avenue at 137th Street. This was a house full of music. Their immediate landlord, a Mr. Anderson, gave dancing lessons with piano accompaniment, and the young Eartha saw some of the great entertainers of the time, like the Nicholas Brothers, Ethel Waters, and Bill "Bojangles" Robinson passing through. Mr. Charles by now was Mamie's steady boyfriend, and Eartha took to calling herself Kitty Charles, rather than Eartha Kitt (indeed throughout her life her friends always called her Kitty, never Eartha).

Eartha's musical talent started to be noticed beyond the confines of school. She took piano lessons and acquired a reputation for her singing ability. But even though Mamie encouraged Eartha in these extracurricular activities, her young charge always felt a lack of warmth there; that her aunt was acting out of duty, rather than love. The clearest example of this came when Eartha starred in a version of *Snow White and the Seven Dwarfs*, put on by her Sunday School at Salem Methodist Church, where she sang in the choir. Mamie made Eartha a beautiful dress for the occasion and the play was a great success. Afterward Mamie seemed happy to accept the compliments from friends and neighbors, but showed no sign of this pride to Eartha herself; refusing even to hold her hand as they walked home together.

Meanwhile, times were only getting harder in Harlem. Eartha and Mamie became dependent on President Franklin Roosevelt's Emergency Relief program, a lifeline but also a badge of shame as far as the young Eartha was concerned. Instead of wearing the same clothes as the other children she wore the dresses handed out by the relief program: one pink with daisies, one blue with daisies. This led to playground teasing, and the harsh realization that even by Harlem standards she was poor.

Not long after this Mamie and Eartha moved into Mr. Charles's own apartment on Madison Avenue, near 116th Street in Spanish Harlem. Relations between aunt and niece got steadily worse as Eartha responded to Mamie's coldness by becoming rebellious. One day Mamie found out that Eartha had skipped her Saturday morning piano lesson in favor of going to a movie, and administered a severe beating that was only brought to a close by the arrival of Mr. Charles.

Again Eartha felt that the only person who was taking notice of what she was going through was her teacher, Mrs. Bishop. And before long it was Mrs. Bishop who was to play a decisive part in Eartha's development. She gave her a poem to learn, and once Eartha had learned it, gave her a dime to take a subway downtown, where Mrs. Bishop had arranged for Eartha to take an audition.

The audition was for the chance to attend Metropolitan Vocational High School, the forerunner of the famed High School of Performing Arts. But where other vocational schools focused on turning out dressmakers or carpenters, this new school also offered music and theater programs. It was founded by the visionary educator Franklin J. Keller, along with a teacher named Edith Bank.

Metropolitan High School was situated at 78 Catherine Street, not far from the Brooklyn Bridge, but it accepted students from all over the five boroughs, subject to audition. Eartha, now thirteen, was terrified, but Mrs. Bishop had arranged for her to have an informal meeting with Edith Bank first, so as to calm her nerves prior to the audition itself. Come the audition, Eartha was still terrified but once again her talent overcame her nerves. When she started reading, she had what she called "an electric feeling," just as she had when she first read to her classmates in Harlem. She was sure she had passed the test, and she was right. Afterward the other kids congratulated her, and a Jewish boy said he looked forward to seeing her next year. She realized at once that she had gained access to a place where the familiar prejudices did not apply.

Eartha's life was starting to change profoundly. She was living in a family unit with Mamie and Mr. Charles. She was enjoying life in their new neighborhood, Spanish Harlem, with its mix of Latin, West Indian, and African-American cultures. And now she was going to be attending a school with young people of all races from all over New York.

FOUR

Metropolitan High

Eartha's new school was a revelation. Every day she took the subway all the way downtown from Spanish Harlem to the Lower East Side, with its thriving Jewish and Italian communities. Eartha wasn't the only black pupil at Metropolitan High, but it was a mostly white establishment. Inevitably it was something of a culture shock for a girl like Eartha, whose entire life had been spent in all-black neighborhoods.

Metropolitan, however, was a genuine melting pot; its students—whether black or white—were all coming out of immigrant ghettoes, and all looking to better themselves. The school's founder, Franklin Keller, had set it up with the explicit goal of helping children from disadvantaged backgrounds.

Eartha's teacher at Metropolitan was Edith Bank, a remarkable woman. An idealist but also a steely realist, she'd grown up on the Lower East Side herself and was determined to help the next generation make their way out of poverty. Shortly before she died she reminisced about her career to one of her former students:

My father had been teaching for many years on the Lower East Side. I grew up there, but my mother thought I should teach at some nice comfortable school in Queens where we'd moved to, but I said I wanted to check this school out. So I went for an interview and I came back and told my mother I'd met this interesting man who wanted me to set up a speech and drama department. Keller represented everything I believed in, encouraging children to become what they could be.[1]

Edith Bank taught Eartha English and a subject called Speech. Speech, or "Elocution," was a fashionable subject in the 1940s. It was based on the idea that, in order to make one's way in the world, you would need to speak in a certain way. It would eventually fall out of favor—why should the poor and the black have to ape the manners of the rich and white to succeed? But among the immigrant communities of the United States in the 1940s pragmatism outweighed idealism. If you needed to speak a certain way to get on in the world then fair enough; elocution lessons were the way to go. And why not? You might not be able to change your obvious Jewishness or blackness, but you could change your voice.

Mrs. Bank didn't just teach her students how to speak, she taught them table manners and took the kids out to a real restaurant, Schlaffly's on Lower Broadway. This was a Jim Crow place that wouldn't have served Eartha and her aunt in a month of Sundays, but when the formidable Edith Bank arrived with a gaggle of Metropolitan kids, the staff gave way. She showed Eartha how to read the menu, how to order food from a waitress, how to hold her knife and fork. She taught her that if you talk a certain way, act a certain way, then people are likely to behave toward you with more respect.

And just as Mrs. Bank's speech lessons opened the doors to the real world, her English lessons opened the doors to all manner of imaginary worlds. Edith Bank didn't just teach Shakespeare, she took her charges to the theater and she taught them the rudiments of acting. She believed that in order for them to become performers they had to change their expectations of life, as expressed in the way they carried themselves. So, just as she'd remodeled their voices, she got to work on their physical bearing:

> They had to develop a bodily freedom; they had to respond to life, to improvise. I made them use their imagination. I'd line them up in class, one behind the other as if they were on a sled, then I'd play music, tell them we're going down through the snow and ice. I wanted them to feel free.[2]

It was a lesson that was well learned by the young Eartha. An adolescent now, she was looking for greater freedom at home too, as she became increasingly enamored of the Latin-flavored street life around her new home. A gang of teenagers would get together each evening, a few blocks from where she lived. The boys would assemble an assortment of improvised percussion instruments and start a Cuban jam session. The girls would dance and sing along. Favored girls like Eartha would then get invited to the weekend dances—fifty cents for girls, a dollar for boys. There was no hard liquor on sale, just soft drinks and beer, and the focus was on the dancing. Eartha soon emerged as one of the queens of this particular scene. She was a natural dancer and quickly acquired the expected Spanish Harlem attitude: ready to cuss out rival girls or pushy boys in either English or *neoyorquino* Spanish.

Between the twin poles of Edith Bank's instructions in etiquette and her street-level education in dancing and flirting, Eartha Kitt was starting to develop her own personality: at once haughty and sexy, sophisticated and wild. It wasn't long before she acquired her first boyfriend, a local boy named Alex, "soft-spoken, handsome, curly haired, brownskin," but also a high-school dropout. Alex was the neighborhood heartthrob: and Eartha was thrilled to be the girl who had him for her own.

Eartha's burgeoning sex appeal had other, less welcome, consequences. She became the object of unwanted advances from the handful of black boys at her school, who had formed themselves into a little gang. It also provoked further conflicts with her aunt, who issued dire warnings against getting pregnant, but nothing in the way of practical advice. Relations were not helped by the lack of money in the household. In an effort to improve her wardrobe Eartha found some of her aunt's old clothes and altered them for herself. Mamie discovered what she had done, gave her a whipping, and from that point on stopped giving her the quarter a day she needed to pay for her lunch and the subway fare back and forth to school.

Without money to eat Eartha quickly learned to hustle. She would show up at her friends' houses around mealtimes in the hope of an invitation to join them. At school she soon realized that if she flirted with the boys she could get them to buy her lunch. Her sex appeal might be getting her into trouble, but it also provided the way out. Nevertheless she could hardly rely on flirting to provide three square meals a day.

Edith Bank soon noticed that something was wrong and took Eartha aside in an attempt to find out what the problem was. Eartha's pride, however, forbade her to tell the truth; instead she took on a part-time job in a stationer's. It didn't end the quarrels with her aunt though, and over the next year or so a pattern was established of arguments and reconciliation, culminating in Eartha running away from home and school. She slept on friends' floors and the roofs of apartment houses for a little while. She did what she had to do to survive, eating from garbage cans, drifting toward the world of prostitution, until she found herself a job in a sweatshop as a seamstress, and a room with a Cuban family in the Bronx.

At this point her aunt showed that she did have some concern for Eartha's welfare, and tracked her down to the sweatshop. Eartha went back home and resumed her schooling, but the arguments continued till she finally told Edith Bank how bad things were at home, and Mrs. Bank had a word with Mamie. There was a short reconciliation, but then Eartha left home for good and went to live with the Cuban family again.

Meanwhile, back at school, Mrs. Bank was busy encouraging Eartha to become an actress. She gave her a ticket to see a production of *Cyrano de Bergerac* on Broadway, starring José Ferrer. Ferrer's performance made a profound impression on Eartha. For the first time she started to imagine that she might make a career for herself on the stage.

Picking up on Eartha's enthusiasm Mrs. Bank pushed her to try for theatrical jobs. The first audition she sent her for was to appear in a production of *Carmen Jones*—the Carmen story transposed to black America. This time, however, Eartha's nerves did get the better of her. She opened her mouth to sing and at first nothing came out. She improved a little thereafter, but didn't get the part. Afterward, though, she felt relieved, knowing she wasn't yet ready for the professional stage.

In the summer of 1944 Eartha left school. She was now seventeen years old. The first thing she did was to head for upstate New York to work in the Women's Land Army of America, the so-called farmerettes, helping out with the war effort by doing light farm work, harvesting cherries and currants. She thoroughly enjoyed the experience. Harsh as her South Carolina childhood had been, it had left her with a lifetime enthusiasm for horticulture.

Eartha came back to New York the following September and very quickly received her first real break: an audition for the Katherine Dunham dance company, the first black modern dance company in the United States.

One afternoon Eartha and her old friend Joyce, Mrs. Wayde's daughter, had gone to see a Carmen Miranda movie. Afterward they were just hanging around in Spanish Harlem wondering what to do next, when a girl came up to them and asked if they knew where a dancewear store was.

The girl was named Othella Strozier. She had recently arrived in New York from St. Louis in order to join the Dunham Company and had been sent up to Spanish Harlem to buy a leotard. The girls showed her the way and asked if she was a dancer. Othella explained that she was with the Dunham Company and the girls were immediately intrigued. They asked if there was any chance they might be able to audition. Othella said no at first, but Eartha was determined. Finally Othella agreed that she could come down the next day and try out for the Dunham School.

This was precisely the break Eartha had been hoping for. The Katherine Dunham Company had brought a new level of sophistication to the world of black dance. They'd been a hit on Broadway, and the year before they'd been in the movie *Stormy Weather*, which Eartha had loved. One of the first Hollywood movies to feature exclusively African-American talent, its stars were Lena Horne and Bill "Bojangles" Robinson, but Katherine Dunham and her dancers were also heavily featured.

So the next day Eartha, accompanied by Joyce, made her way down to the Dunham Company's studio. Once there she borrowed a leotard and watched as one of the Dunham Company leads took a group through a series of exercises. She did her best to memorize the moves that they were making and eventually her chance to try out came. She threw herself into the music with abandon, wiggling and twitching furiously, making sure that her performance was memorable at the very least.

Finally exhausted, Eartha sat back down next to Joyce and waited for the verdict. A tall woman came over to her, most likely the school's leading teacher, Syvilla Fort, and asked if she could come back on Monday morning at ten. Eartha asked why, and was told she'd won a scholarship. It was September 1944, and her path was set.

FIVE

Miss Dunham

Eartha's scholarship consisted of a ten-dollar-a-week stipend, barely enough to get by on. Each day she would arrive at the Dunham School in time to start classes at ten a.m. First they would warm up, then there would be half an hour of straight ballet, and after that there would be an hour and half of work on the "Dunham technique," which Eartha enjoyed very much. This was a fusion of conventional Western ballet techniques with African and Caribbean-derived folk dances and straightforward African-American jazz dancing. It was the vision of Katherine Dunham herself, as was the company, and now the school.

Katherine Dunham, a wholly remarkable woman, was the next great influence in Eartha's life. Like Eartha she was of mixed race, the daughter of an African American and a French Canadian. She grew up among Chicago's black middle class and went on to study anthropology and ballet. Later she spent time in the Caribbean studying the folk dances of the islands and began to develop the Dunham Method.

In 1939 Dunham devised two dance pieces, *Tropics* and *Le Jazz Hot*, which she brought to New York, where they were an immediate hit. This success led to her being asked to take part in a new all-black Broadway musical called *Cabin in the Sky*, also featuring the blues singer and Harlem headliner Ethel Waters.

Dunham took the starring role of Georgia Brown, and was responsible for much of the show's memorable choreography. The show was a great success on Broadway, and Dunham was suddenly a new kind of African-American star: a woman with a doctorate whose friends included Erich Fromm and Igor Stravinsky, but whose dance moves radiated a frank sexuality. The show business world wasn't sure what to make of her. Nor was her costar, Ethel Waters, who was thoroughly put out when she came upon a newspaper profile of Dunham. Dunham recalled what happened next in her memoirs:

> Ethel Waters was in a real state, to put it mildly. She was complaining to Al Lewis, one of the associate producers. She had grabbed him by the coat lapels to emphasize her statement. "Ah don't know nothin' bout no anthropology," she stormed disdainfully, deliberately distorting her language, "but ah sho' knows a lot of naked asses wigglin' when ah see em!"[1]

The success of *Cabin in the Sky* led to the Dunham Company being featured in *Stormy Weather*, which in turn gave her the fame and prestige needed to launch her company's first Broadway show in its own right, *Tropical Revue*.

This was another hit, and Dunham, now riding high, decided to expand her activities. There would be the Katherine Dunham Company itself, which would mount major productions, there would be smaller groups of "Katherine Dunham Dancers," who would appear in nightclubs and bring in steady income, and there would be the Dunham School of Dance and Theater, into which she would pour her profits from the commercial shows. The school would make sure that other African Americans would be able to follow in her footsteps and, at the same time, it would act as a talent-spotting operation to provide new blood for the company.

The school opened its doors in 1944. The first premises were on West 59th Street at Isadora Duncan's former studio, known as Caravan Hall. By the time Eartha joined, they had moved to new premises at the top of the Lyric Theater on 43rd Street. The school was a very basic work in progress, and the students, the scholarship students especially, were expected to do their share of chores around the place.

Eartha had been with the company for a month before she met Miss Dunham herself. In the meantime she had made friends with one of her fellow dancers, a girl called Roxie Foster, and, before long, she moved into Roxie's family's apartment on Convent Avenue, in a smart part of Harlem. She gave Roxie's mother half her stipend as rent, leaving a scant five dollars a week to live on.

When Miss Dunham finally arrived at the school, having returned from Hollywood, she seemed, to the young Eartha, to be an impressive but remote personage. She generally appeared at the school on Sunday afternoons, when potential backers would be invited down to see the new venture in action and members of the Dunham Company would dance alongside the students. Vanoye Aikens,[2] the company's male lead and Miss Dunham's own dance partner, got to know Eartha, or Kitty Charles as she was still calling herself, as one of the first students at Miss Dunham's new venture.

Yes, she was one of the students at the Dunham School, at 220 W43rd St. If we weren't on tour Miss Dunham would have us all come down there every Sunday, as people were invited to visit on Sundays. I don't know how Kitty did at the school as we weren't around that much, we were always touring and then every time you came back to town there was another new group of students . . . I knew she lived with Roxie Foster, they were very close friends. Roxie's family was like Kitty's adopted family in New York—Kitty would call Roxie's mother "mother."[3]

What Van Aikens did notice was that even as a teenager Eartha was very different from her classmates, already holding herself a little apart: "Kitty was not haughty but she was not a gossiper either; she kept her business to herself. She was respected for that. You knew better than to try to get into her business. She was a unique kind of person, she was just always herself."

It may well be that some of Eartha's aloofness was an attempt to emulate her new role model, Katherine Dunham, whose intermittent, rather regal, appearances at the school made her a near-mythic figure to her students. She inspired both love and fear in them. Fear because she had the power to make or break their fledgling careers, and love because even a smart-mouthed teenager like Eartha could see that Miss Dunham was doing something extraordinary, not out of self-interest, or even simply for her company, but for African Americans as a people. She was an inspirational leader, and Eartha and her fellow Dunham students were, for the moment, her devoted followers.

SIX

The Free and Equal Blues

After Eartha had been with the school for six months she had her first chance to dance professionally, as one of the "Katherine Dunham Dancers," in a new Broadway variety show, *Blue Holiday*.

On the face of it *Blue Holiday* should have been great. It was an all-black variety show featuring an extraordinary array of talent. There were songs provided by Duke Ellington and instrumental compositions from the pioneering composer and pianist Mary Lou Williams. Second on the bill was the preternaturally suave blues singer Josh White. And headlining was Katherine Dunham's old adversary, Ethel Waters. There was also a small part for a Haitian-American ingénue called Josephine Premice, who would later become a close friend of Eartha.

The problem was that the show had been thrown together in no time at all by a pair of rookie producers. The cast—talented though they all were—came from disparate backgrounds and the younger elements were flatly disrespectful of old-school Ethel Waters, whose Harlem blues seemed to come from a different era. Katherine Dunham herself had other commitments, so left much of the choreography to one of the teachers from the school. As Eartha once said: "We were helpless little souls, a herd of sheep without our shepherd."

In the absence of Miss Dunham the show came to be dominated by Ethel Waters, whose fondness for modern dance hadn't increased noticeably since her previous brush with the troupe. Eartha later told the story of how she and her fellow dancers were dressed in very scanty costumes and told to wiggle their way across the stage. Before long they heard someone rushing toward them from the wings and then heard the unmistakable voice of Ethel Waters shouting, "I don't want those naked bitches on my stage."[1]

Ethel Waters then went on to take charge of the choreography in an effort to make sure she wasn't upstaged by pretty young girls like Eartha. The result, inevitably, was a rancorous hodgepodge of a show, which attracted terrible reviews and pitiful audiences. At the end of the first week the cast was paid out of the insurance fund insisted upon by the actors' union. At the end of the second week the show closed. It was a shameful waste of talent. Few of the acts were spared by the critics, the principal exceptions being Mary Lou Williams and, particularly, Josh White.

It wasn't only the critics who were impressed by Josh White. Eartha met him for the first time at the rehearsal studio. White walked in with his guitar, stuck a cigarette in the side of his mouth, and started singing the blues. Eartha was immediately and completely smitten, as is very evident from her decidedly lurid description of this first encounter:

> The sound of his music box twanged my womanliness. I watched his hands, as they told of love and hatred, of sensuous love and faithless women. His mouth moved as though he was making love to the words he spoke . . . "There's no woman I cannot have and any woman can have me."[2]

At first Eartha had no idea who this man was, but Roxie Foster quickly filled her in. And Josh himself soon made it very clear that the attraction was mutual. At the time he was a married man with two young children, but he never let that get in the way of his romantic life, and his wife Carol did her best to turn a blind eye to his dalliances.

And so began Eartha's first serious love affair. Josh White fulfilled two key roles for Eartha. He was her lover and her teacher. He was the man who introduced her to the nightclub world and the one who broadened her musical horizons. She could hardly have found a better person to learn from. By the time of *Blue Holiday*, in May 1945, Josh White was only thirty-one years old, but had already done enough to fill several lifetimes. Like Eartha, Josh White came from South Carolina, born in Greenville. When Josh was seven years old his father threw a white bill collector out of his house for being rude. In return he received a beating so severe he never recovered from it and ended up living out his days in a mental institution.

Shortly afterward Josh was engaged by a street singer named Blind Man Arnold, who used the child to collect money and in due course to dance, sing, and play the tambourine. Josh was good at this, and was thus condemned to spend the rest of his childhood trekking around the South in the company of cantankerous, blind blues singers, including Blind Blake and Blind Joe Taggart. He did, however, learn from his employers, and by 1927, just thirteen years old, he became a recording artist himself. In 1930 he signed as a solo artist to ARC Records and moved to New York. On his mother's insistence he only recorded religious numbers, and was billed as "Joshua White—The Singing Christian," before starting a parallel career recording the devil's music under the name "Pinewood Tom."

His career hit a hiatus in 1936, after he contracted gangrene in one hand following a bar fight and could no longer play the guitar. He worked as an elevator operator in New York until his hand healed, and he started making music again, now in a far more sophisticated style, blending blues with elements of folk and jazz and musical theater: a mix more suited to his life in New York.

His reputation grew and before long he appeared in a play called *John Henry* on Broadway, alongside Paul Robeson. He began to move in left-wing circles, collaborating with the folk song collector Alan Lomax on a radio series called *Back Where I Come From*, also featuring Woody Guthrie, Lead Belly, and Burl Ives, and directed by the future filmmaker Nicholas Ray. He had an enormously successful residency downtown at the Village Vanguard. Before long he attracted the attention of the President, Franklin Roosevelt, and his wife Eleanor, and was invited to appear at the Library of Congress, a remarkable honor for a bluesman.

In addition he had a big popular hit record with the tragicomic Depression-era narrative "One Meatball." Like Katherine Dunham and Eartha herself, he was a renaissance person, one who emphatically rejected all the stereotypes people wanted to hang on an African-American entertainer—well, all the stereotypes bar one: like them, he was quite happy to project a very direct sexuality.

White was, by all accounts, quite extraordinarily attractive. You can see his magnetism in the surviving clips of him performing, which also reveal him to have a beautiful speaking voice, clear and melodious with little trace of his original Southern accent. Every woman interviewed for this book who had met Josh White simply sighed when his name was mentioned.

In her autobiography Lena Horne sums his appeal up succinctly: "Josh was a wonderfully sexy man. You used to have to beat your way through swarms of women just to say hello to him." Likewise Josephine Premice, as quoted in Elijah Wald's excellent biography of White: "He was a very impressive man and from age eight to eighty, women were all in love with Josh White. They just swarmed around him like bees to honey."[3]

Men were also fully aware of his appeal. His friend Barney Josephson, who booked him at the Café Society, the Greenwich Village club where Josh made his name, gave Wald a particularly earthy assessment: "He played sex to the hilt. He was bigger at this than anybody else I ever saw in show business. He knew exactly what he was doing—so that when he stroked his guitar strings, the women in the audience just sat there in heat and felt like he was stroking their vaginas."[4]

* * *

In *Blue Holiday* Josh White performed several of the songs that had made his reputation at Café Society—two blues numbers, a song called "The House I Live In," written by Abel Meeropol, the man responsible for "Strange Fruit," and, of course, his hit, "One Meatball." He also led the show's finale, with the entire cast providing the chorus. This was a version of Earl Robinson and E. Y. Harburg's "Free and Equal Blues," a scathing talking blues in which the narrator talks to a doctor about blood plasma and whether it might have a race. The doctor confirms that it doesn't and the song concludes, *Every man, everywhere is the same, when he's got his skin off*. It was a brave sentiment to take to Broadway in 1945.

Each night after the show finished, White would head back downtown to the Café Society to perform a late-night set. Soon he started taking Eartha along with him, much to her delight. Josh was loved by all and Eartha was happy to bask in his reflected glow. And he treated her well, bought her steaks, introduced her to his friends, and made sure the waiters looked after her while he was on stage.

At eighteen Eartha had found her natural habitat: the high-toned nightclubs of the world. But she was never the kind of girl to be satisfied at being there simply as someone else's arm candy. She wanted to be a star in her own right. She soon let Josh know that she could sing as well as dance, and asked him whether he could get her a spot at Café Society too.

Meanwhile, after the rapid demise of *Blue Holiday*, Eartha went back to the Dunham School, which by now was a going commercial concern advertising its services in the trade press. These services included not just dance classes in Dunham Technique, rhythm, tap, and swing, but also percussion, "use of primitive instruments," and, tellingly, speech training. At around the same time, Eartha was called for an audition to become a full member of the Katherine Dunham Company. The company's leading members were currently appearing in another Broadway variety show, running at the

Ziegfeld Theater. Van Aikens remembers Eartha coming down for an audition:

> She auditioned on a Saturday afternoon at Billy Rose's Ziegfeld theater, I'll never forget it. Miss Dunham would always have an audition at the theater between shows and Kitty came along. There were other members of the company there to help with the audition. Anyway Eartha came one Saturday afternoon and she was turned down and she ran off stage crying. I don't think she'd ever been turned down before.

Painful though this setback may have been, it was only a very temporary one. Eartha and her friend Roxie were not rejected outright but put on a kind of waiting list until the company could afford to expand. That time came around very quickly as Miss Dunham secured a Broadway booking for a new solo show by the company, to be called *Carib Song*. It would be closer to a full-scale musical than previous Dunham productions, with dialogue and songs, so the company needed people who could act and sing as well as dance. Eartha and Roxie were duly added to the company and it quickly became clear to Van Aikens that Eartha did indeed have more than just her dancing to offer: "Kitty was one of the most valuable ones because not only could she dance fairly well, but she had a lovely voice. Miss D. was in love with her voice. We had a thing once or twice a year called the *Boule Blanche*, the White Ball, and Kitty would always sing at that ball."

Among Eartha's new colleagues was a young dancer called Gloria Mitchell. Along with Van, she was one of the few company members to get on well with Eartha at the time and also to remain friendly with her over the years. She remembers the young Eartha as talented but decidedly difficult:

> She had been at the school and of course she could sing, so Miss Dunham took her into the company as a singer and dancer. She was always kinda quiet and kept to herself, a little hard to get to know, but she and I hit it off fine—everyone said "Gloria, you're the only one can put up

with her!" She was a different kind of character, she really was. I used to get so annoyed with her because she would carry her personal feelings on to the stage. If she was mad about something, she'd be mad on stage. I used to say "Kitty you can't do that," and she'd just *look* at me.[5]

That *look*—that imperious glower—would become a central part of the haughty Eartha Kitt persona. For now though, she was required to accept her place as a junior member of the company, and not try to impose her personality on proceedings. She wasn't considered to be one of the leading dancers, so her ability to sing was her principle calling card. That and her ability to learn foreign languages. *Carib Song* required a certain amount of French speaking and Kitt volunteered to learn, as Aikens remembers: "Yes, it was when we did *Carib Song* in New York, she was sent to a famous language school and before you knew it she was speaking French. Kitty was a natural linguist."

Carib Song opened at the Adelphi Theater on September 24, 1945. Reviews suggest that it was overlong and the musical and dramatic elements were only patchily successful by comparison with the dance sequences, while the script, by William Archibald, "jumps from bombastic hyperbole to inane drivel." Much of the problem, according to *Billboard*'s reviewer, came down to Dunham herself. "On the terp[6] side La Dunham is in her usual fine form, particularly when she is vamping herself into a pair of new shoes without paying for them. Vocally, however, she is a dead loss and her acting is far from out of the top drawer."[7]

Overall, *Billboard*'s review felt that "*Carib Song* smacks of the faintly arty and pretentious." The public seems to have broadly agreed, as the show closed after a month. However, Miss Dunham was convinced that it contained the seeds of something good and the standout dance sequence, *Shango*, a Haitian-inspired piece, would become a highlight of the Dunham repertoire for many years to come, generally with Van Aikens taking the lead.

As Gloria Mitchell recalls, "*Carib Song* just didn't strike a note with show business at that time. Miss Dunham's thing was not acting. It was her dancing and her beauty: she was a very striking woman." As for Eartha, according to Gloria her presence in the company was a decidedly mixed blessing:

> She had a special part in the show because she sang. But she was very unfriendly at that point. I think the problem was she just hadn't found herself, you know. She wasn't important within the company, she was a lesser member because she was new, and her talent hadn't yet manifested itself beyond the company. She could really be quite an unpleasant person to be around at that time.

After *Carib Song* closed, the company went straight back into rehearsals for the next show. By now, though, there were the beginnings of a rivalry between Eartha, the upcoming starlet, and Miss Dunham, who was in her late thirties. There were also continual money problems, which didn't help the stability of what was already a very rivalrous outfit. What kept them together, in the end, was the realization that they were engaged in something genuinely important, that the Dunham Company were redefining what it meant to be a black American.

This was a timely undertaking. The Second World War was just then drawing to a close, and black Americans were once more wondering just what their place was in their own country. During the war years almost a million of them had served overseas. Their experience of the war had been profoundly confusing. Their own army still enforced a raft of Jim Crow policies and yet the people of Britain and France seemed to welcome black GIs. So who exactly were they fighting for, and why? In the words of a returning black American corporal: "I spent four years in the army to free a bunch of Dutchmen and Frenchmen, and I'm hanged if I'm going to let the Alabama version of the Germans kick me around when I get home. No sirree-bob! I went into the army a nigger; I'm comin' out a man."[8]

Meanwhile, back at home, the war effort had opened up a whole range of better-paying factory jobs to black men and women, which they were now in danger of losing to the returning troops. The mood overall was mutinous but still, ultimately, hopeful. Just as in Britain the returning soldiers voted in the Labor Party in the hope of building a new, more equal country, so now black Americans were ready to work for democratic change. Over the war years membership of the pressure group the NAACP (The National Association for the Advancement of Colored People) had grown from fifty thousand in 1940 to over four hundred thousand in 1946. Much of their struggle was focused on legal challenges; on the whole apparatus of Jim Crow segregation. Their hopes were placed on the next election and the Democratic candidate, Harry S. Truman. On the cultural level, then, the success of a proudly black but undeniably sophisticated outfit like the Katherine Dunham Company was a perfect example of what the NAACP believed in.

However, as far as life in the Dunham Company went, it wasn't all a matter of selfless struggle for the greater good of the race, since the Company was made up of individuals who all had their own dreams of show business success. Even at this early stage Van Aikens could see that Eartha wasn't destined to be a team player, that her future might lie in the nightclubs where her unique personality would be able to come into its own: "I don't think she went trotting after anyone, I don't think she copied, she was an original. Josh White, that's the one person who influenced her. She started singing in Greenwich Village with him. He gave her the best encouragement to be on her own."

So while the company prepared for the new show, Eartha moonlighted down in Greenwich Village with Josh, joining him on stage at the Café Society and, according to Aikens, performing her party piece, a song called "Babalu."[9] This was a Cuban number written by Margarita Lecuona. "That was her signature song," agrees Gloria Mitchell. "We used to tease Kitty about it because wherever we would go, if there was a party or something, she would sing 'Babalu.' Always."

Aside from "Babalu," it was Josh White's material that would become the basis for Eartha's first forays into performing as a solo singer. Josh had long since abandoned the raw country blues of his younger days and concentrated his talent on deceptively smooth renderings of a whole range of songs that certainly weren't blues, and could only very loosely be defined as folk music. Among them were traditional English tunes, like "The Riddle Song," contemporary songs of protest like "Strange Fruit," black pop songs like "Jelly Jelly," and cornball Americana like "On Top of Old Smokey." What pulled this disparate repertoire together was simply the force of his personality and his playing. Add in the combination of worldly sophistication and unashamed sex appeal, plus the ability to master a cabaret room, and you have something like the blueprint for the Eartha Kitt of the future. It would be hard to overestimate the importance of Josh White's influence on the young Eartha, both at the time and in her career to come.

SEVEN

At the Bal Nègre

In 1946 Eartha's professional career still lay with the Katherine Dunham Company, and would for some time to come. Dunham's new show was to be called *Bal Nègre* and, rather than repeat *Carib Song*'s misguided foray into full-on musical theater, this new entertainment put the accent firmly back on the dancing. It was designed to show off the full range of the company's talents, as it moved from evocations of Caribbean religious rituals to the jazz age of the 1920s. It was something of a greatest-hits show: one piece, *Shango*, was reprised from *Carib Song*, others from earlier works. This all augured well for the show's success, but so too did the fact that *Bal Nègre* would see Miss Dunham reunited with two of the key players in her previous successes.

The most important of these was her husband, John Pratt, who had been serving in the army while *Carib Song* was on. John Pratt, or Mr. P. as he was known to the company, was a cultured white man, the scion of a prominent business family, originally from Baltimore and later Chicago. He was a graduate of the Chicago School of Arts and was already fairly well known as an artist and designer when he met Katherine Dunham at a party. Pratt was involved with

Inez Stark, a great patroness of the arts, but soon switched his affections to Dunham. In 1941 they outraged both their families by marrying. Pratt took over as the set and costume designer for virtually every production of the Dunham Company, and was responsible for every costume Dunham would wear on stage and in films. Having John Pratt back on board was important for the balance of the company, as he was a more reassuring presence than the mercurial Miss D. Van Aikens:

> He was the sweetest, kindest gentleman you would ever want to meet, he was one of a kind. We called him Mr. P., she was Miss D. He was the most considerate person, a magnificent costume designer, very intellectual. He was her partner in every sense of the word, except that she was on stage and he wasn't. He was her background.

Similarly Gloria Mitchell recalls that "Mr. P. was a very charming, very smart man. He just knew everything. He could fascinate you for hours on end. He even knew things that you would find it hard to believe he'd know, like all of the songs in the black churches, things like that."

The relationship between Miss D. and Mr. P. was, however, not a conventional one. Both of them were bisexual and had numerous other relationships. According to Gloria, "It was a question of can't live with you, can't live without you. They kind of went their separate ways. Although they lived together and were married, he had his life and she had her life. Of course their common meeting ground was the design of the clothes we wore for the shows."

The other regular Dunham collaborator to return to the fold was a rather less obviously intellectual type, the producer Sol Hurok. Hurok was a Jewish immigrant from Ukraine, an extrovert character who, despite his impenetrable accent,[1] probably did more than any other single person to popularize ballet in the United States. Among his clients were pretty much all the ballerinas the lay person has ever heard of: Anna Pavlova, Margot Fonteyn, Isadora Duncan, and Martha Graham.

Where Hurok differed from other ballet promoters was in his talent for publicity. He wasn't above the occasional publicity stunt. So, in the buildup to launching *Bal Nègre*, he told the press that he had insured Katherine Dunham's legs for $1 million with Lloyds of London. Hurok was also a great believer in taking ballet to the people. *Bal Nègre* would tour for a month around the United States before opening on Broadway, for what was announced in advance as a strictly limited one-month run. And so the show opened in September 1946 in Philadelphia, and moved through New Haven, Indianapolis, and Detroit.

Eartha's own memories of the *Bal Nègre* tour center on an off-stage development: her attraction to a new member of the company, a "husky, brown-haired" white man, who was in charge of electrical engineering for the show. In her book she gives him the pseudonym Charlie, but Van Aikens remembers his real name as being Maury Yaffé—"tall, lanky, a very nice person" according to Van.

Eartha may well have been on the lookout for a new man, because she was disappointed by what was going on with Josh White. That autumn he was heading off on a long nationwide concert tour, and his support act was not Eartha Kitt but another young dancer and singer who had also appeared in *Blue Holiday*: Josephine Premice. Eartha must surely have had her nose put firmly out of joint. And if she'd had any scruples about being faithful to Josh—who was, after all, married—then this news would have put an end to them. It was unlikely that Josh would be celibate while out on the road, so perhaps Eartha now felt free to do as she pleased.

There was an immediate mutual attraction between Maury Yaffé and Eartha that soon evolved into an affair. It began while they were on tour and by the time they arrived back in New York they were, in Eartha's phrase, "deep in caviar."

Gloria Mitchell offers a rather less misty-eyed opinion: "Yes, that was Maury Yaffé. They had quite a romance. But he was married and all that stuff. He wasn't anything special that I recall: very tall, very thin. I guess he had a particular charm."

Eartha's fondness for Maury's particular charm must have provided a welcome distraction from the less than idyllic aspects of touring life for a black dance company. While on the road the Dunham Company had a constant struggle to find decent accommodation in this era of Jim Crow laws and policies. They were regularly refused admission to hotels, or sent to a floor reserved for "coloreds" only. These accommodations were always substandard and, on occasion, actually rat-infested. Depressingly, the North was generally no better than the South. As Dunham told her biographer, Joyce Aschenbrenner: "You'd think it would be better the farther north you go, but it's not true."[2]

Gloria Mitchell elaborates:

> It was difficult when it came to places to live and restaurants to eat in. There was subtle—well I guess it wasn't too subtle!—discrimination. If there was a restaurant next to a theater where we were appearing, well, the audience was happy to come see us as stars on stage, but they did not want to eat with us afterward. I remember one time we were in East St. Louis, there was a drugstore a couple of doors from the theater and I went for a cup of tea and they didn't want to serve me, so I threw the cup of tea across the counter . . .

Nevertheless, *Bal Nègre* did well on the road, and when they arrived in New York the reviews were far more positive than for *Carib Song*. "*Bal Nègre* socks over with a bang," said *Billboard*, while the *New York Times*, in a piece about Miss Dunham with a headline that posed the question, "Schoolmarm turned siren or vice versa?" concluded that "over the show as a whole, including the many parts of it that are not new, is a new dignity, an absence of sensationalism, a new taste, that certainly interferes not at all with its values as theater entertainment."

The show was a considerable hit. The company's reputation began to spread further afield as the world outside the United States, now emerging from wartime, woke up to this new American dance talent. European backers started to express an interest in taking the

Dunham Company across the Atlantic. More immediately Dunham's new friend, the tobacco heiress Doris Duke, arranged an introduction that led to the company being booked to appear in Mexico the following summer.[3]

The show helped lift Eartha's profile too. As well as dancing, she had a role as one of the three "Sans Souci Singers" who made regular contributions to the show and attracted very favorable notices. These led to a flurry of attention for Eartha personally. This came as no surprise to Gloria Mitchell:

> Kitty definitely had something that the rest of us didn't have, I'll say that. I used to tell her "you're different from us, you know." I knew she had something. I didn't know how it would manifest itself, but she was definitely different. And she had that singing style already; she had that from the get-go.

After *Bal Nègre* closed, the company had a couple of months off to rehearse before their next engagement, in Mexico. Around this time Miss Dunham started to show off her undeniably "different" protégée around fashionable Manhattan. Another company member, Julie Robinson (of whom more later), told me that she used to play the conga drum to accompany Eartha while she sang at cocktail parties. "I would get the chills," she remembered, "as Kitty had a sound no one else had."

This kind of informal exposure led to a brief profile in *Glamour* magazine, which commented that:

> Miss Kitt, after a year and a half at the Dunham School, speaks Spanish, sings in French and French Creole, understands the words and the deeper cultural import of the songs in her repertoire and has a dancer's control of her body. When she is judged ready, she will have a great deal more to offer than a pretty face and a nice body.[4]

This was followed up, in what was now the spring of 1947, by what would seem to have been a concerted effort by Eartha to launch herself as a solo act. On March 8 a picture of Eartha was syndicated to the black press with an announcement that she would be headlining at Jock's Place, one of the great old Harlem bars. A couple of weeks later there was an intriguing announcement in *Billboard* magazine. It simply said Eartha Kitt would be making her café debut at the Village Vanguard on April 7.

This is interesting for several reasons. The Village Vanguard was absolutely Josh White territory, so Eartha's appearance there suggests that, however infatuated she may have been with Maury Yaffé, her relationship with Josh was still going on. More than likely the show was booked for her by Josh's agent, Mary Chase. It also makes it clear that Eartha had ambitions for a solo career, and had some kind of a stage act, as far back as 1947, which flatly contradicts her own accounts in which she claims she only thought of becoming a solo performer on arrival in Paris, a couple of years later.

There's no record, sadly, of how her appearances at Jock's Place and the Village Vanguard went, and perhaps it's not surprising that it seems subsequently to have slipped her mind, because by the end of the month Eartha and the rest of the Dunham Company were heading abroad for the first time: to Mexico.

EIGHT

En Route to the Casbah

The train journey to Mexico City took four days. Eartha would remember it as a romantic journey, a time when she and Maury were deeply in love but attempting to keep it secret from the rest of the company.

In Mexico City they appeared at the beautiful Palacio de Bellas Artes, a turn-of-the-century building every bit as palatial as its name suggests, its interior swathed in murals by Diego Rivera. It was a wonderfully prestigious venue for the Dunham Company and they easily lived up to their surroundings, despite the fact that their first performance had to be given in a mixture of their street clothes and whatever John Pratt was able to improvise, as their costumes had been held up by customs.

Mexico offered the company a respite. Here they could stay in the best hotels and eat in the best restaurants, all a considerable contrast to their experience of touring in the United States. They appeared for four weeks in Mexico City and then Guadalajara. The original plan was that they would head on to Hollywood, where they'd been asked to appear in a new film called *Casbah*, a musical reworking of the French film, *Pépé le Moko*. But when the news came though that filming had been held back for a few months most of the company were very happy to stay on in Mexico, where they could live cheaply, rather than go back to New York. Maury, however, was one of those who decided to head back to the States. It was a heartbreaking and seemingly inexplicable decision as far as the young Eartha was concerned.

Funds were short, so Dunham rented a house called Villa Obregon for the eight girls in the company and found hotel rooms for the boys. The girls were given twenty-five dollars a week between them to live on, administered by Lucille Ellis, "the company's Mother Bee" as Eartha described her.

For all Eartha's heartbreak, life at the Villa Obregon was actually a lot of fun. The girls gave parties every Saturday, went to the bullfights on Sundays, and rehearsed all week. She got a little black dog and named it Babalu after her party piece. Maury wrote her a letter a day and eventually came back down for a visit, only to reveal the real reason for his return to New York. He had a fiancée there (actually a wife, according to Gloria) and was in agonies of indecision over whom to choose. Finally the lovers agreed to postpone the decision and to meet again in Los Angeles, when the *Casbah* job finally got under way.

Luckily financial salvation was at hand, as the Dunham dancers got a booking at Mexico City's smartest nightclub, Ciro's, that ended up running for two months. During that time Eartha struck up what she later described, with typical coyness, as "a very warm friendship" with the Mexican actor Pedro Armendáriz.

Gloria Mitchell, her roommate for much of the Mexican trip, laughs at this. "Yeah, she liked to make out she was the Virgin Mary. But she had something all right, men were crazy about her. Even the ones that you would least suspect, like Pedro Armendáriz."

Armendáriz was a major film star at the time, a kind of Mexican Clark Gable. He's now best remembered for his role as Kerim Bey in *From Russia with Love*.[1] He was another man to make a big impression on Eartha, taking her out for meals and introducing her to Mexican culture, driving her out into the countryside to see the real

Mexico, and so forth. She was particularly impressed when he took her to see a preview of his latest film, a John Steinbeck adaptation called *La Perla*. The relationship was clearly seen by both of them for what it was, a brief affair that would be over when Eartha went back to the States. After all Armendáriz was also, like Maury, like Josh, married to someone else.

Finally the call came from Hollywood. Filming on *Casbah* was ready to begin, and the company prepared for this fresh excitement stronger and more unified after their sojourn south of the border. The Eartha Kitt that made the trip to Hollywood was significantly older and wiser than the one who'd left New York.

The journey to Los Angeles took three days and on arrival the company found itself with accommodation problems again. Katherine Dunham had the loan of a house in Beverly Hills for herself, but the rest of the crew had to make their own arrangements.

Two of the dancers, Dolores Harper and Richardena Jackson, found a room in a boarding house that catered for black entertainers. Eartha moved in with them for a while, sleeping on the living room floor until the landlady took a dislike to her, ostensibly because Eartha made a mess of the bathroom.

Eartha herself put this down to one more example of black people being prejudiced against her because of the lightness of her skin. This recurrent complaint is puzzling, as she was in fact darker than many others in the company. Katherine Dunham, for instance. Yet there is no suggestion that Miss D. suffered because of her light color. Gloria Mitchell was also lighter skinned than Eartha. She finds the idea that Eartha was the victim of skin-tone discrimination most unlikely: "Well, I always found that a little strange, I mean she wasn't near white. Maybe something else was going on . . ."

Eartha found another place to stay, just down the street, and before long Miss Dunham took her to the film studios to meet the director, John Berry, along with Jesse Hawkins. Miss Dunham was hoping to get Eartha and Jesse, the company's two star singers, their own cameo in the film. The three of them sat in the director's trailer waiting for Berry to appear.

When the director arrived, preceded by his dog, Eartha was immediately and thoroughly smitten. John Berry, then thirty-one years old, was a New York Jew who'd been a child actor and a boxer before becoming a comedian and then working as an actor with Orson Welles in the Mercury Theater. In 1942 he'd appeared in Welles's production of Richard Wright's howl of African-American rage, *Native Son*. Touring that show around the United States had allowed Berry to experience what he described as "the enormous prejudice, the overpowering sense of white superiority that existed everywhere."

After working with Welles, Berry had moved to Hollywood, and *Casbah* was to be his fourth feature film. It was almost certainly Berry who asked for the Katherine Dunham Company to appear in the film, as an ostensibly North African troupe of dancers. Certainly, Berry went on to work with an array of black talent.[2]

After their initial meeting Eartha contrived accidently to leave her coat in the director's car. Sure enough Berry brought it along to the first day's shooting and that evening he took Eartha out to dinner and bought her the best steak she'd ever eaten. They continued to go out for dinner together throughout the making of *Casbah*, though keeping it quiet from the rest of the company. Typically Eartha insists that, despite the initial rush of mutual lust, he was another "perfect gentleman" at all times, content with a peck on the cheek at the end of the evening, though Gloria Mitchell remembers otherwise. "Yes, John Berry had a little thing for her. It was very hush-hush, but it did happen." Gloria also confirms that it was not only when it came to her autobiography that Eartha preferred to keep the details of her love life to herself. "No, that's how she was. As close as we were, she was not a typical girlfriend; she didn't share her secrets with anyone."

Clearly Eartha was fast discovering just how powerful her sex appeal was. Throughout her adult life she'd been able to get every man she wanted. She'd moved seamlessly up from Alex, the handsomest kid on the block, to Josh White, the handsomest black man in New York show business, to Pedro Armendáriz, a Mexican film star, and John Berry, a white Hollywood director. Her sexuality was getting her places that a young black woman in the late 1940s could never have expected to go, but she knew instinctively that to keep the momentum, discretion and secrecy were vital.

Casbah itself was a kind of musical thriller starring Tony Martin and Yvonne De Carlo and featuring a clutch of Harold Arlen songs. The rather bland Martin was Pépé le Moko, a French jewel thief hiding out in the Casbah of Algiers, while a detective played by Peter Lorre tried to lure him out. Eartha had one line to deliver; during a dance sequence she snapped her fingers in Tony Martin's face and said, "Come on Pépé." In the final cut, however, Eartha's line proved to be inaudible and Katherine Dunham overdubbed it. One might suspect that this was a further sign of burgeoning rivalry between the two women, especially as close-up shots make it obvious that Miss Dunham, who had a fair amount of screen time in her role as the barkeeper Odette, was pushing forty, while Eartha, though only visible on screen for a few seconds, glowed with all the blazing luster of youth.

Gloria Mitchell remembers the shoot itself as an unsatisfying experience:

> We had a difficult time because they didn't know what to do with us. They hired us because of Katherine, so we were dancers in the Casbah. Yet they didn't want us to be dancers, they wanted us to be waiters and waitresses. I refused to carry a tray on film. I said "I don't know how to do that!" I don't remember it being a very pleasurable experience because making movies is very boring. You think you're going to be seen and it's left on the cutting-room floor.

Away from the set, however, the Dunham Company mostly enjoyed their time in Hollywood, not least because they were earning more than ever before: 150 dollars a week each. While off duty the Dunham dancers roamed the studio lots. Edward G. Robinson and Burt Lancaster were filming *All My Sons*, Louis Jourdan and Joan Fontaine were making *Letter from an Unknown Woman*, and Deanna Durbin and Vincent Price were on the set of *Up in Central Park*. The other girls may have been swooning over the Hollywood stars, but by now Eartha had not only John Berry to deal with, but also the return of Maury.

This relationship was becoming ever more tortured. At first Eartha was determined to reject him out of hand, but after a couple of days she relented. However, it soon became clear that things had changed. In public there was none of the affection he'd shown her in Mexico. Finally, after dinner one evening, Maury explained what was going on. He was an ambitious man and he felt that if word got around that he was having a relationship with a black woman it would be bad for his career. In particular he believed it might cause people to suspect him of communist leanings (at the time this was not such an absurd notion as it might seem today, given that US Senator Joseph McCarthy was just beginning his Hollywood witch hunt). Therefore he was happy for the relationship to continue, but only on a clandestine basis—Eartha could be his mistress but never his publicly acknowledged consort.

Eartha, unsurprisingly, was terribly hurt by this all-too-revealing assessment of their relationship. She couldn't believe that Maury wasn't prepared to fight against the prejudice of the times. More than that, she was outraged by his idea of a compromise: that they should carry on seeing each other but keep it all undercover, as if he were ashamed of her.

Eartha was not prepared to put up with this. She finally ended the relationship, telling Maury that she "would not be tied down to hate." She didn't see him for another week. Then, after John Berry had dropped her off at her lodgings and kissed her goodnight, a crazily jealous Maury banged on the door then threw her to the floor when she let him in, accusing her of two-timing him—a reasonable enough claim, as it happened. They had a full-on fistfight which ended in lovemaking.

However, the reconciliation was only temporary. After filming finished the company began the new year, 1948, with a two-week booking in the Los Angeles Ciro's, and then they headed off on a tour of the northern cities with an updated version of Dunham's 1943 show *Tropical Revue*, starting in Chicago. Maury stayed in Los Angeles. The relationship was over.

This was Eartha's first experience of having a relationship effectively terminated by racism, of being told that she was welcome to be a mistress but never a wife, and it would not be the last. Perhaps it's because it was a harbinger of things to come that Eartha makes so much of this affair with Maury in her autobiography, and so little of her other early involvements with men, particularly Josh White, a crucially important figure in her life, yet one she pretends she never had a sexual relationship with.

There seem to be two possible reasons for this. One is a desire to portray herself as a good girl. As Gloria Mitchell puts it: "She liked to make out she was the Virgin Mary." This is understandable. No woman of the time wanted to be seen as promiscuous, but for black women it was particularly important—as they had all manner of racial and sexual stereotypes with which to contend.

Yet that still doesn't explain why she should admit the affair with Maury and deny the much longer involvement with Josh White. Could it be that she denied the sexual relationship with Josh White because he was black? It's possible, given that Eartha always had a predominantly white audience, and she may have been worried about alienating them. Certainly the accusation that she wanted to distance herself from her fellow black people was one that would be made again and again throughout her career. And if there's some truth to it, there are also valid reasons for it. Eartha Kitt, even at twenty years old, knew she was not prepared to settle for life as a second-class citizen. She wanted to enjoy everything the white world had to offer. If other black stars preferred to stay in a black world that was their business. Eartha was never scared of being different.

Chicago in January was a harsh place to be: freezing cold and thoroughly segregated. The company had to stay in lodgings on the South Side, miles from the theater. To make matters worse, Eartha nearly got raped on a blind date with a medical student. She was seriously contemplating going back to Hollywood and trying her luck there, when news arrived that the company had been offered a trip to Europe, starting in London.

Eartha was initially dubious, preferring the certainty of a sunny Southern California over the unknown of postwar Europe. The deciding factor was the influence of her latest boyfriend, the company's new stage manager Dale Wasserman.

Wasserman, like so many of the people in the theatrical world of the time, had his own colorful history. He grew up in Wisconsin as one of fourteen children born to Russian immigrants, was orphaned before the age of ten and then escaped the orphanage in favor of a Depression-era adolescence spent riding the rails as a hobo. He ended up in Los Angeles and eventually found a job working for Sol Hurok, which in turn brought him into contact with the Dunham Company.

Wasserman was a charismatic ladies' man who had already had affairs with several of the dancers and, unsurprisingly, soon became involved with the company's emerging starlet. It was Wasserman who persuaded Eartha that she could go to Los Angeles any time, but that this trip to Europe was a once in a lifetime deal and not to be missed. Eartha finally gave in and traveled back to New York with the rest of the company at the end of the tour. They had ten days to prepare themselves for the boat journey to England.

In New York, Eartha went to see her Aunt Mamie for the first time in a while. They had been on bad terms when Eartha left home, but had been partly reconciled when Mamie came to see her perform in *Carib Song*, and since then they had communicated by letter while Eartha was away in Mexico and California. It was a sur-prisingly warm reunion, and Eartha went to stay with Mamie up in Spanish Harlem until she left for Europe. Mamie helped her get a passport and shopped for luggage and clothes for the adventure. Finally, she revealed that she had been putting aside money for Eartha ever since she came to Harlem. It came as a profound shock to Eartha to discover that her skinflint, unfeeling aunt had always been looking to her future. At last she felt that her Aunt Mamie, whom she'd always referred to as her "mother," was truly a mother to her.

Later in life Eartha would wonder if her "Aunt" Mamie was actu-ally her real mother, and had fled to New York in shame follow-ing Eartha's birth, leaving her to be brought up by her sister. This theory had an obvious appeal. If it was Eartha's aunt rather than her mother who gave her to Aunt Rosa when she was little, then it would have been a lesser, more comprehensible, betrayal.

On the other hand, if Mamie really was Eartha's mother, then it's very hard to imagine why she didn't tell her so. They were living in Harlem, nearly a thousand miles from the gossips of South Caro-lina, so there was no reason for Mamie to fear any disapproval. So, in the absence of any really compelling evidence to the contrary, it's reasonable to conclude that Mamie was indeed Eartha's aunt, but nevertheless a surrogate mother to her.

The following day Mamie brought Eartha down to the docks to board the SS *George Washington*. Eartha introduced Mamie to the rest of the company and then they said their goodbyes. It was the last time Eartha would see the woman who'd raised her.

NINE

Foggy Days in London Town

After a week of seasickness the Dunham Company docked at Southampton, gateway to the old world. It was late spring, 1948. They took the boat train to London and were met at the station by a representative of the Prince of Wales Theater, where they would be performing. The company members were shown to their various digs around London. These were not segregated, as in the United States, but that was about all that was to be said for them. They were cold and grim, and Eartha, along with her designated roommate Julie, thought she could do better.

Julie Robinson was the newest member of the company proper, finally making the step up after some years at the school. She was the first white student at the Dunham School and now the first white member of the company. The child of artistic Jewish parents, she had grown up in Greenwich Village and had found her way to the Dunham Company through her interest in modern dance.[1]

She would go on to marry Harry Belafonte, but at the time she met Eartha, however, Julie had another illustrious boyfriend, a young actor who was to become even more famous than Belafonte, and went by the name of Marlon Brando.[2]

Having Julie assigned as her roommate was a stroke of luck for Eartha. Julie was more a woman of the world than the other dancers, and was able to secure the two of them an apartment in Manchester Square, a grand address next to the Wallace Collection museum and near the high-end department store Selfridges. However, they soon realized that a fancy address still didn't mean that it was warm, as Julie recalls: "In the apartment it was so damp and so cold I slept on the floor by the heater, you had to put a shilling in, and I had to keep turning around in the night like I was roasting myself!"[3]

Eartha remembered this as an exciting time: the two of them setting up housekeeping and negotiating the rationing system, with its limits on the meat, eggs, cheese, milk, and sugar, etc., that you could buy. Gradually they learned to supplement their rations by making black market connections or by getting food parcels sent from home. Clothing, too, was rationed, which came as something of a shock to the fashion-conscious Dunham dancers. Nylons were another commodity that had to be sent from America. Postwar Britain was in a seriously enfeebled state.

London did have nightlife though, if you knew where to look for it. And the Dunhams certainly did. As Julie says, "In the company, you know, we really lived life! So, very often, after a rehearsal or whatever we'd go out dancing."

And there was nowhere better go out dancing in London after the war than Soho's Caribbean Club, just off the busy thoroughfare Piccadilly, well within walking distance of the Manchester Square apartment. One of its old habitués, the veteran jazzman Kenny Gordon, told me about the mix of people you got there: "Showbiz people, society people, an interesting mix. Sidney Poitier came down when he was filming *Cry, the Beloved Country*. So did Canada Lee, people like that."[4]

The quality of the house band, a fine jazz trio, ensured the Caribbean's popularity, not only with visiting black stars but also London society folk. Its atmosphere is well captured in Stanley Jackson's *An*

Indiscreet Guide to Soho, written a year or so before the Dunham Company arrived:

The Caribbean is on the second floor of a building that seems crowded with little drinking clubs of one kind or another. You ring the bell and a shutter-window slides open to reveal a dark cropped head. If you are a member you are admitted; otherwise you are politely but firmly turned away. There is no touting for custom. They already have three thousand members.

As soon as you walk in you're conscious of something vital in the atmosphere. The bars are crowded with people, mostly whites, who are laughing and joking. The whites are pretty mixed, as you might expect. A little shopgirl with a silk dress clamped over her buttocks is drinking whisky . . . with a ferrety little man who looks like a warned-off jockey and wears pointed shoes, a diamond ring and a pearl in his over-gay tie, he keeps one hand in his pocket like George Raft in a gangster film. Two officers with fair Guardee mustaches and Sandhurst voices are discussing the new Rattigan play with two young women who look very Kensington Gore. A couple of black American sergeants chew big cigars and gulp down gin at an alarming rate while they try to flirt with the pretty colored barmaid. Two colored RAF pilots, one wearing the DFC and bar, come in and order pints of bitter. They become involved in an argument but it's not over the golden-brown Creole who's giving them the business with her eyes. You discover they are discussing Ibsen! Nothing surprises you here.

The dance floor is dimly lit, the floor tiny and surrounded by check-clothed tables. The three-piece band is pulsing with joy and freedom. Even Eton and Kensington Gore have taken fire and are wriggling and jiving in a way they'd never do at the Dorchester.[5]

This was the world the Katherine Dunham Company had landed in; one in which West Indians and their culture were still seen, in these days before mass immigration, as enlivening rather than threatening. And London was a war-weary city ready and waiting for a production as vital as the Dunhams' *A Caribbean Rhapsody* (basically a revamped version of *Bal Nègre*) to make its debut on the West End stage.

The show opened on June 3, 1948, and duly received rave reviews, including this one from *The Times*, which is worth quoting in full to further understand just why the show caught on so fast and so emphatically:

> From rhythm in the raw to hot rhythm, with dances sung by negroes to white man's words of Spanish, French, and English, *A Caribbean Rhapsody* proceeds with the art of the music-hall, high-pressure American production and real musical feeling to present a show which is more than revue and different from ballet.
>
> Miss Katherine Dunham, with Mr. Vanoye Aikens as her principal partner and a highly efficient company in support, makes good her claim to present ideas, customs, and dances which came to the West Indies from Africa at once authentically and artistically. Behind all the arts of entertainment there is a solid core of knowledge and, better still, sympathetic understanding of cultural anthropology; in consequence the art does not violate the authenticity. No doubt African drummers drum even more elaborate counterpoints of rhythm than were heard over and above the crude, monotonous, maddening beats which produced dramatic tension in the theater, but there was plenty of rhythmic subtlety as well as primitive persistence in *La Comparsa*. Then again *L'Agya* was not a folk tale but a mime play of Miss Dunham's own contriving, but no pundit of folklore would complain of outrage to his science in this powerful sketch.
>
> The third part of the program was lighter, but it too had its basis of sociology—for dancing is a social phenomenon and no performing musicians are so enthusiastic for history as the practitioners of jazz. And so we had passed before us a survey in sequence of Ragtime, Tango and Turkey-trot, Charleston, Blackbottom, and those gay exuberances that prove the world once to have been a gayer place than it is now. No wonder Miss Dunham called this turn "Nostalgia" and the audience welcomed it with the sentimental rapture of happy memory.[6]

Eartha was now clearly one of the stars; featuring as one of the Sans Souci singers, performing a duet with Jesse Hawkins, and taking a major part in the showstopping *Shango* routine.

Sadly there's no film footage available of the *A Caribbean Rhapsody* show as performed in 1948, but there is a book of evocative photos, taken by Roger Wood. Also Pathé News did film the company on their next visit to London, without Eartha, in 1952. The clip shows them performing *Shango* and, even without Miss Kitt, it's still stunning to watch. The Dunham Company in full flow offered an effortless demonstration of Afrocentric culture, two decades ahead of their time.

As the *Times* review suggests, *A Caribbean Rhapsody* was remarkable in that it was a success both commercially and artistically. It worked for the regular theatergoer expecting a showbiz revue, and for the serous balletomane. This was something the *Observer* picked up on, in a wildly enthusiastic profile:

> Miss Dunham's success has been acclaimed on all sides, from the *Daily Express* to the highbrows of classical dance. The former calls her show "the fastest and most colorful London has seen for many years" and has booked it for an Albert Hall festivity. While one of the latter remarked that her barefoot company made classical dancers seem like waxwork figures; and another compared the impact of her company's visit to the arrival of Diaghilev's ballet in the year 1908.[7]

It's significant, though, that the *Observer* profile was of Miss Dunham alone, rather than of the company as a whole. The journalist commented that:

> The extraordinary fact about this diverse and brilliant show is that it is entirely the work of one person. A "star" who is capable of more than executing her own part is rare: one who can write produce and direct the work of a whole company and do so with

originality—without ever using clichés—must be something of a genius.[8]

This is telling because it pointed to an ever-wider divide in the company between its "genius" leader and the rest. Miss D. and Mr. P. had their own place in London during the show's triumphant five-month run and became café society darlings. Miss Dunham was invited to give a lecture to the Royal Anthropological Society. She duly came up with an intriguing subject: on the theme of "The Occurrence of Cults among 'Deprived' (i.e. traditionless) Peoples." London saw Miss D. flying high.

Meanwhile the Dunham troops were living in rather less high-falutin style. They were enjoying the nightlife but, in Eartha's case at least, also wondering whether they were expected simply to bask in Miss Dunham's reflected glory. Eartha was starting to challenge Miss D.'s hitherto undisputed starring role in the company. Their incipient rivalry came to something of a head when the company had a royal visitor to the show.

Beforehand Miss Dunham had agonized as to whether or not, as a proud American, she should curtsey to a British royal. Eartha was impressed by the elegant compromise Dunham came up with, waiting till she was facing the royal box, then nodding her head in time with the drums, so that her minimal act of deference was barely distinguishable from the rest of the dance.

Next came Eartha's own spot in the limelight, and she was determined to outdo her mentor. In a clear act of defiance to the queenly Miss D., she began by customizing her outfit. Instead of having a bandanna covering her hair, as usual, she pinned it to one side. When Miss D. didn't complain about this small liberty, Eartha was emboldened to try out a scene-stealing move at the end of the *Shango* routine. She stood on the shoulders of two of the male dancers, then dived to the floor and slithered from one end of the stage to the other.[9]

This seemingly simple act, as delivered by the young Eartha was, according to all those who saw it, absolutely hypnotic. One of her contemporaries, the singer and actress Annie Ross, told me that she still remembers it vividly over sixty years later: "She did a slow walk in just a kind of short sheath, just from stage left to stage right. She moved very slowly, just to drums, and she was mesmerizing. It was fantastic and yet she didn't do anything!"

Sure enough, this kind of talent wasn't going to go unnoticed for long, and nor was Eartha the kind of person who was happy to play second fiddle. She had already given solo shows in New York and by the end of the run at the Prince of Wales she was openly weighing up her options.

The American tap dancer and later choreographer (most famously for the Motown groups of the sixties) Cholly Atkins was in London that summer, touring the provinces with his dancing partner Charles "Honi" Coles. It was a miserable tour, tap-dancing on unsuitable music hall stages (on one occasion right after a donkey act had left the stage liberally dotted with their leavings). Whenever possible the pair hightailed it back to London and hung out with the Dunham dancers:

> Their company manager had rented a big house right there in the city for the whole cast. Most of the black theatrical people in London were in contact with one another and that house became our main hangout. Since Dunham and her husband, John Pratt, were housed in a different place, we didn't see much of them, but we became pretty close to several people in the cast, especially Eartha Kitt, one of the chorus kids. She had a spot in the show where she hit a high C while doing a cartwheel— broke up the house every time! Eartha was thinking of leaving the company at that time. So she had long conversations with us about pursuing a solo career.

Word of this obviously got to Miss Dunham, as in the company archive there is a signed note from Eartha confirming that "With reference to the forthcoming Continental season, I understand and give my assurance that I can accept no engagement other than with your company."

Miss Dunham may have staved off Eartha's departure for the time being, but the company's emerging starlet still wasn't exactly a happy camper, and certainly not always a happy roommate, as Julie remembers:

> She was a rather temperamental person: she could faint at a moment's notice to draw attention. Sometimes in the early morning I'd hear doors slamming. Wham! Wham! I'd just wait and then when her fit was over I'd hear her start humming to herself, so then I'd go out and say "Good morning!" And start the day.

Her increasingly difficult behavior was starting to alienate the rest of the company. Julie again:

> Kitty was her own worst enemy and there were a lot of older members of the company who did not like her. I was kind of in-between because I found her very interesting, and I knew her from before so I had a little history with her. Also by that time I had a few years of therapy myself! So I remained her roommate.

Julie is at pains not to be too damning of the young Eartha; the two remained close right up until Eartha's death and she was able to see that her friend's erratic behavior was more to do with her insecurity than anything else. She also admired Eartha's intelligence and her eagerness to learn: "Kitty always had a quest for knowledge, a very sincere one. My parents would send me the Sunday [*New York*] *Times* and she'd always say, 'When you get through with the paper, can I have it?'"

Self-education was Eartha's new obsession. She had recently become an avid reader and would remain one for the rest of her life. Hers was a genuine, if sometimes naïve, quest for knowledge. In the early years of her fame hardly an interview would go by without her telling the reporter about all the improving texts she had been reading.

This thirst for learning had started in Hollywood when she found herself surrounded by people who would be discussing the state of the world—Stalin and Roosevelt and the emergent Cold War—when all she felt qualified to talk about was the latest fashions or dance styles. "I was constantly amazed at myself because I had not taught my mind to think enough of me to read the proper books, or think there was any more to a newspaper than Dick Tracy and Little Orphan Annie."

Maury, for all his other faults, had played an important part in encouraging her to start reading seriously. He had recommended books for her, and when there was something she didn't understand, they were close enough for her to be able to admit her ignorance and ask him to explain matters.

Eartha Kitt at twenty-one was something of an intellectual sponge. She soaked up London culture and visited all the great historical sites. Not that her life was all self-improvement: like the rest of the company she dated her share of Englishmen—and of course, according to her, they were all perfect gents. However, the notion that all the relations between the Dunham dancers and their English beaux were courtly in nature is refuted by one of their number. She didn't want to be named but disclosed the fact that several of the girls had to make the acquaintance of a London society abortionist during their stay.

By the time the run at the Prince of Wales came to an end, the company had already secured its next major booking, at the Théâtre de Paris. Eartha was off to the city that was to act as her finishing school.

TEN

Springtime in Paris

Julie's mother, a much-traveled painter, had recently been in Paris and she recommended a place to stay to her daughter. This was the little Hôtel les Acacias, just off the Champs-Élysées, and close by Maurice Chevalier's nightclub of the same name. Julie and Eartha booked a room there and their fellow dancers, Othella Strozier and Richardena Jackson, decided to follow suit, taking the room next door.

For their first evening in Paris the four girls decided to go out and explore and, sure enough, starting as they meant to continue, they ended up being bought dinner and plied with champagne by a wealthy American and his bodyguard. All was not quite as auspicious as it seemed, however, as the American turned out to be a Chicago gangster lying low. Similarly, the young women who congregated around the hotel's bar turned out to be there for business rather than pleasure, as Julie remembers: "Oh yes, we stayed in Les Acacias and of course the prostitutes became our best friends."

The girls' friendship with the prostitutes swiftly led to them being embroiled in a brief French farce, as they got caught up in a police raid on the hotel. The French press, already fascinated by the arrival of this much-heralded new dance troupe, got wind of the story and sent photographers down to the theater to take pictures of them at rehearsal. As Eartha recalls, "Our rehearsal clothing being scant, not revealing but scanty, it was just what the cameramen wanted. We were posed this way and that." Miss Dunham was less than impressed by the subsequent photo spreads in the paper and lectured Eartha and the others on the need "to protect ourselves from vulgarity."

This was a lesson that Eartha clearly took to heart. Whatever might go in her private life, from this point on she was always very careful to appear as respectable as possible in the press.

A few days later the show was due to open at the Théâtre de Paris. Miss Dunham decided to make the opening night something special. To that end the lobby was decorated along a jungle theme and a stage was set up to provide pre-show entertainment for the audience. She asked Eartha, as the company's singing star, to perform a few songs. The rest of the company was in no doubt that this was a sign of Eartha's new status within the outfit; as Van Aikens remembers: "Miss Dunham really recognized her talent by that point, so when we first opened in Paris at the Théâtre de, Kitty was placed in the lobby on opening night to sing."

The evening was a triumph, as Eartha recalled: "If we never danced before, we did that night in Paris." The audience was enraptured and the show ran for three months of sold-out houses. News of the triumph swiftly made it back to New York, as *Billboard*'s Paris stringer contributed a rave review:

> Katherine Dunham and her company have captivated Paris. This producer-choreographer-director-star has earned unequivocal praise from press and public . . . An evening with this company is a unique experience and French audiences are packing a 1,300-seat theater every night to prove it.[1]

Paris had long had a lure for African-Americans, both for its own sake and as a place to escape from the racism of the United States.

It's a tradition that goes back at least as far as the nineteenth century when the slave-turned-abolitionist Frederick Douglass arrived and commented that he was "enjoying what the wisest and best of the world have bestowed for the wisest and the best to enjoy."

It was during the interwar period, however, that black Americans came to Paris in numbers, and in some cases to stay. Among these pioneers was the celebrated club owner Ada "Bricktop" Smith, a woman who, so legend has it, F. Scott Fitzgerald and Cole Porter fought over.[2] But the most famous of the interwar arrivals was the singer-dancer Josephine Baker who arrived in 1925 to appear at the Théâtre des Champs-Élysées. Her frankly erotic, if dubiously "exotic," routines were an immediate hit and she decided to stay. She became the star of the Folies Bergère and muse to any number of writers and artists, among them Ernest Hemingway, who called her "the most sensational woman anyone ever saw." During the war she worked for the French Resistance and subsequently received the Croix de Guerre from Charles de Gaulle.

Baker was still in Paris in 1949 and had been looking forward to Dunham's arrival, having heard much about this woman who was offering a more scholarly, less populist, take on black dance than that which had been so successful for her. She showed no jealousy toward her younger rival. Instead, as Dunham dancer Tommy Gomez remembered, "She came backstage to Dunham's dressing room to see her after the show, with Chevalier, Marais, Cocteau and Mistinguett; and she congratulated the whole company . . . The next day there was a handwritten note from Baker saying how wonderful the show was and thanking every member of the company."

Maurice Chevalier, the actor Jean Marais, the polymath Jean Cocteau and the actress Mistinguett—this was pretty swanky company to be keeping. Just as she'd conquered London, Katherine Dunham was now all over Paris society. And, again, taken seriously as an intellectual: her university thesis on Haitian dance was picked up by a French publisher and issued with a preface by Claude Lévi-Strauss.

As well as hosting black American entertainers, postwar Paris was used to providing a haven for black intellectuals and writers. Richard Wright, of *Native Son* fame, arrived in 1947 and wrote in his journal, "How calm I've felt here in Paris! No more of that tension that grips so hard . . . I walk down a street and feel my legs swinging free." Wright's young rival James Baldwin arrived the following year, just in advance of the Dunhams, later commenting that "It wasn't so much a matter of choosing France—it was a matter of getting out of America."

There was no shortage of places to go for the nighthawks of the Dunham Company. There was Chez Honey, a club-cum-gallery near Montparnasse, where Kenny Clarke and Duke Ellington played, and Lena Horne and the Peters Sisters sang. You could get fried chicken and jazz at Chez Inez, near the Sorbonne, recently opened by the singer and former secretary to Duke Ellington, Inez Cavanaugh. Chez Inez was the favored hangout of American expats like Terry Southern, George Plimpton and Orson Welles. Or there was La Rose Rouge which opened in 1948 on the left bank and was run by African dancer Feral Benga and Greek-Ethiopian Nikos Papadakis.

In May 1949, just as the Dunhams were coming to the end of their run, the first Paris International Jazz Festival took place. Among the American contingent, brought in by promoters Charles Delaunay and Eddie Barclay, were Charlie Parker and a young Miles Davis, who later remembered that: "Early in 1949, Tadd [Dameron] and I took a group to Paris, France, and played opposite Bird, just like we had done at the Royal Roost. This was my first trip out of the country and it changed the way I looked at things forever. I loved being in Paris and loved the way I was treated."[3]

As for Eartha, the delights of Paris were coming thick and fast, as men queued up to shower favors on her. She did her best to act as if she were unimpressed, later describing just what a drag it was to be wakened each morning by gifts of perfume, flowers, and champagne, or just the offer of a date for lunch. However, she also had to confess that she didn't turn many of these invitations down: "I didn't want to Miss anything."

There are two versions of Eartha at war in this remembrance: the young American who doesn't want to Miss anything and the Continental sophisticate who affects nothing but boredom in the face of more champagne, more perfume. One suspects that at the time Eartha was more the former than the latter. Nonetheless the blasé pose would soon become the basis of her stage act.

It was clearly a head-turning time to be a beautiful young black woman in Paris. That same spring of 1949, a would-be actress called Dorothea Towles arrived in Paris and was taken up as a model by Christian Dior and Elsa Schiaparelli. She was the first black woman to appear on the Parisian catwalks. "If you're beautiful, they don't care what color you are," she said later. "I got invited out all the time, I was the only black model in Europe and I just thought I was an international person."[4]

The company embarked on a tour of Europe, but on their return Eartha's thoughts were again turning toward a solo career. She'd made friends with an expat American piano player and singer called Hugh Shannon who was playing at Bricktop's new café as well as an expat joint called the Mars Club. Eartha had been playing some impromptu spots there, with Shannon backing her, and now he was quietly looking out for opportunities for her. This despite the fact that Eartha had signed the contract promising not to take on any outside work.

This wasn't the only respect in which she was skating on thin ice with regard to Katherine Dunham. While in Paris Miss D. was being paid court by the famed playboy, diplomat and racing driver Porfirio Rubirosa.[5] Rubirosa had been married to an old friend of Miss D.'s, Doris Duke, who was said to be the richest woman in the world. She had inherited a tobacco fortune when she was twelve, and devoted much of her time to her twin passions for modern dance and jazz. She and Rubirosa had recently divorced, and as part of the settlement Rubirosa had been given a house in Paris. Exactly what his relationship with Miss Dunham was, it's hard to be certain, but in the course of his visits to see the Dunham Company during their new season, Rubirosa's eye was caught by Eartha Kitt.

He invited her to dinner at Maxim's. Eartha briefly considered the likelihood that Miss D. would be monumentally put out by this and accepted anyway. Even before their dinner Rubirosa bought Eartha a couture dress and string of pearls. And yes, afterward, according to her, he behaved like a perfect gentleman. She later claimed that he "thought I was too young," which given that she was by now a pretty worldly twenty-two year old seems unlikely.

Still, having got away with encroaching on Miss Dunham's territory, Eartha was clearly emboldened to make her move for further independence. She accepted her first nightclub booking for a solo show. This was at a fashionable place called Carroll's. Hugh Shannon had brokered the deal. Carroll's resident Cuban vocalist was leaving and they needed a replacement. Frede Baule, who ran Carroll's, was already aware of Eartha. She was a great Parisian clubland character: an elegantly mannish lesbian, who was rumored to have been Marlene Dietrich's lover. Frede certainly made a strong impression on Eartha, who was fascinated by her look, her tight bob, and tailored suit.

Frede was just as keen on Eartha and offered her a job on the spot. And as for the matter of her being under contract to the Dunhams, Frede went on to say that she was happy for Eartha to continue to perform with the Dunhams, then come over to Carroll's to give a late-night solo show. With this in mind Eartha went to see Miss D. just before the evening's show. Miss Dunham said she would have to take it up with the show's producer, the impresario Fernand Lumbroso.

After the first act Eartha was ushered in to meet Lumbroso. He explained how much he and his agency had done for the Dunham Company. Indeed they were about to book a South American tour for them. Hearing this, Eartha was initially repentant. Then, however, Lumbroso's tone changed. He became more threatening as he told her that "If you dare accept a job in any part of this country, other than with this company, you will not be able to obtain a working permit and I shall have you deported."

Eartha did not take kindly to being bullied. She left the meeting and wrote out a brief note which is still filed with Katherine

Dunham's papers. It simply says, "Miss Dunham. You have my two weeks' notice as of November 9th 1949. Eartha Kitt."

After the show Miss Dunham assembled the company together and announced that Eartha was leaving and would be replaced immediately. Van Aikens remembers it well: "Miss Dunham always said that if you find another job, you have to leave the company. So, when Kitty got the job with Frede, we were all called on stage to receive the news. It wasn't so much of a surprise, we'd heard a rumor that Kitty had already had a dress made for her."

ELEVEN

Paris is Always Paris

Both women were upset by their parting. Two days later, Katherine Dunham wrote the following to her lawyer, Lee Moselle, in New York:

> Due to another casualty in the company—Eartha Kitt has abandoned us for Paris night life . . .—I am expecting Frances Taylor[1] to get in touch with you. I have offered to pay half of her plane fare over as we feel that we should have her over here immediately. We have already been negotiating with her, but I felt that it was to replace Othella Strozier—who has married[2]—but this new development with Eartha Kitt means that I will have to have her right away.
>
> For a long time I have tried to put the company on an honor system and test their confidence in me. In the case of Eartha Kitt it did not work out as she is here under a labor permit for M. Lumbroso . . . He has every intention of giving her some trouble but of course these things are very unpleasant and I prefer simply to withdraw from it . . . The whole thing is against my principles and a little insulting to me personally in view of the many unnecessary protections that I give the company, but I see there is nothing to do about it.[3]

Years later, talking to her first biographer, Ruth Beckford, Miss Dunham was able to take a more considered view of the situation:

> It was a very awkward time in Paris when Eartha Kitt left. I was extremely upset because I thought she could at least have completed our season. But now, reflecting on it, I realize it was her time to go. She had seen London and Paris and, in observing me, knew what being a star was like. She was also aware of her own talent as a dancer. Her acting talent was something that was noticed later, but certainly her mime talent, her dance, and much of her vocal talent had been put before the public—at least in the beginning—by us. She had really become a featured part of the company, so it was very difficult for us to have her leave with practically no notice.[4]

For her part, Eartha was shaken by being cast out into the cold. She had expected to have two weeks' notice to work out; time to plan her solo show. Instead she was suddenly on her own. She asked Hugh Shannon what to do and he took her back to see Frede. Frede took the situation in hand. She advanced Eartha enough money to have a new dress made and said she could start as soon she wanted to, for 10,000 francs a night—nearly three times as much as she had been getting with the Dunham Company.

In three days' time Eartha was ready to go. She rehearsed a short set of mostly Cuban material with the band, and she had a new dress: a strapless white silk number with a large pink rose. It was customized on opening night by Frede, who decided it was altogether too chaste, and ripped the seam so that it was split to midthigh.

Despite Eartha's first-night nerves, her opening set was a great success, especially the final number which featured one of her Spanish Harlem moves, a hip-shaking dance with a Cuban twist, the hip movements getting smaller and smaller, more and more intense, until she broke the spell with a shrug of the shoulder. Then the spotlight immediately blacked out and the audience erupted in applause.[5]

It's a number that was captured on film for a French-Italian co-production called *Parigi e Sempre Parigi*, in which a collection of visiting Italians tours Paris, falling in and out of love and visiting plenty of nightspots along the way. One of these nightclub scenes features the young Eartha, and watching it, it's clear to see why she was such an immediate hit. Her singing, in Spanish, is fine, but her dancing, a mix of Dunham technique and her own Spanish Harlem moves, is downright incendiary.

Eartha stayed at Carroll's for three months, through the winter of 1949–50. Word soon got around that she was something special. Orson Welles, who was in Paris to talk about putting on a new theatrical extravaganza, came to see her twice. Another regular visitor to her show was that winter's other great café society sensation, the chanteuse Juliette Gréco who was performing at nearby club, Le Boeuf sur le Toit. As she remembered:

> Well, you know, there were such interesting people. There was this young girl, Eartha Kitt, she sang so beautifully, and there was this young man who was so in love with her, a very handsome boy called Marlon Brando. He lived in the same part of St. Germain des Prés as me, and he often gave me a lift home on his bicycle.

It may be that Ms. Gréco had confused Eartha with Julie Robinson as the object of Marlon Brando's affections. But there was certainly no shortage of eager suitors to be found for Eartha. Chief among them was a rich young Californian called Bayeux Baker, who met her one night at her regular after-hours watering hole, the Café de Paris. The next morning he threw pebbles at her hotel window until she came down to let him in, and so began one of her happiest love affairs.

It was during this time, on January 31, 1950, to be precise, that Eartha went into a recording studio for the first time. The session was produced by Charles Delaunay and saw Eartha backed by local jazz musicians on bass and piano plus the expat American trumpet player Doc Cheatham. They cut four standards, including Cole

Porter's "What Is this Thing Called Love?" and Duke Ellington's "Solitude." However, they weren't released at the time and you can hear why. Eartha sings nicely enough, and there are glimpses of her potential as a song stylist, but overall the tracks sound tentative, with the young Eartha still not sure whether she should sound like a conventional jazz singer or just be herself.

This pleasant period in Paris came to an end on February 26th, 1950. One night Carroll's impresario, Eddy Marouani, sought Eartha out and gave her a message from America. Her aunt was very ill. She should call Mrs. Wayde at once. Eartha made the call only to find out that Mamie had died six days earlier. Mrs. Wayde said she would get money from Mamie's life insurance and send Eartha a ticket home. A few days later the ticket duly arrived.

On the day of Eartha's departure there was an impromptu send-off party. As a result she was uncharacteristically drunk on champagne and blackberry brandy by the time she arrived at the airport, and proceeded to fall asleep on the plane. She came to briefly as the plane stopped in Newfoundland, before coming back to full consciousness on arrival in New York where two of the Wayde children, now grown up, were waiting for her. They took her back to her old apartment where Mrs. Wayde explained what had happened. Mamie had died during an operation to remove a stomach tumor. She had indeed left Eartha some money, but first the funeral expenses would have to be paid. The funeral itself, according to Mamie's wishes, was to take place back down South, at St. Peter's Church, just outside North.

The next day Eartha went to see a lawyer, who told her that she had been left the remarkable sum of ten thousand dollars. However, and somewhat to Eartha's displeasure, the funeral would cost some two thousand dollars. She went from the lawyers to the funeral home, settled the expenses, and made arrangements for the body to be shipped down South and the funeral to take place a few days hence. Then she called an old friend and lover, the man she felt she could rely on in her time of need: Josh White. He was delighted to hear from her after a long separation and the following day she went downtown to meet him. A couple of days after that she took the train down South, accompanying the coffin. It was the first time she had been back to South Carolina since she had left fifteen years before.

Eartha did not enjoy her return to the South. When she arrived at the station in Orangeburg she failed to recognize any of the waiting friends and family. And when they introduced themselves she scarcely acknowledged them. She had worked hard to make herself into Eartha Kitt, star of the Parisian cabaret, and she had no intention of being dragged back into the land of King Cotton.

She was taken in a rattletrap old car to a relative's house, down a track through a cottonfield, past the creek, and into a field where stood what she described as a "shambly shack," before adding, "the scene was so miserable it was funny." Eartha slept that night in the shack and helped out with breakfast in the morning, all the while painfully aware of the gulf between her life and that of her kinfolk, who no longer understood her accent.

Later that morning she went into town and bought new clothes and a month's supply of food for her relatives, who praised her generosity, telling her she was just like Mamie, who, it transpired, had also made regular charitable visits back home. The family washed in a tin basin and dressed for the funeral, Eartha in a black suit from Paris. And then just to confirm that she was now a big shot, a brand-new Oldsmobile drove up. Inside was Josh White, no less.

Josh had promised Eartha he would come to the funeral and he'd delivered, driving seven hundred miles from New York, further clear evidence of how close their relationship really was. Together, they headed to the church. The service only reinforced Eartha's feeling of alienation from this world that she'd left behind. Her aunt might have been close to this community, but she was not.

Toward the end of the funeral Josh White came forward to sing a spiritual, but, to the horror of the congregation, he accompanied himself on the guitar, which they considered the instrument of sin (perhaps with some justification in Josh's case). So the congregation steadfastly refused to join in. For Eartha this chimed perfectly with her own sense of isolation. The woman who had brought her up was dead, and the people she came from were strangers to her. And, of course, she had recently made the break from her mentor and role model, Miss Dunham.

Josh and Eartha left the church together, got into his Oldsmobile and drove back to New York, where she would rejoin her new life. It would be several decades before she could bring herself to return to South Carolina.

TWELVE

Helen of Troy

Back in New York Eartha considered her options. Rather than return to Paris, she decided to stay there for the moment, with a view to trying her luck in the clubs. She moved back in with the one last maternal figure available to her, Roxie Foster's mother, and did her best to sort out Mamie's affairs. Assorted friends and relations clamored for financial recognition for the help they swore they'd given Mamie over the years and, rather than argue, Eartha paid them off. Katherine Dunham, meanwhile, sent her a kind note of condolence, showing that she, at least, was over the initial bitterness of the split.

Eartha got back in touch with Josh's manager, a former actress called Mary Chase, who had been representing her, on and off, for several years. Chase secured Eartha a booking at the Blue Angel, Herbert Jacoby's decidedly swanky nightclub on 55th Street. She was initially booked for a tryout on a Saturday night, with a further run to follow if she passed muster.

At the last moment, however, Eartha decided to cancel her show at the Blue Angel and booked herself a boat ticket back to Europe. She wasn't ready yet to risk rejection at the hands of her home town.

She may also have been influenced by the fact that Josh White was about to head over to Europe for an extended tour.

Back in Paris she booked into the smart Hôtel Gallia, just off the Champs-Élysées, and phoned her friends to let them know she was back. One of them, Jesse Hawkins, her fellow singer-dancer from the Dunham Company, told her that Orson Welles had been asking after her. He was about to open a new show at the Théâtre Edouard VII and wanted Eartha to audition.

Eartha refused to believe this at first, but consented to meet Jesse at Chez Inez for a meal. No sooner had they arrived than the proprietor, the singer Inez Cavanaugh, confirmed Jesse's story. Orson Welles was indeed looking for her. They agreed that Eartha should go down to the theater the following day.

This was a wonderfully exciting prospect. In the summer of 1950 Orson Welles was just thirty-five years old, but had already had a remarkable career. He'd grown up in a wealthy but troubled family in Chicago, made his theatrical debut at the Gate Theater in Dublin at age sixteen, and had a huge hit with his Mercury Theater company in his early twenties (most notably with the famous panic-causing radio adaptation of *War of the Worlds*). He'd made his film debut as the star, cowriter, and director of the then controversial and now classic *Citizen Kane* in 1941, age twenty-six, and had gone on to make a series of further movies in Hollywood and a Broadway adaptation of *Around the World in Eighty Days*, featuring songs by Cole Porter. In 1948 he'd headed to Europe, horrified by what he saw as the philistinism of the American movie world.

In Europe he'd had his biggest popular success to date with his appearance in *The Third Man*, but had spent the last year or so working on a more troublesome project, a largely self-financed film of Shakespeare's *Othello*. This featured Welles himself as Othello, his old Irish actor friend from the Gate Theater, Micheál Mac Liammóir, as Iago, and a young French-Canadian actress named Suzanne Cloutier as Desdemona.

Othello had been a huge strain to make—at one point Welles had resorted literally to throwing himself at the feet of the movie producer Darryl Zanuck to beg for funding—and most of the actors had yet to be paid. So, as something of a relaxation (and a way of generating some quick cash), he had decided to debut two short plays at a theater in Paris and then tour them around Europe. The project would be relatively low-key and a chance to focus simply on acting for a change. At least that was the idea.

The two plays were an anti-Hollywood satirical squib called *The Unthinking Lobster*, with Suzanne Cloutier starring opposite Welles, and an extremely loose adaptation of Christopher Marlowe's *Dr. Faustus*, titled *Time Runs*. This would feature Orson again, plus Hilton Edwards (Mac Liammóir's partner in both life and work) in the role of Mephistopheles. Duke Ellington had agreed to provide the music. The play also required an actress to play the part of Helen of Troy, a timeless embodiment of female beauty. Welles had trouble deciding whom to cast for this part. He'd tentatively offered it to several different actresses before he had the notion of asking the young woman he'd seen dance with Katherine Dunham and perform in cabaret at Carroll's club: Eartha Kitt. He'd done his best to get hold of Eartha, but had been told she was still in New York. So he'd found another potential Helen instead, the Anglo-American singer and actress Annie Ross.[1]

But Orson was a capricious employer and when Eartha showed up at the theater he decided that she was after all his perfect Helen of Troy. She was in and Annie Ross was out. Annie duly received the bad news:

> I realized I hadn't been given a rehearsal call, so I rang the theater a couple of days later. This voice said "I'm his secretary." I said, "Can you tell me when my call is?" and he said, "Mr. Welles last night rewrote the whole play and he's cast somebody else," so I said "Oh what a drag." I was really disappointed. And that person turned out to be Eartha.[2]

Not only did Eartha have the part, but it was now a rather bigger one than originally planned. Orson rewrote the play overnight, prompted by his enthusiasm for his new Helen. As he told his biographer: "Eartha Kitt was obviously a star. You could tell that."

Rehearsals were to start the following day, a Tuesday. According to Eartha, the show was due to open the following Saturday. However, an examination of Micheál Mac Liammóir's published diary suggests this to be an exaggeration. His entry of May 28 reveals that Eartha had already been cast and the opening night was not until June 19. So there was probably something closer to a month's preparation. Meanwhile there was scenery to be painted and costumes to be sewn. Some of this Eartha was used to, thanks to her time with the Dunhams, but the acting was a whole new challenge for her. Orson Welles recognized this and would stay late at the theater with her, helping her with her lines.

Mac Liammóir's diary offers a vivid picture of *Time Runs'* genesis:

[*Time Runs*] is based on the legend of Dr. Faustus . . . it is as strangely moving in its way as one expects from Orson; it also has a dark malevolent glitter that causes the flesh to creep. The stage is populated by actors in the role of students of the Jean-Paul Sartre order conducting brisk debate on damnation with a young colored girl (her name is Eartha Kitt, discovered by Hilton and Orson in some nightclub in the rue du Colisée, a tiny, curious, bitterly-smiling fascinating creature), who at given moments flashes an electric torch on the audience as she sings in a husky amber voice about Satan, Hell and Eternal Damnation (swing). Music, however, not yet written, so at present Eartha K strings notes together herself, often with lovely haphazard effect. Who's going to write it?[3]

The answer to this last question was meant to be Duke Ellington, who had met Welles in 1941 and was currently touring Europe. Unfortunately the demands of touring meant that Ellington himself was unable to devote much time to the project. However he was able to send his regular cowriter, the wonderfully talented Billy Strayhorn, to Paris. Strayhorn was happy about this, as his long-term lover Aaron Bridgers had recently moved to the city and just been hired as the pianist at Eartha's favorite hangout, the Mars Club. Strayhorn was given four Orson Welles song titles (though no actual lyrics) to work with: "Me Is the Trouble," "Zing, Zing," "In the Dungeon of Guilt" and "Song of the Fool."

Close to showtime Welles still hadn't written any lyrics and was considering cutting the songs altogether. At one point he sent Hilton Edwards to Stockholm to meet Ellington and ask for a number of pieces of incidental music. Nothing appears to have come of that mission however, at least not for the show.[4] Instead Welles went out with Strayhorn to the Café de la Paix and over several drinks came up with the odd, haunting words for "Me Is the Trouble" (words surely inspired by his enigmatic new star): *"Hungry little trouble, bound in a bubble, yearning to be, be or be free/All that you see, is all about me/Hungry me."* Strayhorn gave them a mournful blues setting and hoped for the best.

Meanwhile Welles was rehearsing the show in his own inimitable fashion. Mac Liammóir continues:

> Rehearsals never begin until two or three (or thereabouts) in the afternoon: they then work on till past midnight, frequently till two or three (or thereabouts) in the morning, and then Orson gazes triumphantly on the actors now stretched motionless on the floor, says, "Gosh! They look tired! Come on, Hilton!" and then the Night Life begins. Did this myself for two nights and then went on strike. Champagne was endlessly guzzled among inane inferno of noise in one dimly glittering haunt after another, and the sun rose high in the heavens as we staggered back to our hotel in the Boulevard Montparnasse with hours of work to face on the following day.[5]

Eartha's own account offers a rather less jaundiced view of proceedings. For her, this whole time was like being at some extraordinary finishing school. She had been yearning after culture, busily educating herself, and now she was in the company of the absolute titan of self-education. She worshipped Orson and Hilton Edwards and loved being part of the cast of writers and artists they would carouse with at the Mars Club or Bricktop's. They would eat huge meals and the men would discuss Plato or Camus and get up from the table to declaim speeches from Shakespeare. For her part Eartha was content to keep quiet and learn. Indeed she later suspected that it was her rapt silence, rather than anything she actually said, that Welles took as the sign of a keen intelligence and prompted him to call her "the most exciting woman in the world."[6]

As for the late, late nights, these were heaven too. Eartha and Orson would walk together through Paris, and watch the sun come up over the Champs-Élysées, as they finally headed back to Eartha's hotel.

It's easy to speculate as to what would quite likely have happened next, especially given Welles's reputation for womanizing, but according to Eartha, he was (oh yes!) a perfect gentleman. "He would take me to my door, ring the bell and say, '*A demain*.'" It's safe to say, though, that all those who were involved in the play took it for granted that Eartha and Orson were having an affair. It's a shame that her urge to appear respectable prevented her from giving a more honest and intimate account of another pivotal relationship with a genuinely remarkable man.

Work on the play carried on right up until opening night on June 15. *The Unthinking Lobster* played first, followed by an intermission. Then the curtain came up on a dark stage. Three girls wearing street clothes, slacks and shirts or a sweater, wandered out of the audience, discussing which of them would be playing Helen of Troy in the school play. The three girls are an unknown called Rosalind Murray, the underused black American actress Tommie Moore (who was in her early thirties then, but always looked remarkably young), and Eartha herself. Eartha shone a flashlight around the stage and let it light on an apparent statue of Faust—actually an immobile Orson. Two of the girls left and Mephistopheles appeared. Eartha sang "Me Is the Trouble" for the first time. Eventually Faust anointed girl three, Eartha, as Helen of Troy, the most beautiful woman in the world. He took her in her arms and said, "Is this the face that launched a thousand ships?

Helen, make me immortal with a kiss," and then kissed her hard. And so on. Eartha sang "Me Is the Trouble" a couple more times and the play ended with her leaving a ticking box on the stage, the ticking growing ever louder till the curtain came down.

Critical responses to this odd theatrical evening were mixed. No one much liked *The Unthinking Lobster*, but *Time Runs* intrigued people, and Eartha positively bewitched them. It was soon clear who the real star of the show was—and it wasn't the big man.

If reviews were mixed, audiences were positively meager. Still, *Time Runs* ran for more than a month with Welles ceaselessly tweaking the show in the hope of attracting a bigger audience. Mac Liammóir was dispatched to London to see about a run there, but by the time he got back Welles had changed his mind again. They would go to Germany next. Meanwhile he was busy finding ways to avoid being upstaged by his young protégée. On occasion, Eartha told Welles's biographer, he would simply station himself in front of her so that her words seemed to be coming from his body.

Relations between star and protégée were further strained a couple of weeks into the run, when Josh White showed up in town, taking some time out after a brief US government-sponsored European tour in the unlikely company of Eleanor Roosevelt. Whatever may have been going on between Eartha and Orson, the presence of Josh White threatened to put an end to it, and Orson was none too happy. He made his move on stage, one night when Josh was in the audience. Eartha immediately sensed that something was up, that Orson wanted to show Josh who was boss. Suddenly her casting as Helen of Troy was all too appropriate.

The tension built as the play wore on. Both Orson and Josh were accustomed to being the focus of attention: the man the women all gravitated toward. Neither was used to having any serious competition. But that was exactly what was happening here. Josh was in the front row waiting for Eartha, and Eartha was on stage with Orson. And Josh would certainly have known Orson's reputation; they'd both moved in the same liberal circles in New York.

Finally the play drew to its climax: the moment at which Orson was going to kiss Eartha, but this time Orson didn't just kiss her, he sank his teeth into her lip and bit her hard, so they both tasted her blood in their mouths.

Eartha was a pro. She didn't let out even a whimper. She didn't want Josh fighting Orson. But she was, of course, outraged. After the final curtain she rushed up to Orson, punched his chest and kicked him. It was all to little effect, given the difference in their sizes. Finally she asked him what he was playing at. "Oh, I was just in that mood," he told her, and walked off.

Eartha got changed and went to meet Josh at a nearby café. When he saw her swollen mouth he asked what had happened. Eartha tried to pass it off as an accident and said she'd tripped and fallen. But then Josh overheard one of the other actresses relaying the rumor that Orson had bitten Eartha and he jumped up from the table and ran around to the theater, arriving just as Orson was getting into his car.

Orson had his driver speed the wrong way down a one-way street to get away from the enraged Josh. He might have been physically bigger than Josh, but he wasn't about to take on a man who'd spent his childhood leading blind blues singers around the juke joints of the South.

Over the following days Eartha stuck to her accident story, but Josh didn't believe her and, for the rest of his time in Paris, she kept away from Orson's dressing room and gave him orders to keep away from hers. Then she accepted a late-night booking at Carroll's, so after each night's performance she went off to sing and left Orson to his own devices, for the time being at least.

At the beginning of July, Josh headed back to London where he was starting to make quite a name for himself, but he promised to come back to Paris as soon as he could. By then plans were starting in earnest for the German tour. This was now to be billed as *An Evening with Orson Welles*. *The Unthinking Lobster* was out, *Time Runs* was in, but was to be entirely rewritten for the German audience. Eartha would still be Helen and Orson would still be Faust, but Mephistopheles would now be Mac Liammóir ("should obviously be the other way round," he noted in his diary, referring to his and Orson's parts, "or is Type-Casting definitely thing of the past?"). Hilton Edwards would now be the director.

At some point Mac Liammóir must have queried Eartha's role as he records the following response from Welles: "Helen of Troy has got to be colored; no, dearest Micheál, no, please don't ask 'why' with that apparently intelligent but in fact totally moronic expression on your face; it is obvious to anyone why Helen of Troy was colored. You'll be asking me next why the horse was wooden, Goddammit!"

The other girls, however, were cut from the cast. The only other members of the touring party would be what Orson referred to as "The Mob." This was a compact mob consisting of three people: Sandy Matlovsky, the musical director, and two actors, Lee Zimmer and Janet Wolfe. Wolfe, who was to be Eartha's roommate for the tour, was memorably described by Mac Liammóir:

> A thin, nervous, small-boned, powerfully-built, wiry, jumpy, young woman with brown, fiercely curling hair, an inquisitively snubbed nose a wide, tragic generous mouth . . . and greenish-blue eyes full of a secretive astonishment like two oysters whose shells, just having opened, are seeing for the first time what sort of world confronts them. Really extremely attractive, yet she alternatively staggers and bounces through life under the fixed impression that she is the world's ugliest woman and is despised and rejected by men.[7]

Apart from *Time Runs*, the show was initially slated to include a condensed version of *The Importance of Being Earnest*, followed by Orson lecturing on "Life today, yesterday and tomorrow." (Mac Liammóir commented "'Tis Hilton's idea: personally think it will be bloody awful.") The evening would finish with a Shakespearean extract. There would also be a brief performance of songs by Eartha. Mac Liammóir again:

> She has extraordinary talent and extensive repertoire, which includes gay and mournful trifles with rather pessimistic titles such as "Lonely and Blue," "Warum bin ich geboren?," "Nobody Wants you when you're Down and Out," and a more hopeful one in Spanish called "Yo quiero bailar con todos los hombres" (this, surely, more the spirit?).

It's evident from this account that Eartha had grown enormously as a solo artist over the previous months, both in terms of her performance and her ambition. The musical sophistication she'd learned from Josh White had melded with the controlled sexuality and starry demeanor she'd learned from Katherine Dunham, plus the intellectual reach and ambition she'd seen in Orson Welles.

By July 27 the run at the Théâtre Edouard VII had come to an end. Orson was ill in bed but still making plans for the German tour. Orson's latest idea, much to Mac Liammóir's horror, was to perform a selection of conjuring tricks. "Orson, are you out of your mind?" he asked. "Of course I am, didn't you know?" replied the great magician.

With Orson laid up, rehearsals carried on rather more smoothly than normal, give or take some displays of artistic temperament from their ramshackle revue's new star. Mac Liammóir again:

> Eartha has moments of rebelliousness during which she coils and uncoils like a young resentful snake audibly hissing, but these are only moments and are due to the fact that her fiancé is in Paris and naturally enough Eartha wants to be with him all the time. But Hilton who admires and loves her very much, can quench her with the blanket of a smile or a frown as he thinks best, and the fire-serpent is changed in a twinkling back to a child.[8]

It is reasonable to assume that the "fiancé" Mac Liammóir refers to was Josh White, who'd taken time out of his British engagements at the end of July to pay a trip to Paris. He cannot have been actually engaged to her, as he was still married to Carol, his wife and the mother of his children, but it's possible that he was at this stage proposing to divorce Carol and marry Eartha.

Why didn't it happen? The reason, in the short term at least, was probably simple enough. When Josh returned to London from his Parisian idyll with Eartha, he received a panic-stricken phone call from Mary Chase. A McCarthyite newsletter had identified Josh as a communist, which was potentially disastrous for his career. He had to come back to the United States immediately and deal with this new crisis.[9] Eartha, meanwhile, was off to Germany.

THIRTEEN

C'est Si Bon

The German adventure began in Frankfurt. The Welles troupe had made it there in a series of cars laden down with cases of Nuits-St.-Georges and champagne because their French producer was convinced that postwar Germany would be a barren wasteland with none of the essential creature comforts. In fact the new Germany, firmly under Allied control, was by now well stocked with clothes and provisions.

On arrival in Frankfurt they discovered they would be performing at a theater in the woods outside the city, a venue more commonly used for circuses and the like. Which was not entirely inappropriate, as it happened.

Mac Liammóir was concerned on arrival to discover that their advance man had plastered the city with posters claiming that Orson Welles ("*Die dritte Mann Personlich!*") would be performing Goethe's *Faust*. Given that Frankfurt was Goethe's hometown, and this was very much Welles's personal take on Faust, Mac Liammóir anticipated disaster even though Orson did his best to explain matters at a preshow press conference.

Sure enough, much of the audience on opening night arrived clutching bilingual editions of Goethe's *Faust*, hoping to follow the play. Instead they looked at each other in bafflement as the latest Welles version began with Eartha and Mac Liammóir wandering on to the pitch-black stage, turning flashlights on and off from time to time, and singing a kind of spooky madrigal: "*Hallelujah, fool ya/ Doodle-de-doo!/Pay close attention/This could happen to you-hoo.*" Goethe this was not.

However, by the time Eartha launched into her second song, "Me Is the Trouble," the audience realized that they were watching something very different from the original and started to relax. As it turned out, they enjoyed *The Importance of Being Earnest* and the *Henry VI* extract, they loved Eartha's song recital, and they absolutely adored Orson's magic show. And so it was clear that, bizarre as it might be, and high art though it mostly wasn't, Welles's company did after all have a show.

Orson's assistant in his conjuring act was Janet Wolfe. Wolfe, by then in her early thirties, provided comic relief both on and off stage, telling tales of her ever more unlikely misfortunes. Typically, her bags had been confiscated at the German border after an incident which had culminated in her throwing them one by one at the customs officer. After-show parties were regularly enlivened by her drunk act, which would be provoked by the merest sip of a drink.

By the time the tour made its way across Germany to Berlin, via Hamburg, Munich, and Dusseldorf, it was clear that the purpose of the trip was for Orson to kick back a bit and enjoy himself. This was never more apparent than at his press conferences. In Munich he threatened to hang the next journalist who asked about *The Third Man*. In Berlin there is a wonderfully eloquent photo of Orson addressing the assembled press, a big man in a dark suit and striped tie, his right hand making a fist, his mouth wide and smiling, clearly caught midanecdote. Eartha stands next to him, wearing a demure but stylish dress buttoned almost to the neck, with a big coat worn over the top as if she has just come off the street on a cold day.

She is giving Orson a sidelong look with the expression of someone who can't stop herself from smiling though she knows it's somewhat against her better judgment. In fact the press had just asked him if he planned to return to Hollywood. "I am not planning to die," he replies, "but both are inevitable—and equally horrible."

After Berlin the troupe headed back to Paris and then off to Brussels for a last hurrah. This was the end of the Orson Welles adventure, an occasion for mixed emotions.

Back in Paris Eartha was laid up for a month suffering from menstrual hemorrhaging, a complaint that would recur a few times over the years. She was looked after by Bayeux Baker, her on-off boyfriend. Meanwhile the exotic Frede was promising Eartha a lucrative booking at her new venture, a classic club called Le Perroquet which was being refurbished. The opening was put back repeatedly so Eartha was broke again by the time opening night finally came around. Thankfully it was a triumph: Le Perroquet was packed, and with a gratifyingly high celebrity factor. Among the audience was Orson Welles's ex-wife, Rita Hayworth, and another of the great playboys of the era, Prince Aly Khan.

Eartha had prepared a new set for the occasion, working with the club's Cuban bandleader and her friend Hugh Shannon. It featured a mix of the Latin material she'd started out with, plus the jazz standards she'd added for her last run at Carroll's, and the more cosmopolitan material she'd been performing with Orson. One completely new addition to her set was a French song, a catchy number called "C'est Si Bon." It was written by Maurice Chevalier's pianist Henri Betti, with lyrics by André Hornez, and had been a hit in France for the great Yves Montand. The song had been translated into English in 1949 and this thoroughly asinine version had been recorded by everyone from the very bland Johnny Desmond to the ineffable Louis Armstrong.

Whether Eartha was familiar with the English translation or not, she wisely chose to stick with the original French lyrics with their fluent celebration of the simple joys of life and love, punctuated by backing vocals declaring "C'est Si Bon!"

When she first performed it on stage, however, she got halfway through the song and forgot the words, so she improvised instead. Adopting the character of a gold-digging sophisticate, she turned the song from a hymn to the simple joys into a request for the expensive joys. It was delivered with cartoonish sexiness as she told the listener that "*Je cherche un millionaire/Avec un grand . . . Cadillac car*," etc.

And this was the eureka moment, the point at which Eartha Kitt went from being an intriguing possibility—a Harlem girl who could dance up a storm while singing anything from Josh White folk blues to Cuban novelties to German melodrama—to a fully-fledged artist: one who could do all the above but imbue the whole range of material with a single indelible personality. It was the moment Eartha Kitt became "Eartha Kitt," the sophisticated sex kitten who seemed to come from everywhere and nowhere. From now on it was evident to anyone who saw her perform that Eartha was a star, it was just a matter of waiting for the world to wake up to this fact.

"C'est Si Bon" became Eartha's signature song. It would be one of the first numbers she recorded when she finally got a recording contract a couple of years later, and she would sing it almost every time she gave a concert for the rest of her life.

Eartha stayed in Paris till the end of the year, moving from Le Perroquet back to Carroll's after a while. Her reputation was spreading in international nightclub circles and offers of work were coming in from far and wide. She considered going back to New York at this point, but decided she was still not quite ready. Instead she accepted a series of European bookings: she would go to London first, then, for the hell of it rather than any likely career advancement, she would go to Istanbul. Meanwhile Bayeux headed back to America after telling her, in what was starting to become a familiar refrain, that he would love to marry her, but his family would never stand for it.

In the case of Bayeux himself, this was not that big a deal, but a pattern was being set. The men Eartha fell hardest for from now on were mostly men like Bayeux: young white men from well-established, wealthy families, eligible bachelors, if you like. In the words of one of her most famous songs, she was looking for "an old-fashioned millionaire." It would be easy to stereotype this as simple gold-digging, but in fact her motivation seems to have been rather more complex than that. Eartha wasn't so much after these men for their money—though she was as partial as the next girl to a diamond necklace—as for the absolute respectability and security they represented.

Perhaps her ambition was less to marry into money than into a family that could offer her all the things her own childhood had so utterly lacked—and there were not a lot of black millionaires from old-money families to be found. There were successful black men in her world, of course, and they could buy her diamond rings too, but they hardly represented security. Eartha had already been in show business long enough to know that. Security was what she really wanted, and in the fifties the white world had a monopoly on it. She might have more in common with a fellow black artist than with a rich young WASP, but was that really enough?[1]

Meanwhile, however, Eartha was becoming all too well aware of the inconvenient truth that while there were plenty of rich young men who liked her, their families tended to be markedly less enthusiastic. And for all Eartha's ambitions to find herself the right white husband, she was still far more involved with Josh White than she cared to admit.

Eartha arrived in London on January 5, 1951, after a two-year absence from the city. The last time she'd been in Britain she was just another member of the Katherine Dunham Company. This time she was front-page news. Clearly Churchill's Club, where she was scheduled to be performing, had an excellent PR person, because Britain's biggest circulation daily newspaper, the *Daily Mirror*, had a picture of this new cabaret star on its front page. It was captioned "Eartha—Star of the Savage Songs." The piece continued:

> Colored Cabaret star Eartha Kitt, 22, who arrived in London yesterday, has come here to sing "some of the world's most barbaric songs." Eartha

will put on her brand of barbarity at a London nightclub. To soften the blow she says she will wear the very latest in sophisticated Paris gowns. Eartha was "discovered" by Orson Welles, who said she was his "feminine ideal." He took her on a tour of Continental night clubs and everywhere they went she stopped the show with her savage songs.[2]

This talk of savage songs and barbarity sees another central element of the "Eartha Kitt" act being put into place. "Savage" and "barbaric" would soon translate into "feline" and "exotic"—the crucial thing being the stress on her difference from the norm. In a world where popular female singers were supposed to be demure, there had to be some explanation for Eartha's evident lack of modesty, and that explanation was her mysterious otherness. And this was something she was happy to play up to for the press: to discuss her "barbarity" or, more gently and with less obviously racist overtones, her "feline" nature.

Two weeks later she was the subject of a very brief interview in Britain's leading music magazine of the time, *Melody Maker*. Here, for once, it's only Eartha's music that is of interest. And it's clear that serious music lovers saw her first and foremost as a protégée of Josh White, who had become enormously popular in Britain over the past year. The piece was headlined "Josh White Taught her the Blues," and Eartha is quoted as saying that she is interested in New Orleans jazz, jazz on a Cuban theme, and all real Cuban music, "and American folksong, particularly when Josh White sings it."

A few years later Bruce Brace, the promoter responsible for booking Eartha, reminisced about her stint at Churchill's:

> She was with me for a month. Fantastically good some nights. Diabolically bad others. Couldn't care less. Would turn round, frown and mutter at the band. My star at that time was Josh White. I was paying Josh White £300 a week. Josh said to me, "That girl's good. She'll go far," But I couldn't see it. She wanted me to be her manager, run her career. I could

have signed her up for 25 percent commission, anything. But being an agent wasn't my line of country. My job was running nightclubs.[3]

Churchill's Club on Bond Street, fronted by the flamboyant and luxuriantly mustachioed Harry Meadows, was London most sophisticated nightspot of the time: all white banquettes, champagne, and celebrity visitors. It had a resident Latin band, elaborately costumed dancing girls, and an array of supporting attractions including the likes of Ella May Wong, the famous contortionist, and Joan Rhodes, "the mighty mannequin," who would rip London phone directories in half.

The singer with the resident band at the time of Eartha's engagement at Churchill's was a black Londoner called Lauretta Boston, whose career stretched back to the 1920s when she made her debut, age nine, singing at a temperance rally in her native Paddington, billed as "the little colored nightingale." She loved working at Churchill's, not least because of the clientele, a who's who of the entertainment world of the time: musicians from Frank Sinatra to Louis Armstrong, actors from Elizabeth Taylor to Errol Flynn, who would sit in with the band, playing the bongos. Eartha Kitt, however, was rather less convivial than Mr. Flynn. She might not have been a household name, but she already seemed very sure of herself. "She just came in, did her show and left, didn't talk to us at all," Lauretta told me, "but stars have to be a bit like that, a bit aloof."

Eartha's own recollections of her run at Churchill's confirm this impression: "That audience consisted of royalty and important figures. I met and made friends with quite a few. One was a Maharajah who invited me to his establishment one night for late tea." The girl from South Carolina via Harlem was getting used to the high life.

While in London Eartha made her first attempt at gaining a recording contract. According to Francis King of the *Sunday Telegraph*, she was introduced to a British record label and recorded versions of "Love for Sale" and Josh White's faux folk number, "The Cherry Song," in their studios. However the label's A&R men were bemused by her unorthodox style and declined to take matters further. It seems odd that she didn't record "C'est Si Bon." Perhaps she had yet to understand her own strengths.

After her sojourn in London Eartha headed to Istanbul. When she arrived at the hotel she was thrilled to find that her old friends the Nicholas Brothers were staying there too. The Nicholas Brothers, Fayard and Harold, were the greatest of all the midcentury African-American dance acts.[4]

Istanbul was another very new experience. Eartha liked the museums and the culture, but understandably disliked the fact that she was unable to go out alone without being pawed over. The night-club shows, at a brand-new joint called the Kervansaray, in the city's emerging business district, went well. She stayed for two months and, during her run, began to add some Turkish songs to her set. Her ability to sing in different languages was becoming another cornerstone of the Eartha Kitt act.

One Turkish number in particular was an immediate hit. "Uska Dara" is a typically saucy trifle, based on a Turkish folk song called "Kâtibim," about a woman traveling to Üsküdar with her male secretary. Musically it's a brash but effective East-meets-West number, no doubt the product of Eartha working with a Turkish band whose knowledge of American music was fairly approximate. So, out of necessity rather than design, she came up with a pioneering piece of what we would now call world music. As with "C'est Si Bon," Eartha personalized the song with a stream of asides delivered in sex-kitten character—"Oh those Turks!"—and thus it was that "Uska Dara" became a regular feature of her live set for years to come.

After Istanbul Eartha headed to Athens and arrived back in Paris sometime in the late summer. She made plans to return to the States in late November. In between times she went back to London for a run at Churchill's in early October.

At the same time Josh White was coming and going between America and Europe, and between London and France. A lot of his time that year—from January to April and from September to December—was spent in the UK, capitalizing on his success of the year before, and getting away from the America and its politics. And whenever possible he hooked up with Eartha. One man who witnessed Eartha and Josh's relationship at close quarters was the radio producer, Charles Chilton.

Chilton was the producer and presenter of any number of classic programs from Britain's golden age of radio.[5] He met Josh White after the war and before long they collaborated on *Walk Together Chillun*, a radio program devoted to spirituals. This they followed up with a show called *Glory Road*, featuring a wider range of songs. It stretched to two series; one recorded during Josh's spring visit and the second in the autumn. While they were preparing the second series in late 1951, Josh persuaded Charles that they should look across the Channel for more contributors. Charles was happy to go along with the plan: "We went over to Paris to record the great number of American jazz artists who were there at the time, some of them very famous. These were people who wouldn't just do anything for anybody, but Josh used to persuade them to do it."[6]

Once in Paris and ensconced in a hotel, it soon became clear to Charles that Josh had an ulterior motive for visiting the city:

> It was during that time I first met Eartha Kitt. Because the minute we got to Paris he sought her out. She'd been his mistress for some time and so it was a reconciliation for those two. Josh asked me if I could move out of the hotel room we were sharing so she could move in! Then, of course, Josh said why don't we use her in his show? So when Josh came back to London Eartha came with us; that was when I used her on the BBC.

The Eartha Kitt that Charles met may not have had any hit records yet, but she was already an imposing presence, with a strong sense of her own status. This haughty manner of hers rubbed a lot of people up the wrong way, but Charles takes a more sympathetic view:

She wanted to be treated like a star, she was making a great effort to be treated well because all her life she'd been treated badly. She was looking for comfort and Josh gave her plenty. She already seemed successful to me, as my view of her was through Josh White's eyes. Josh White was obviously in love with her, but he had a wife in the States and he had two children . . . He had dozens of girlfriends, women fell for him, hook, line and sinker, but Eartha was his special one.

Musically, too, he could see the links between Eartha and Josh: "Eartha sought out sophistication, she didn't really want to be thought to have anything to do with folk music: that was the 'nigger music,' she wanted to be a lady. Josh was maybe a bit more naïve: he felt like that too but he didn't go about it in the same way."

Back in London to do some recordings, Josh's complex love life once again came to the fore. He was involved with an English woman called Rene Dannen, and so had some serious juggling to do. By this stage, however, Eartha was clearly used to Josh's way of carrying on and, besides, she was hardly waiting faithfully for Josh to come back to her, as Charles remembers:

Oh yes, Josh was off here and there, but Eartha was involved with someone as well when she was in Paris, some rich industrialist. She was very well off at the time—not her money of course! As I say we recorded in Paris and then when she came to London I used her again. She already had this distinctive, rather odd style. And I would have to go to her hotel to talk to her now and again, and she'd say come up to my room and she'd be in bed with this girl, someone who worked for Mary Chase.

This was not as surprising as it might appear. Showbiz circles of the period were easygoing when it came to flouting sexual norms. The world of jazz and blues was even more so; its stars being beyond the social pale in the first place. The out-and-proud Gladys Bentley sang in the Harlem juke joints of the Prohibition era, and her contemporaries like Bessie Smith, Ma Rainey, and even straitlaced Ethel Waters, all had lesbian dalliances. As the Harlem Renaissance painter, Richard Bruce Nugent, put it: "You just did what you wanted to do. Nobody was in the closet. There wasn't any closets."

Katherine Dunham, in many ways Eartha's role model, was well known to have had affairs with women. So, too, was the new black star whose success Eartha aspired to: Lena Horne. But where Eartha differed from Horne was that there was no obvious gap between her onstage and offstage sexual persona. Horne played it straight on stage, but Eartha gave the clear impression that she was ready for anything, that any conventional norms were of absolutely no interest. More than any other performer of her time, once on stage she was not "straight" or "gay," just omnivorously sexual. Whether dancing with the Dunhams or singing in nightclubs, no matter how sophisticated the material she was delivering, Eartha had never lost the direct nothing-to-lose sexuality she'd learned on the streets of Spanish Harlem. It was that element of the untamed, the farouche, that marked her out from her cabaret peers.

While this made her a captivating performer it inevitably led to complications in her personal life. There was evidently an extremely tangled set of relationships between Eartha, her lover Josh, their joint manager Mary Chase ("very hard" according to Charles Chilton), and Mary's assistant. It was a mixing up of personal and public lives that was never likely to work out well.

Eartha didn't stay long in London. "I don't think she liked England much," says Charles Chilton. Instead, she went back to Paris, saw a little more of her Belgian steel magnate boyfriend Michel De Merbes, and then decided that she was ready to return to New York, where Mary Chase had a booking ready for her in early December. She decided to sail on the RMS *Queen Elizabeth*. The only question that remained was whether fifties America would be ready for her.

PART TWO

America's Mistress

FOURTEEN

Monotonous

On arrival in New York Eartha went back to stay with Roxie Foster and her mother, who were both happy to see her. Her opening at La Vie en Rose, a nightclub on East 54th Street, was set. Roxie helped make her some new gowns, and meanwhile Eartha worked with the club's owner, Monte Proser, on her show. Proser, who also launched the Copacabana, was something of a nightclub visionary, and he had his own ideas as to how to present this new attraction. He encouraged Eartha to sing in all seven of the languages she knew. Meanwhile, the choreographer insisted she self-consciously up the raunch factor with his constant refrain, "Be sexy, Kitty, be sexy."

What the choreographer failed to understand was that Eartha's version of sexy was entirely her own creation, not a set of mannerisms. Indeed "Eartha Kitt" was entirely her own creation. She had influences all right—like Josh White and Katherine Dunham—but she didn't, and never would have, any kind of Svengali directing her career. Eartha never really had a manager: she trusted no one but herself to make decisions about her career.[1] This was mostly a good thing, but it didn't make her life easy, especially in these early stages when she was coming up against American showbiz for the first time, with its conventions as to what did or didn't work on stage.

By the time opening night came along Eartha was terrified, and not sure whether she was doing what she wanted or what Monte Proser wanted.

Eartha's main memory of what followed is of a blonde eating at a ringside table and looking at her in increasing disbelief as she ran through songs in English, French, Turkish, and then German, after which she turned to her friends and said, "Now really, what is that? An educated nigger?"

From then on Eartha was convinced that she was a disaster— "I knew I was a flop before I went into my last song"—and goes on in her books to detail the humiliation she felt after the show: the few words of reassurance from the friends who dared to come backstage and so forth. Not to mention the terrible reviews she claims to have received in the press.

Actually, while her run at the La Vie en Rose wasn't a commercial success, as the uptown audience certainly didn't get her at first sight, the reviews really weren't that bad. Both the main trade papers, *Billboard* and *Variety*, reviewed the show and they were far from damning. *Variety*'s review was, however, thoroughly patronizing:

> Miss Kitt seems to have plenty of confidence but she lacks pace and needs to be sharply routined. Her voice is good enough without being socko. It might be a good novelty for her to stay within the milieu of French song repertory, since she could conceivably build a rep along novelty lines . . . One number, "C'est Si Bon," in which she casually tosses off some asides, indicates that she has a light touch and can work up a French chantoosey idea . . .[2]

It may well be that such faint praise hurt Eartha more than outright criticism. As she told the *News Chronicle*, she could understand that people might not like her—that was true to her whole experience of life—but the notion that they might find her merely ordinary was unbearable. The *Billboard* review, however, should have cheered her, as Bill Smith gave her a firm thumbs-up:

> This spot has found a real talent in Eartha Kitt, a pretty American Negro gal, ex-Katherine Dunham, who acquired her rep singing in Paris. Miss Kitt is a dramatic song seller reminiscent of the Edith Piaf school. Showing an ease and assurance, she went through French, German, Afro-Cuban, Spanish, English and even Turkish songs with a strange intensity which kept the overflowing room spellbound.
>
> On some numbers she leans against the stage frame, on others she gets the audience with French singing questions, directing them via a pair of intensely dramatic eyes and graceful arms and hands. That few people here could understand the language didn't dampen the enthusiasm . . . Miss Kitt is a class act capable of working any intimate room where Jim Crow doesn't exist.[3]

This review finished, however, by informing readers that Miss Kitt had had an accident a few days later and cabaret regular Thelma Carpenter was filling in. Eartha's accident involved her tripping over and injuring her jaw. To her it seemed a merciful release, and provided a convenient excuse for all concerned to bring her run at the club to a swift end.

Thus it was that a week before Christmas Eartha was out of work and in a tricky situation. She was outstaying her welcome at Roxie Foster's, but didn't have the money to go anywhere else. Mary Chase wasn't having any luck finding her any more work (her contacts were presumably limited as her only client of any real note was Josh White). However, she could see that Eartha had potential and was smart enough to ask for help. So she called Virginia Wicks.

Virginia Wicks worked with virtually all the big stars of the mainstream jazz world—bandleaders like Benny Goodman and Artie Shaw, singers like Ella Fitzgerald and Nat King Cole. It was she who discovered Harry Belafonte. Her relationship with Eartha was remarkably close, at times more like that between a mother

and daughter than between a publicist and client, even though
Virginia was only five years older than Eartha. She told me how
they met:

> A woman called Mary Chase, who I did not know, called me and said
> she was representing somebody that she thought deserved publicity.
> This somebody had been appearing in Europe with Orson Welles but
> she wasn't working now. I said "Ask her to come round," so Eartha did
> and I was fascinated by her: her looks, her attitude, how different she
> was from anyone else. I was handling the best singer—Ella—and I didn't
> know how Eartha could sing or anything, at that stage, but she told me a
> bit about her past and Orson Welles and Katherine Dunham and I took
> her on immediately because she was so interesting.
>
> She had no money, she was living with a cousin or something like
> that in a black section of New York, and I got the feeling she was
> hungry, and so the first thing I did was get her fed. Back then if you
> did radio interviews in the morning, they gave you breakfast. So we
> went to this restaurant, Sardi's—that was the traditional place where
> show people went to eat after the shows and read the reviews—and
> she ate up a good breakfast and then they interviewed her on the
> radio station.
>
> Afterward I called the people at the Village Vanguard and they
> agreed to try her out. She was such an interesting personality and
> singer, not like anyone else, such a very, very strong personality. So
> they took her.
>
> La Vie en Rose had let her go, they didn't understand her. The only
> people who did were Artie Shaw and Judy Garland, of all people. They
> came in one night and they thought she was terrific, but the rest of the
> people were like "huh?" They didn't get it but the Vanguard did—that
> was the start and then it all began to happen.[4]

In fact Max Gordon at the Village Vanguard remembered Eartha
from her brief appearance there five years earlier ("Max liked what
he heard and especially I guess what he saw of Eartha," recalled his
wife Lorraine in her memoir). Here, back in Greenwich Village, in

a club that had long supported Josh White, she felt among friends and able to be herself. She reverted, more or less, to the set that had served her well in Paris and London, one that still had strong traces of Josh White's influence. There was the folk song "If I Had a Ribbon Bow" and, as her closing number, a spiritual closely associated with Josh, "I'm Gonna Live the Life I Sing About, Down in My Soul."

Eartha opened at the Village Vanguard on February 25, two hungry months after the La Vie en Rose fiasco. She took over there from another of Virginia's clients, a fledgling Harry Belafonte, an artist whose career would crisscross with Eartha's over the years, and who later became the husband of her friend and fellow dancer, Julie Robinson. Eartha and Harry, though, were never destined to be close, according to Virginia Wicks: "They didn't get along, both with their separate egos."

Eartha was an immediate hit at the Village Vanguard. Her initial two-week run eventually stretched to ten. Word began to spread of this exotic new chanteuse in town. The week she opened, Dorothy Kilgallen's syndicated column was tipping this "sultry singer"—"an import from Paree"—as "tops in town." By mid-March the doyen of gossip columnists Walter Winchell was taking note of her, also announcing that she was soon to marry one of her old Parisian boyfriends, "Belgian Steel King Michel De Merbes."

Another visitor to the Village Vanguard was the veteran Broadway producer Leonard Sillman. He was best known for his series of *New Faces* revues which went back as far as the thirties. His last couple of theatrical ventures, however, had been spectacular flops. Sillman was a determined fellow though, and given that the *New Faces* format had been converted into a successful radio show, he was determined to try it on Broadway one more time. The format was simple: find a dozen or so talented unknowns and put them together in a revue-style show.

Sillman's initial idea had been to recruit talent from abroad. To that end he'd toured the cabaret joints of Europe during 1950 and while he'd narrowly missed out on signing up an English unknown called Audrey Hepburn, he had been very struck by Eartha Kitt, as he recalled in his memoirs:

> In Paris I had been hearing sharply divided opinions on Orson Welles' production of *Dr. Faustus*. I wanted to see it but could find nobody willing to go with me, so I went alone, a practice I abhor, and was prepared therefore to spend a miserable evening. I was not disappointed. *Time Runs*, which was the title Welles gave his adaptation, turned out to be a pretentious piece of fakery. Its one redeeming feature was a wisp of a colored girl who played Helen of Troy. I fell wildly in love with her and sent a mash note backstage to ask if she'd be interested in coming to America to appear in the next *New Faces*.
>
> I got no answer from the lady with the unlikely name of "Eartha Kitt" during the rest of my sojourn in Europe, so I gave her up for dead, or discourteous, or just plain dumb, but when I got back to America there was a letter waiting for me. Eartha had written to say she was interested in my offer—and that's how it all started.[5]

In the intervening period Sillman had assembled the bare bones of a show. In particular, he'd found an actor, comedian, singer and writer called Ronny Graham to anchor the show. The excellent Art Siegel was to write the music and Sillman's sister, the equally excellent June Carroll, the lyrics. The four of them—Sillman and Graham plus the songwriters Siegel and Carroll—were the show's brain trust and audition panel. Sillman took them to the Village Vanguard to see this Eartha Kitt that he'd been raving about.

Unfortunately Eartha at this stage was still a relatively raw solo performer. Her set was a rather haphazard affair, a ragbag of material she had picked up for here and there and wasn't always able to pull together. And she was still an artist who was at the mercy of her own emotions; she could be great one night and terrible the next. Sillman and his cohorts clearly turned up on one of the off nights:

> I told my writers of the fantastic talents of this young unknown, built them up to a point where they were gasping for a sight of her, then took

them down to the Vanguard. My writers sat through her act and looked
at me as if I'd lost my mind. This was the great Eartha Kitt? This under-
sized, unsexy kid with the lousy material? My creative artists looked at
each other during her act and I could tell exactly what they were thinking. They were retelling each other, telepathically, that I had lost the one
really sure touch I had ever possessed, to pick stars out of the blue . . .
To tell the truth, my own ego began to falter a little. Eartha was pretty
bad that night. But on the way out of the club June said to me, "I've got
an idea for a song for her. It'll be called 'Monotonous' . . ."[6]

June Carroll had picked up on the way Eartha's ad-libbing
enlivened a song like "C'est Si Bon"—the way she implied a whole
character—and saw the possibility of expanding the ad libs into
a song which properly showed off this persona. She met up with
Eartha and talked to her about her continental adventures, then
used them as the inspiration for a set of lyrics to be sung in the
character of the most jaded of sophisticates, a woman who's been
wined and dined by film stars and maharajahs and now affects to
find the whole business a frightful bore.

The lyrics allowed Eartha to detail her improbably exotic suitors and the lengths they'd be prepared to go to for her—*T. S. Eliot
writes books for me*[7]*/King Farouk's on tenterhooks for me*—before
dismissing then with the single-word refrain, *Monotonous!*, and
reflecting that *I could not be wearier/Life could not be drearier/If I
lived in Siberia.*

Art Siegel added the tune and Eartha was presented with a showstopping number that both fit her perfectly and was impossible to
imagine anyone else attempting. It offered her not only another
signature number, but a chance to take her offstage personality
and dramatize it onstage. No longer did she have to hide behind
attempts at straight blues or jazz: with "Monotonous" she had the
makings of a style and an act that was completely her own.

In the short term it had the effect of making her an indis-
pensable part of the *New Faces of 1952* project. All concerned
could see that Eartha singing "Monotonous" was going to be

something special, and from this point on she was inked into the cast.

And so, barely a month after opening at the Village Vanguard, Eartha was rehearsing for a Broadway show, and this time as a featured act in an otherwise all-white revue, rather than as just another dancer in an all-black show.

FIFTEEN

New Faces of 1952

Eartha's fellow New Faces were an oddly assorted bunch. Ronny Graham, the nearest thing the revue format permitted to the star of the show, was a good-looking piano-playing comic from a vaudeville family, who would go on to have a long and varied career in show business doing everything from writing episodes of *M*A*S*H* to appearing in *Murder She Wrote* and collaborating on several Mel Brooks movies. Robert Clary was a diminutive French singer and comic actor who'd spent his early childhood in a concentration camp, and is best known for appearing in the sixties sitcom *Hogan's Heroes*. Then there was the comedienne Alice Ghostley, who would go on to achieve TV immortality as Esmeralda on *Bewitched*, alongside another New Face, Paul Lynde. Other female roles were taken by Virginia De Luce, as an absurdly dumb blond, and June Carroll herself, pressed into action by Sillman to perform her own deceptively sweet songs. The stage design was courtesy of Broadway great Raoul Pène Du Bois, and the direction by Ziegfeld veteran John Murray Anderson. Among the sketch writers was a young comic called Melvin Brooks.

New Faces of 1952 was a mixture of songs and sketches, all very tenuously linked by brief skits featuring Ronnie Graham as the producer and Virginia de Luce as the producer's bimbo girlfriend. The writing was consistently more highbrow than you'd expect for a mainstream Broadway show. Sillman had consciously decided to take the kind of material that was assumed to work only in a Greenwich Village nightclub and take it to a mass audience. So the sketches included parodies of Clifford Odets and Truman Capote, and the songs ruminated on sophisticated themes such as the love life of a Boston bluestocking ("we were drunk on love . . . and cheap muscatel") and the ennui of an international courtesan.

Eartha had two numbers more or less to herself and a featured role in another, plus a few supporting roles in the sketches. The shared number was a relatively straightforward ballad, "Love is a Simple Thing," written by Siegel and Carroll; her first featured number was a French song, "Bal, petit bal," written by Francis Lemarque, and a hit for Yves Montand while Eartha was in Paris. Finally, there was her intended showstopper, "Monotonous."

After much ado with performers and fundraisers dropping out at the last minute, the show was finally ready to go. They would open in Philadelphia on May 1, for two weeks of out-of-town tryouts, and then hit Broadway on May 16. At last everything was running smoothly, or almost everything, as Sillman remembers:

But there were things wrong with it, as there always are in out-of-town tryouts, and one of them was Eartha Kitt. She had the surefire number of the show, in the best of all spots to sing it—the number before closing. All through rehearsals I knew she'd kill the customers with "Monotonous" and stop the show cold. Then we opened in Philadelphia and nothing happened. She sang to nothing but polite applause. Murray tinkered with the number and I tinkered with it but nobody could figure out what was wrong till June, who had written the song, came to me with fire in her eyes. "Listen—the name of the song is 'Monotonous.' It's supposed to be sung by a gal who's jaded, who's bored to death. Why do you let Eartha keep *smiling* all through the number? Wipe that smile off her face! Tell her to look bored—tell her to sing as if she hates the song!"

That was it of course. For the next two weeks Murray and I tried to persuade Eartha to get the hap-hap-happy look off her face. She wouldn't. She kept right on going as if she were doing a double impression of Mistinguett and Bojangles.[1]

Finally, so Sillman tells it, he persuaded Eartha to act like a cat— "make claws of your hands! Spit the damned song out!"—and the song was finally fixed.

Eartha tells the story rather differently. According to her, the staging of "Monotonous," which involved her slinking her way across a series of chaise longues, was all her idea. And it was she, too, who realized that the song wasn't going over as well as it might in Philadelphia. "I couldn't afford to be good, I had to be better than good." She blamed the choreography for the problem and claims that when they got back to New York, for a few days' final rehearsal before the Broadway opening, she took over the choreography herself.

It's hard to know who's right. Eartha certainly had a unique talent and a remarkably strong sense of self, but she was sometimes slow to acknowledge when she'd been given a helping hand along the way.

The show finally opened at the Royale Theater on Broadway on May 16. It was, as Sillman remembers, an immediate hit:

At 8:30 I stood in the back of the house looking over the audience. The beginning was strangely auspicious. It was a distinguished audience and a quiet one . . . And the curtain went up and Ronny walked out on to the stage alone and started to talk and I knew we were in. I could feel it from that first moment.[2]

Afterward the show's principal backers, Jean and Walter Chrysler, threw a lavish party well attended by, in Sillman's words, "All the stars of stage, screen and radio, all the columnists, several of my friends and all my enemies, and four hundred people I had never met before. It was the party of parties on the night of nights."

His one remaining worry was whether the critics would agree with the first-night audience:

> For the first few hours of rejoicing I suffered from the gnawing sensation at the heart that every producer feels before the morning papers come out . . . At midnight John Beal came panting up the staircase with the morning papers. He stood on a chair and started reading to the crowd. John Chapman in the *News* loved us. Robert Coleman in the *Mirror* loved us. Walter Kerr in the *Tribune* loved us. But it wasn't till John got to Brooks Atkinson's review that my pulse reached the bursting point. Mr. Atkinson loved us too, but he said one thing that meant more to me than all the high praise that had gone before. He said that we were "a literate revue."[3]

Brooks Atkinson was the *New York Times*'s eminent drama critic. Brightest of all the show's new stars, according to him, was undoubtedly, "Eartha Kitt [who] not only looks incendiary but she can make a song burst into flame."

Another highlight singled out by Atkinson was the sketch spoofing Clifford Odets, which was written by Mel Brooks. But while the reviews may have shared the praise around the various cast members, it soon become clear to Mel Brooks who the real breakout star was:

> Eartha Kitt rapidly became a star by word of mouth. Of all the people in the show who became stars it was Eartha first, Paul Lynde second and maybe Alice Ghostley third, but Eartha was above and beyond. It wasn't just the reviews, but the word of mouth which went around that that here was something incredibly special.[4]

The rest of the cast, according to Brooks, took their teammate's success in good part, none more so than Ronny Graham.

Let me tell you a story: Ronny Graham and I used to wait for Eartha after the show. She used to sign a lot of autographs and finally Ronny would come out of the dressing room last. Nobody was there, but Ronny would open the stage door and say, "Get the fuck out of my way! Give me a break! I'm a human being just like you! I have to leave!"—and of course there was no one at all there! He wasn't insane, he was just amusing himself. He'd do it every night. But Eartha, well she would sign a hundred autographs every night. They would all take pictures and pose with her.

Brooks himself enjoyed hanging out with the new star:

I spoke a little French and she loved that. Robert Clary was in the cast and he spoke French so the three of us would go out sometimes after the show and they'd speak a lot of French and I'd chip in with my Brooklyn twenty-five-cent French, you know . . . I'd heard she'd been in Europe. There was a kind of Josephine Baker glow from the fact she had done clubs in Paris.

And again Brooks stresses that *New Faces* did not so much create a star as acknowledge that there was one there all along. It was just that now people were noticing her.

Strangely enough she was a big shot of a star when she was unknown. She thought she was hot stuff and the amazing thing was—she was hot stuff! She didn't change much with success. She was arrogant, had a lot of hubris from the beginning. Her attitude was "I'm great. Fuck you if you don't know it, it's your problem." For a New Face she had a total command of the stage. She came out and looked the audience straight in the eye and she kind of said, "I'm good. I don't need you. You're lucky to get me, this is going to be a treat." It was like Fred Astaire saying I can dance, I'm not worried about your approval. She was like that. She was—that poor cliché—one of a kind: she's one of the few people that phrase really fits.

Indeed, Brooks notes that it was a measure of how starry Eartha already was that her big hit number was one written in the voice of someone already bored with fame.[5] "By far the bravest number they wrote was 'Monotonous.' They could have been shot down for being actually monotonous, but it turned out to be anything but— especially the way Eartha delivered it."

For the Broadway run Eartha tweaked the lyrics, adding a new suitor to her list as she crooned that *Sherman Billingsley even cooks for me.* This was an especially audacious line. Sherman Billingsley was the proprietor of the Stork Club, an upscale joint that had recently been accused, by Josephine Baker, no less, of running a racist admission policy.

It was the show's one carefully coded allusion to the fact that their star was an African American. By and large it was something she herself, along with her fellow New Faces, preferred to ignore, but, America being America, it couldn't always be avoided, as Sillman remembers:

Five of us were sitting at a table discussing the state of the world. From this world we went to the next. We started talking about space travel and flying saucers and how one day we'd be invaded by the Martians and that would be that. And then we got to talking about racial prejudice. We were on that subject, gleefully tearing it apart in natural tones when it suddenly dawned on four of us at the table—simultaneously it seemed—that the fifth member of the party was colored. We just never thought of Eartha as being colored, but now the awful subject had flared up like spontaneous combustion and we were all, suddenly, horribly aware of it. There was dead silence for a long moment while we all pretended to be unaware of the whole thing. In the midst of that silence Eartha suddenly turned her wonderful smile on my sister June. "June," she asked, "Would you mind terribly if your daughter married a Martian?"[6]

It's a revealing story. It demonstrates the way the white world— or at least the fashionable metropolitan world—related to Eartha: "We just never thought of her as being colored." You can be pretty sure that no one ever said that about Bessie Smith (who famously decked a society hostess who attempted to hug her).

A more telling comparison would be with Lena Horne, the biggest-name black female entertainer of the time as far as white audiences were concerned. But the white world was always very aware that Lena was black, for all that she was elegant and well-spoken, with notably Caucasian features. The difference was that Lena, though only seven years older than Eartha, had come up during the prewar era. She had danced in the Cotton Club chorus and sung in any number of nightclubs where the black performers, no matter how classy, always had to enter by the back door, while the white patrons, no matter how trashy, came in through the front. Lena always knew that she was effectively always on display, she was always concerned to be a credit to her race. In a sense she was so concerned to act "white" that you could never forget she was black, because somewhere beneath the grace and grooming was a burning rage born out of too many years of smiling in the face of prejudice. Eartha, however, was different: she had little interest in being a credit to her race; she just wanted to be her own unique person.[7]

And in Manhattan, in a popular show, surrounded by smart liberal white people, Eartha was able to be something like her own unique self, or at least the self she aspired to become, and to be appreciated for it. The next step was to discover how far she might go. To see whether the appeal of a multilingual black woman with unconventional looks, and a musical style that owed more to Marlene Dietrich than Bessie Smith, could reach beyond Broadway.

SIXTEEN

I Want to Be Evil!

New Faces of 1952 ran on Broadway for nearly a year, closing at the end of March 1953 after 365 performances. And the only reason it closed then was because Sillman had decided to take the show, with its original cast, on tour around the United States. By the time the Broadway run ended, Eartha Kitt was a fully-fledged star. Much, however, had happened in the intervening twelve months.

Appearing in *New Faces* hadn't put an end to Eartha's nightclub career. She had doubled in Paris while appearing with Welles and she proceeded to do the same thing in Manhattan. Following her success at the Village Vanguard she was now a bankable nightclub attraction and so, within a week of opening *New Faces*, she began a season at the Blue Angel, the uptown sister establishment to the Vanguard, a much swankier joint, overseen by Gordon's partner Herb Jacoby and, with a whopping $5 dollar cover, well out of reach for the Greenwich Villagers. Eartha was second on the bill, sandwiched between a comedian named Orson Bean and the headliner, none other than Josh White himself.

This must have been a poignant engagement. Josh was still a star attraction, but he was also pushing forty and relying on the same set he'd been playing for years, whereas Eartha was an overnight sensation and new offers were arriving daily. It was the last time they'd share a bill. One of Eartha's longest lasting relationships had finally run its course.

Eartha was obviously destined to be a bigger star then Josh had ever been. Virginia Wicks was doing a fine job for her new client, who had turned out to be a publicist's dream. Record companies vied to sign her up. Doubleday was rumored to be publishing her poetry. On June 1 she was on the *Ed Sullivan Show* for the first of many appearances. In a clear indication of the eccentricity of the variety shows of the time, she was featured alongside Errol Flynn, Yehudi Menuhin, and Baudy's Greyhound and Monkey Act. Magazines queued up to take her picture and repeat her stories of living *la vie en rose* with Orson Welles et al. back in Gay Paree.

The August edition of *Life* magazine devoted four pages to Eartha, mostly taken up with snaps from her globetrotting career to date: a picture of her with Rita Hayworth in Carroll's club; another of her jitterbugging with the Nicholas Brothers in Istanbul; one of her dancing with members of the Swedish ballet; and one in a bikini, taken in Stockholm of all places. Alongside these were a set of photos specially taken for *Life* by Gordon Parks, a young black photographer who was breaking some color bars of his own (and who would later direct the film *Shaft*). These are defiantly anti-star shots of Eartha in tomboy shorts and shirt, with natural hair, cycling through New York, swinging on the branch of a tree in Central Park and, rather implausibly, playing baseball. They were relaxed snaps of a sort that the ever-glamorous Lena Horne would never have contemplated.

The accompanying text, meanwhile, admires her command of languages and range of musical styles before observing that "Eartha does not dance much now, but when she sings every muscle in her lithe elfin body sways and ripples in a ballet of its own." Not bad, they conclude, for a girl, "who at the age of eight was picking cotton in South Carolina." Overall you sense that the wider world had woken up to Eartha, and was fascinated by her, though it didn't have a clue what to make of her. And that went for the black press too, just as much as for *Life* and the syndicated gossip columnists such as Walter Winchell who were now regularly speculating on the new starlet's bound-to-be-exotic love life.

The black press of the 1950s consisted of local newspapers like the *Pittsburgh Courier* and Harlem's *Amsterdam News*, plus a new breed of black general interest magazines, mostly published by the Johnson Publishing Company. Johnson's flagship magazine was *Ebony*, a glossy tabloid-sized affair, an obvious black take on *Life*, which peddled a relentlessly upbeat vision of black advancement, liberally sprinkled with ads for whiskey and skin-lightening creams. Lena Horne had personified the *Ebony* vision since the magazine started in 1951: she was its feminine ideal, a product of the black bourgeoisie whose image precisely embodied their values. Eartha was something else: she was certainly aspirational, but how did she relate to the mass black audience? Was she part of the black bourgeoisie, or was she thumbing her nose at them? *Ebony*, and its more down-market sister magazine, the cheaply printed weekly news digest *Jet*, didn't know. But they were determined to find out.

Eartha's doings through the early fifties are covered in considerable detail by the two magazines. She came across their radar with her appearance at the Village Vanguard and, once *New Faces* had opened, barely a week went by without an Eartha story. That summer *Ebony* devoted a three-page photo spread to this exotic new star and her adventures in Paris. The photos are great: Eartha on the rooftop of her hotel, the Élysée Palace, Eartha in an artist's studio, Eartha at the Café de Flore, Eartha backstage being served tea by a black man wearing a fez. Many of the stories concerned her various boyfriends. *Jet* repeated Walter Winchell's claim that she was about to be engaged to the "Belgian steel king." In August came reports that a besotted admirer had given her a yacht. It was said to be moored in San Francisco and Eartha was alleged to be looking forward to inspecting it in due course.

In October, however, there was a more substantive story about Eartha's love life. *Jet* reported the following: "Eartha Kitt's blue-blooded suitor, John Ryan, hopped to London for his sister's forthcoming wedding to a nobleman—but he sent Eartha a beautiful string of pearls to celebrate her Blue Angel opening and give her something to remember him by (as if she didn't already have a mink coat)." The following month Mr. Ryan had a full name—John Barry Ryan III—and was clearly back in New York, as he was said to have given Eartha "an aquamarine ring set with forty diamonds."

This John Barry Ryan III was the scion of a New York banking family. Eartha met him at the Blue Angel, introduced to him by the maître d', who told her that this young man had come in alone every night just to see her. Eartha agreed to talk to the young man, who made an unconvincing play of being in showbiz. A few nights later they ate together at the club. The next day he invited her to meet in the afternoon, at which point he whisked her down to a jewelers, and bought her a thousand-dollar antique diamond ring. As ever, Eartha's own accounts are completely unforthcoming as to the sexual relationship. She resorts instead to using her favorite euphemism, declaring that the two of them became "inseparable." As for Ryan's particular charm, she gushes that "never had I met a boy so wonderful."

Ryan was twenty-two, four years younger than her, and he bought her jewelry in profusion, paid her bills, and bought her a new wardrobe, mink coats and all. None of which was quite so monotonous in real life as she affected to find it all on stage, especially once Ronny Graham had filled in her new boyfriend's background for her, telling Eartha that he'd recently inherited around eight million dollars and belonged to one of America's richest families.

John Barry Ryan III's family was not just rich, it was also eminent. His paternal grandfather was Thomas Fortune Ryan, an Irish millionaire financier. His maternal grandfather was Otto Kahn, a German-born banker who had done much to secure the development of the American railroad system. The Ryan family's properties included their very own castle on Long Island. To cap it all, John's sister Virginia had just married a member of the British royal family, David Ogilvy, the Earl of Airlie.

Once she'd found all this out, Eartha stopped thinking of Ryan as a "boy." Instead, "He was everything I thought I could want in a man." Later in life she would refer to Ryan as one of her two great loves. But with love came danger. The ice-woman of the *New Faces* songs was far more vulnerable in real life than onstage. It was only in a Broadway theater or the rarefied environs of the Blue Angel that she might seem to transcend race. In the outside world there were inevitably going to be problems. When it came down to it Eartha was black and in showbiz, while John Barry Ryan III was a rich man from a WASP family. Apart from anything else, the gulf between their origins made their affair catnip to the gossipmongers.

Carl Van Vechten,[1] the society photographer with a particular interest in portraits of African-American stars, had inevitably taken an interest in Eartha and photographed her in his studio. In a note to a friend, dated December 1, 1952, he remarked that "The rumors are Miss Kitt will marry an ofay [white] millionaire."

Clearly that was what Eartha was hoping for, but, following her experience with Bayeux Baker, she must have known the odds were stacked against her; after all in many US states interracial relationships were still illegal. And all this publicity and gossip was starting to place a strain on the young lovers. Eartha generally felt that all publicity was good publicity, but in this instance she was concerned at the possible reception the news stories might have in the Barry household. Would her new love's parents be prepared to consider her as a possible daughter-in-law?

The short answer to this was no. They were great patrons of the arts, but there were limits. In the New Year Ryan's mother, Nin, decided to take matters into her own hands. She was friendly with the film director John Huston, who was just about to start filming *Beat the Devil* on location in Italy, with a starry cast including Humphrey Bogart and Gina Lollobrigida. Nin knew that her son had ambitions in the movie world so she persuaded Huston to offer Ryan a job working on the film. He understood what the offer meant, all right: it was a bribe to persuade him to leave Eartha behind. He took it and left for Italy.

Eartha was devastated. Fortunately Virginia Wicks, who was fast becoming her surrogate older sister and confidante, as well as her agent, was there to sympathize and to reassure.

This wasn't easy, as inside Eartha felt "unwanted, unpretty, uncharming, unattractive, uneverything." Virginia Wicks well remembers her charge's devastation: "She was shocked, but it was just unthinkable evidently to John Ryan's family. He stopped seeing her, though I think he did care for her."

Racism was also causing Eartha more practical problems. Once she started earning, her first priority had been to move out of Roxie Foster's place. She found a small apartment on Manhattan's Upper West Side, in a very nice block on Riverside Drive at 99th Street, overlooking the Hudson, which she sublet from a fellow performer, but she soon ran into trouble with the landlord, who was unhappy about the presence of a "Negro" in his apartment block. Eartha responded with a charm offensive and, in this instance at least, managed a small victory. Not only was she allowed to stay in the building, but she was soon offered the penthouse apartment with wonderful views of the river.

Her professional life, meanwhile, was going very well indeed. The Blue Angel residency went from strength to strength. Josh White had left in September, pleading poor health, and had checked into a sanatorium (something he was prone to do, more to cope with exhaustion than any more complex medical problems).[2] He had also invited his English girlfriend, Rene Dannen, over to New York, perhaps out of pique at Eartha taking up with Ryan. Eartha was promoted to headliner, and was now earning considerably more for her cabaret performances than from *New Faces* itself.

Her next step was to get a recording deal. Earlier in the year she had recorded a couple of Latin songs for a small New York label called Seeco. One was a Chano Pozo tune called "Caliente," the other a song called "Tierra Va Tembla," that she had learned in her Spanish Harlem days. These were released as a single, but sank without trace. After the success of *New Faces*, however, the big record companies started to take notice of her. Several labels came down to the Blue Angel to see her perform, but none of them could figure out how to market such an unorthodox talent. The one exception was RCA.

RCA had already issued a soundtrack album for *New Faces*, and in December they put out a single featuring the show's two most popular tunes: Alice Ghostley singing the "Boston Beguine" and Eartha singing "Monotonous." The disc got great reviews in the trade press and spurred the label into having another look at Eartha.

She was initially wary. Always sensitive to rejection, the fact that the other labels had turned her down clearly rankled and she responded by feigning indifference. So, when Dave Kapp from RCA came to see her after the show, she was immediately on the defensive: "I said, 'Mr. Kapp, there's no point in talking to me. Everybody's refused me. I know what you're gonna say—you saw my act and you want me to sing some stupid song like "My ma gave me a nickel to buy a pickle."'[3] He said, 'Oh, no. We'd like to record you exactly as you are.'"[4]

Dave Kapp, then in his late forties, was one of the great record industry pioneers.[5] He immediately saw Eartha's potential. From the start, he gave her the respect and star treatment usually reserved for white artists. Black artists were generally confined to the ghetto once known as "race music," subsequently referred to as "rhythm and blues," but Kapp was convinced that Eartha could appeal to a "pop" (i.e., white) audience.

Eartha's first session for her new label took place on January 13, 1953, in a studio in the Manhattan Center, a former opera house on 34th Street. She recorded three songs under the direction of staff producer Hy Grill. Two of the songs, "Two Lovers" and "Lovin'," are lost, the other, a sentimental trifle called "Annie Doesn't Live Here Any More," survives. A Guy Lombardo hit from the thirties, with a Johnny Burke lyric, it tells the pitiful tale of one Annie who waited and waited for her lover to come back but eventually gave up and left in the company of a gentleman in a top hat (presumably intended to be an undertaker, though, in Eartha's version, it's somehow easier to imagine a rich suitor instead). Despite the obvious resonance for Eartha, whose own lover was en route to Italy, it's a disappointing recording. Not only is the material hackneyed—really not that far from "My ma gave me a nickel" territory—but Eartha herself sounds girlish and unformed, while the overall production is a little thin.

Evidently all concerned had a rethink as Eartha's next session was not until two months later. Hugo Winterhalter, the bandleader last time, was now the producer, and the former bandleader turned RCA house arranger, Henri Rene, was brought in as the orchestra leader. The sessions took place on the afternoons of March 12 and 13, 1953, between 2:00 and 6:00 p.m. These were far more successful. On the first day they recorded four songs including two cornerstones of Eartha's musical career: first the live favorite "C'est Si Bon," and then a novelty called "I Want To Be Evil."

This number is sung in the persona of a girl who's "prim and proper" and thoroughly tired of it, she's "petted stray dogs and shied clear of dope," but now she wants to go to the devil. It's camp through and through, and absolutely ideal for Eartha as it allows her much commented on "feline" sexuality to become cartoonish and unthreatening, a PG-rated version of evil. It's only at the very end that there's something of the real Eartha, as she vamps out on the lines, "*I wanna be evil, little evil me/Just as mean and evil as I can be.*"

During that first, very productive afternoon in the studio they also recorded James Shelton's crazily melodramatic show tune, "Lilac Wine," and had another shot at "Two Lovers." The next day, clearly emboldened by their success, they ventured further into Eartha's foreign-language material and recorded five songs, including her Turkish favorite "Uska Dara" (with lyrics newly corrected by Ahmet Ertegun, the expatriate Turk who founded Atlantic Records); the lovely Mexican song of racial protest, "Angelitos Negros";[6] another French song, "Avril au Portugal"; and two less successful, though interesting, numbers, "African Lullaby"[7] and the Chinese-inflected "Mountain High, Valley Low."[8]

The two sessions had produced a bewildering array of material; a collection that's impossible to imagine being put together by anyone other than Eartha Kitt. The question facing RCA was where to start. Which of these nine songs was the American public most likely to take to its heart?

The answer they came up with was a single featuring "Two Lovers," with "Uska Dara" on the flipside. The press release extols "Two Lovers" as a "salt-flavored sea ditty which Eartha projects with a maximum of feeling and style." The flipside is described as having a "truly oriental arrangement," while Eartha's "atomic-powered delivery is unique in pop music."

What no one was expecting was that it was "Uska Dara" and not "Two Lovers" that became an immediate jukebox hit. It's given a jaunty, ersatz Middle Eastern orchestral treatment with a spoken section in the middle, in which Eartha informs her listeners that "Uska Dara" is the name of a little town in Turkey, and in the old days many women in Turkey had male "secretaries." "Oh well, that's Turkey," says Eartha, apparently dismayed at the unfairness of not having such a secretary herself. A further spoken section ends with a sighing "Oh, those Turks."

In later years Eartha would claim that RCA released "Uska Dara" in the hope that it would fail and enable them to end her contract. This is obviously both nonsensical and untrue. "Uska Dara" was originally seen as the flipside of "Two Lovers," but the popular taste of the early fifties was far more eclectic than one might imagine, and it ended up at No. 23 on the charts, going on to sell a very healthy 120,000 copies.

Confident now in their unorthodox new artist, RCA released the other March recordings on a mini album called *RCA Presents Eartha Kitt*.[9] Sixty years later Eartha's first album still sounds profoundly odd and completely compelling, unlike anything else from its time. It's hard now to imagine any major record company getting behind an artist with an image and voice as unique as Eartha's, and a song repertoire spread over four different languages and as many different styles. That this should have happened in the early fifties is remarkable, and that it should have been an enormous popular success is positively extraordinary.

"C'est Si Bon" was released as the second single and was a huge hit, selling a quarter of a million copies in the first two months of release, and remaining on the singles chart till the end of the year. Then *RCA Presents* was released, and it too sold well in all its various formats, making its way into the top ten album bestsellers and staying there for six months.

At first Eartha hardly had time to notice her new success as a recording star. *New Faces* finally finished its Broadway run in March 1953, and immediately went on the road. They played three weeks in Boston and then settled into Chicago at the end of April for what was initially meant to be a one-month run but ended up being nearer six, such was popular demand. It was while she was in Chicago that Eartha realized she was suddenly famous in the wider world and not just in theater circles. Kids came up to her as she sunbathed in the park and asked if she was the famous Eartha Kitt. Being recognized in public was a novelty she would soon get used to. "Uska Dara" and "C'est Si Bon" became jukebox and radio staples and people would call out "*C'est Si Bon!*" when they saw her around town.

What really pleased Eartha was that her album was doing just as well as her singles. A couple of hit singles didn't mean too much; you might still be a flash in the pan, but album sales implied an artist who was here to stay. As Eartha observed a little while later, "albums are security, like annuities. A single record makes money fast, but can die fast."

This was perceptive of her. The recording industry was changing. The new long-playing discs were reshaping the music business: no longer did everyone have to chase after an individual hit, instead they could build up a mood over a set of songs. Frank Sinatra would come to understand this better than anyone in the pop field, but Eartha's first albums were also pioneering works. From the early fifties onwards singles were aimed at younger record buyers, while albums were angled at older, more sophisticated listeners, who were also interested in buying the new hi-fi setups that the big record companies were starting to market. And in America in 1953 Eartha Kitt pretty much defined sophistication.

Eartha's fame wasn't confined to stage and recording. During the early fifties television ownership was increasing exponentially, and Eartha was a natural for the new medium. She had already appeared on the *Ed Sullivan Show* in the first flush of *New Faces'* success, and that led to a string of further spots on variety shows like those hosted by the comic Red Buttons and the singer Perry Como. Then, in April 1953, she was offered her first TV acting role.

This was an appearance in a series called *You Are There*, filmed in the CBS TV studios, which dramatized key moments in American history. Each episode was introduced by newscasting legend Walter Cronkite. Eartha appeared in the tenth episode of the first series, *The Conquest of Mexico.*

Intriguingly, this was directed by the future Hollywood director Sidney Lumet, and written by the screenwriter Abraham Polonsky. This was remarkable because, at the time, Polonsky was on the McCarthy blacklist. But the show's producer Charles Russell was a committed liberal and, at some risk to his career, gave Polonsky a series of writing jobs masked by the pseudonym "Jeremy Daniel."

In the show Eartha played the part of Doña Marina, a fifteen-year-old Aztec princess who became a slave to the Spanish conquistador Hernán Cortés. Doña Marina sided with Cortés, becoming his right-hand woman and helping to bring about the fall of the Aztec empire. It was a wonderfully resonant part for Eartha, who would spend much of her life and career feeling torn between different worlds.

Eartha's success was bringing her to the notice of America's black intellectuals. The best known of these, Langston Hughes, who had a syndicated column in the black press, was a huge fan: "Eartha Kitt looks like a cat, purrs when sings, slinks when walks and I'm wondering what she does when she talks," he wrote in March 1953. Where other black commentators were dubious about Eartha's high-toned image and apparent ease in white society, Langston saw it all as positive. He saw her as someone who was ready and able to break through the entertainment world's color bars. "Where does the Negro stand in entertainment?" he had asked in another article that May. "He stands on one leg with the other tied behind him by Jim Crow."

For her part, Eartha was happy to be included in the black intellectual world. She had her portrait painted by fashionable young artist Lady Bird Cleveland. In March 1953 she appeared at an NAACP gala in New York[10] with Lena Horne and Erroll Garner. In Chicago two months later she attended an opening for the painter Stan Williamson along with the likes of Gordon Parks, who'd photographed her for *Life*, and Ralph Ellison, whose new novel, *The Invisible Man*, won the National Book Award that year and became one of the key texts of African-American literature.

Summer in Chicago stretched into autumn, and Eartha began to grow impatient with the restriction of having to appear in *New Faces* every night. *Jet* wondered if she might be having an affair with her neighbor, the actor Herb Jeffries (known as "The Bronze Buckaroo" for his roles in black cowboy movies). As her records climbed the charts, offers started to come in from nightclubs around the country. For the moment her *New Faces* contract forced her to turn them down. Most persistent was the prestigious Mocambo in Los Angeles. Eartha promised to appear there just as soon as the Chicago run ended.[11]

Meanwhile negotiations were afoot for a film version of *New Faces*. At first it was to be filmed onstage in Chicago, but then the producers decided to film it in the studio in Hollywood, and in CinemaScope. The filming was set for three weeks in November, and after some hard bargaining it was agreed that Eartha would film by day, and appear at the Mocambo by night for a startling $2,500 a week. As soon as the filming was done the show would carry on touring.

Once the Chicago run finished in early October Eartha headed back to New York where she appeared on a radio show called *The Golden Treasury*, reading a favorite poem, and then she went back into the recording studios for two more sessions for RCA.

There was potential trouble here. There had been a shake-up at the label while Eartha was in Chicago. Following an internal power struggle Dave Kapp had left, and was preparing to set up his own label. Eartha was now to be looked after by Manie Sacks, an industry veteran who had previously been at CBS. Worryingly, Sacks was less than wholehearted in his enthusiasm when talking about her to the press: "Eartha's a great stylist. She can't compete with a Doris Day or a Dinah Shore on a pop record. She needs special material and a big city audience. But with the right song she comes through on wax so you never feel you've been cheated out of a performance."[12] With this talk of "special material" and "a big city audience" it's hardly a ringing endorsement. Sacks, it seems, saw definite limits to Eartha's potential—for all that her remarkable sales over the past year might have suggested that a mass audience was hers for the taking. Joe Carlton, who replaced Dave Kapp as her A&R man, was similarly guarded: "She's a sound, a very singular sound. There are better voices around. But no matter how fast you spin your dial you identify her immediately."

For the moment, however, things were reasonably serene. Over the two recording dates Eartha recorded ten new songs. Eight of them would make up her next album, to be called "*That Bad Eartha*" (with quotation marks—an early example of conscious irony in the popular music industry) and released in the new year. The other two songs would be her new single, a double-header featuring "Under the Bridges of Paris" and a sexy Christmas number called "Santa Baby."

By now Eartha was getting used to the recording studio and in particular to working with her arranger, Henri Rene. Rene clearly loved working with Eartha, as he told *Collier's* magazine the following year.

She never makes a grand entrance. No working temperament. She just sneaks into the sound studio in slacks and sits in a corner or else gets up and prowls around, talking to the musicians, trying to play the horns, full of chatter and curiosity until we're ready to go. Then she bears down. Eartha's very expressive physically when she sings. That makes for a lot of green notes in the background. The musicians can't watch her and the music at the same time. We always work out our arrangements together, tossing ideas back and forth. Lots of ideas, like that muttered Cadillac business in "C'est Si Bon," have been hers.[13]

Despite all Manie Sacks's caveats, RCA clearly recognized that "Santa Baby" was an obvious hit. At the end of the month there was a "hi-fi symposium" in New York. The label pushed their new line of hi-fi equipment and "Santa Baby" was the track chosen to illustrate the new possibilities of high fidelity in the home.

It was released uncommonly early for a Christmas record, at the beginning of November. At the end of the month it had sold 200,000 copies. By that time Eartha was in Los Angeles, filming the *New Faces* movie, and appearing to sold-out audiences at the Mocambo. She was the girl who had it all, except perhaps a lover to share it with. But that, too, was about to change.

SEVENTEEN

Santa Baby

November 1953 in Hollywood was a perfect time in Eartha's life. By day she was filming *New Faces*, and it was now clear that she was the star of the show. Several of the original sketches and songs were dropped, and in their place came three more numbers for Eartha, her two big hits from earlier in the year, "Uska Dara" and "C'est Si Bon," plus her new release, "Santa Baby." None of the other cast members were featured in these sequences: they were in effect wonderfully lavish music videos.

The film of "Santa Baby" seems extraordinarily raunchy for its time. Eartha is pictured standing by a window, waiting for Santa. She's apparently naked, her modesty protected only by a large white fur stole which she toys with suggestively. All the while she's purring away about all the things she hopes Santa Baby might bring her: "a yacht, and really that's not a lot," and so on. The single itself with, again, a remarkably provocative sleeve—depicting a stocking-clad Eartha in the arms of a burly white Santa Claus—was climbing the charts perfectly well on its own, but the *New Faces* footage helped to ensure that it became a Christmas standard.[1]

Eartha's season at the Mocambo was another big step up the ladder. Charlie Morrison, the owner, had a huge banner announcing her presence strung across Sunset Boulevard, and ensured that her dressing room was full of flowers and champagne. She was an immediate hit. She stayed for three weeks, drew sold-out crowds and more advance reservations than the Mocambo had ever had for a show. Visitors ranged from Hollywood stars to Eartha's old friend from the Dunham days, Gloria Mitchell.

All this was helped by some smart publicity maneuvering from the Virginia Wicks crew, including a slew of headlines detailing the alleged offense caused by Eartha's general sultriness at a benefit performance in front of royal visitors, King Paul and Queen Frederica of Greece. The Los Angeles mayor Norris Paulson professed himself to be outraged by Eartha's performance, and the result was all good publicity for the Mocambo shows. Eartha herself responded to the mayor's criticism by telling the press, tongue firmly in cheek, that "I can't understand it. I'm just an innocent little girl. I didn't think it was possible to shock politicians."[2]

Toward the end of her stint at the Mocambo Eartha was sitting at a table with Charlie Morrison and his wife when she was introduced to a young man named Arthur Loew, Jr., who made an immediate impression on her and vice versa. For his part, he was simply bowled over by her performance that night. As for Eartha, she was thrilled to be in the presence of Hollywood royalty.

Arthur Loew, Jr. was the scion of not one but two Hollywood dynasties. His maternal grandfather, Adolph Zukor, had founded Paramount Pictures, while his paternal grandfather, Marcus Loew, was behind both MGM Studios and the Loew's cinema and theater chain. At the time he met Eartha, his own father, Arthur Loew, Sr., was president of MGM.

Arthur Jr. was a year or so older than Eartha. He was tall, thin, and good looking, shy with people he didn't know, funny with those he did. He had once had acting ambitions and had appeared in walk-on parts in a number of Hollywood movies, but by the time Eartha met him he had turned his attention to film producing, an easy enough jump given his family connections. In truth, though, he had no need to work as he had already come into a huge trust fund at the age of twenty-one, so his film producing was little more than a sideline and a further excuse to meet the actresses he liked to go out with. Mostly his reputation was as a playboy around town. Before meeting Eartha he had dated a whole string of starlets: among them Debbie Reynolds, Janet Leigh, and a striking young Italian actress called Pier Angeli, who would later date one of his best friends, James Dean. With his money, his connections, his looks, and his sense of humor, Arthur Loew, Jr. was about as eligible as bachelors could get.

He was exactly the kind of man Eartha was looking for, and when he made his play for her, she fell for him very hard indeed. She wasn't one for protracted courtships; when she came up against someone she liked she had no inhibitions about letting them know. For the next week, following their meeting at the Mocambo, Eartha and Arthur were, as she coyly put it, "inseparable."

This honeymoon period ended a week or so later when the Mocambo run ended and *New Faces* went back on the road. Next stop was San Francisco for a short pre-Christmas run. Eartha was staying at the Huntington Apartments across the way from the Fairmont Hotel. Arthur Loew phoned her every day and life was good.

Appearing at the Fairmont at the time was the Will Mastin Trio, a black variety act that had taken the nightclub circuit by storm over the past few years. Their star attraction was a young dancer-comic-singer called Sammy Davis, Jr.

And so began one of the odder relationships in Eartha's life. Eartha and Sammy were photographed in the press that December, dancing cheek to cheek. They both appeared on a TV show in San Francisco that month. By this time *Jet* magazine was eagerly reporting gossip that Sammy had proposed to Eartha and these two rising stars of black entertainment would be married the following summer. And even though that didn't happen, this was a story that wouldn't go away. There would be regular speculation about the pair in the press and Sammy, at least, seemed to be besotted with Eartha. Over the next few years he periodically burst into Eartha Kitt's dressing room and proposed marriage, only to be turned down.

As to just how much of this was real, and how much publicity hype, it's hard to be certain. There doesn't seem to have been much real feeling on Eartha's part when they first met. For her, the whole affair provided a convenient smokescreen. She had just embarked on the relationship with Arthur Loew and, after what had happened with John Barry Ryan, she wanted to keep things quiet. Having the press follow a wild goose chase involving Sammy Davis must have suited her very well. Virginia Wicks, however, confirms that it wasn't all a setup, that Sammy at least was genuine about his feelings:

> Sammy Davis, Jr.? He wanted to marry her. I was walking down the street near the nightclub where she was working and he caught up with me and gave me a ring to give her, an engagement ring, and I was excited and I thought "My goodness!" So I gave it to her in her dressing room and she said, "I don't want it, I would never marry him!" So it wasn't PR from me. I was very surprised at her absolute flat refusal to take the ring.

This story is echoed from Davis's side. Three years later he told the *New York Post* that he had proposed marriage to Eartha, giving her a seven-carat diamond ring, which she initially accepted only to hand it back a couple of days later. At first, according to the *Post*, Eartha had agreed to wear the ring as a token of their "friendship," on the understanding that Sammy accepted that they were not actually engaged. Sammy had failed to accept that and Eartha sent the ring back, saying, "He's a sweet boy, but he gets mixed up."[3]

Eartha's own account of her relationship with Davis portrays it as a simple friendship, one that began in San Francisco when she met this obviously talented young artist and was dismayed to discover that he only ever read comic books, of which he had a huge collection. She decided to take him in hand and introduced him to modern art and literature with some success, as Davis was known as a great book-buyer ever after. She is adamant, however, that there was no romantic component and in this instance—when she had so recently met Arthur Loew, Jr., a man who had the potential to give her rather more than Davis could—there's no reason to disbelieve her.

After San Francisco, Eartha headed back to Los Angeles. *New Faces* was booked in for a short New Year run at the Biltmore Theater, and Eartha was again to double at the Mocambo. Her relationship with Arthur Loew was flourishing and all was well, apart from her increasing exhaustion as a hectic year drew to a close.

It had, in fairness, been one hell of a year. *Cashbox* magazine anointed her the number one female newcomer in the music industry (not in rhythm and blues, or jazz, or any other marginal category but, quite simply, the number one female). The other music business trade paper, *Billboard*, offered a more sober, financially based assessment of her success. It reported that she had started on *New Faces* at $350 a week and was now on $750. Her first run at the Mocambo had earned her $2,500 a week, but now she was on $5–6,000, and her latest booking, at the Sahara in Las Vegas, was for an impressive $10,000 a week. She no longer needed Santa Baby or even Arthur Loew to buy her diamonds: she could afford her own.

The new year began with the release of Eartha's second album, "*That Bad Eartha*," which immediately took over from *RCA Presents . . .* in the top ten, and remained there for most of 1954. It's a more restrained and frankly more forgettable set than its predecessor. It's telling that, a couple of years later when the two albums were combined to produce one twelve-inch album, only three songs from the original "*That Bad Eartha*" survived. The highlight is a playful rendition of "Under the Bridges of Paris," while there are perfectly creditable run-throughs of standards like "Smoke Gets in Your Eyes," and a winsome "Let's Do It." A version of Duke Ellington's "Blues" shows a little more serious intent, while "Sandy's Tune" has to be the worst song Eartha ever recorded. It's a mock Caledonian confection that she sang in a ludicrous Scottish accent and has to be heard to be believed.

January also saw a new single from Eartha, a calypso tune called "Somebody Bad Stole de Wedding Bell." For some unaccountable reason the song was a big favorite that month, as Eartha's version was chased up the charts by rival covers from such noted calypsonians as Georgia Gibbs and Sylvia Syms. Eartha's version is fun, but no more than that. Clearly poppier than her previous releases, and rather less successful in the charts, its release was a sign that RCA was no longer quite sure what to do with their unexpectedly hot property.

Eartha herself had little time to consider such matters. She plugged the new record on the *Colgate Comedy Hour* with Dean Martin and Jerry Lewis, and hammed it up with Jimmy Durante, then went from the Biltmore back to San Francisco at the end of the month for two more weeks with *New Faces*. Arthur Loew came up to join her for a few days. Eartha, Arthur, and Ronny Graham spent an enjoyable afternoon visiting Hoagy Carmichael. Eartha was by now completely smitten with Loew.

As far as she was concerned she had met the man she wanted to share her life with. He was smart and funny and, of course, he was rich, but beneath the urbane exterior Eartha detected a kinship between them. No matter how different their origins, they were both loners at heart. Loew's money, she felt, had stopped him from really committing to anything or anyone. He had been given life on a plate and found it hard to take it seriously. In fact Eartha felt she was the luckier one because she had goals to strive toward. It was her mission now to bring him fully to life.

Interestingly Christopher Isherwood, who met Loew around this time, noticed some of the same qualities but had a rather more negative reaction, as he wrote in his diary: "As for Loew—didn't like him. He's one of the ones who 'continually deny.' Always sneering at himself and his work—and therefore at everybody else."

It is perhaps not surprising that Isherwood didn't take to Loew. As this reminiscence from one of Loew's many Hollywood girl-friends, Debbie Reynolds, suggests, he was very much a woman's man: "He was a friend to all of us, and he loved women and he loved to be your boyfriend without taking you to bed. He really wanted to hold your hand and be the gentleman, take you out and teach you about all the good things in life. Arthur, who was a very, very rich man, was the sweetest."[4]

Despite Eartha's best efforts, word of her relationship with Loew was starting to get around: toward the end of January *Jet* was reporting that the Sammy Davis romance was stillborn. *Jet* quoted Hollywood columnist Harrison Carroll as saying that "La Kitt has a secret love, but she's afraid to call his name. It would stand the town on its ear and the guy's family would kick up a beeg fuss."[5]

The attention of the gossipmongers wasn't the only thing threatening Eartha's relationship with Arthur, however. More immediately problematic was her relentless touring schedule. After San Francisco the *New Faces* caravan headed on to St. Louis and Detroit before finally closing in April, nearly two nonstop years after their original opening. And still there was no rest. She flew into New York for a couple of days for another *Ed Sullivan Show,* and then she was off to Las Vegas to open as a solo attraction at El Rancho.

Las Vegas in the fifties was a tricky prospect for black entertainers. On the one hand it paid more money than anywhere else; on the other it treated them with less respect than most. This was a Jim Crow town through and through.

The Las Vegas hotels were happy to book black entertainers who appealed to a white audience—including the likes of Lena Horne, Pearl Bailey, and Duke Ellington—but they refused to allow them to do anything more than perform on the premises. It was the Cotton Club all over again: black acts generally couldn't eat, drink, gamble, or even sleep at the places where they played. And the audiences were of course all white. In an effort to redress the balance an integrated casino, the Moulin Rouge, was opened in the Westside the following year, but closed six months later.

Sammy Davis, Jr. became a Las Vegas favorite and was more outspoken than most in his opposition to the town's color bars. On one famous occasion, while performing at a hotel on the Strip, Sammy decided it was time for him to personally integrate the swimming

pool by jumping in. In a startling display of the petty ferocity of fifties racism the hotel had the pool drained and scrubbed by a clean-
ing crew the next morning.

Eartha Kitt, however, was able to rise above most of this. El
Rancho, and its owner Beldon Katleman, were exceptions to the
racist norm. Black artists were treated relatively well there: Eartha
had a cabin by the pool and free-flowing champagne every night.
It may, of course, have helped that she had as powerful a boyfriend
as Arthur Loew flying in to see her there. On stage, meanwhile, she
was a hit. Even hard-to-please *Variety* declared that she possessed
"an unmatched sultry sexiness," while her show was "strictly boffo!"

Racial questions were very much in the news in the summer of
1954. On May 17 the Supreme Court finally gave their verdict on a
long running case known as *Brown v. Board of Education*. This was
a case that challenged the legitimacy of racially segregated schooling
in America. It was a crucial test case because, if it was deemed legally
unacceptable for schools to be segregated, then the same obviously
went for lunch counters, restrooms, swimming pools, and so on.

When the news broke that the Supreme Court had ruled against
segregation it was a momentous event. The starter's whistle had
effectively been blown for the civil rights movement. The nation's
justice system had finally made a stand. Now what remained was
for the people themselves to make sure the Supreme Court's pretty
words had real meaning on the ground. It would, of course, be a
long and hard struggle.

There was still no letup for Eartha. Leonard Sillman had been
talking for some time about finding a new Broadway role for her,
and now he had one in development. This would be Eartha's first
straight acting job, in a brand-new "play with music"—rather than
a musical—called *Mrs. Patterson* and written by black playwright
Charles Sebree. It would launch in the coming autumn.

In the meantime Eartha was deluged with lucrative nightclub
gigs and took on as many of them as she could: the Latin Casino
in Philadelphia, the Cal Neva in Lake Tahoe, and then back to New

York for an engagement at La Vie en Rose, where she had the chance to make up for her previous failure of a couple of years earlier. It was a ferocious workload, and Eartha was becoming increasingly reliant on regular shots from a doctor who specialized in keeping flagging entertainers on the road. These shots were most likely a cocktail of vitamins and amphetamines. Throw in the fact that she was separated from her new love for weeks at a time, and it was hardly surprising that she was becoming more stressed than ever.

Somewhere in the midst of this ceaseless activity Eartha was the subject of her first really in-depth magazine profile. This appeared in the June edition of *Collier's* magazine. The writer, Richard Donovan, began by setting out the extent of her recent success—one of RCA's five bestsellers, with sales of more than two million records, and in the top ten on the nation's jukeboxes—before moving on to give the following portrait of her home life:

> Real life for North, South Carolina's only international chanteuse, centers around her headquarters—a softly decorated, picture and book-lined, four-room terraced apartment overlooking the Hudson in upper Manhattan. When the pressures force her to take time off, she vanishes for days into this apartment, wandering silently around, listening to the music of Bartok and Bach and Ravel, rereading various king posts of literature, with emphasis on Ibsen, Shaw and the Russians, sewing a few personal touches into a gown by Dior or a hat by Dache . . . On such retreats she may appear at midnight in a bathrobe at the lower-floor apartment of her friend Mrs. Marki in search of aimless talk and some of Mrs. Marki's matzoh-ball soup.[6]

The Mrs. Marki in question was one Dolores Marki, who, coincidentally enough, had once been a concert pianist with the Dunham Company. She offered Donovan her own take on Eartha's success: "Eartha never did slow down. She worked like she was possessed. It was that drive plus her great natural talent that made her one of the few in her group who pulled out on her own." Mrs. Marki stressed the importance of Eartha's sojourn in Europe: "It was as though she only had a year to grow up in."

Elsewhere in the profile Eartha is keen to stress that she was actually still something of a child beneath the glamour. Thus she tells Donovan that she likes to put on jeans and a sweater and join in the kids' baseball games in Central Park, where she is apparently considered "a good shortstop and a fair switch hitter."

In later years Eartha would often refer to herself as being two people in one—the star called Eartha Kitt and the little girl called Eartha Mae. This interview suggests that the split was there from the very beginning of her stardom. Whether or not she actually played much baseball in the park—it seems unlikely given how little time she was spending at home—it's still a revealing glimpse of Eartha's confused self-image.

Rather more in keeping with her sophisticated persona, and obvious ambition, are other claims made in the article. An anonymous friend of Eartha's tells Donovan that "A while ago she took up painting as a hobby and ended up at the Art Institute of Chicago, studying like crazy. She also decided to relax with golf, and the first time out was struggling furiously to break 100."

The article notes that Eartha could be imperious. Her friend Jimmy Shelton, the songwriter who wrote "Lilac Wine" and was now commissioned to write the songs for her forthcoming Broadway show, commented that "Eartha can't help playing the great lady with strangers." However the childlike side of Eartha reappears later in the article. First there's the story of her reaction to Virginia Wicks becoming seriously ill.

When Miss Wicks was very ill and being fed intravenously in hospital, Miss Kitt arrived with a mutual friend, gave the press agent an airy "Well, how long are you going to be in here?" for a greeting, conversed distantly for a few minutes and left without a good-bye.

"That performance might have retarded my convalescence" says Miss Wicks. "But the friend called later to say that Eartha had cried all the way home and into the night. When I asked her about it finally, she said, 'Ginny, I can't show emotion. But you're supposed to know how I feel.'"[7]

Virginia goes on to comment that "Eartha is a child of nature." Donovan picks that observation and runs with it, retelling an Eartha tale that had lately done the rounds in showbiz circles:

A reporter who interviewed Miss Kitt in San Francisco recently had occasion to observe this child of nature bent. Miss Kitt, drawn to a fine edge from overwork, was sitting alone in her dressing room, reading Dostoyevsky's *Notes from the Underground*, and weeping quietly. The reporter asked what the trouble was. "My tongue is coated," said Miss Kitt, sorrowfully sticking it out. Her tongue was coated. Positive he was closeted with something catching, the reporter hurried his questions which she answered vaguely. Then, without warning, Miss Kitt stood up, slipped suddenly and startlingly out of a quilted robe and began to walk around absolutely unprotected from dangerous drafts, her mind faraway like nature's child. The reporter felt his brow. He had a fever, all right.[9]

What was the reporter meant to make of this performance? First Eartha presents him with her intellectual side, then she's acting like a child, sticking her tongue out and removing her clothes as if her nakedness were no more than a sign of her affinity with nature. Was he being teased? Seduced? Or was she really so discombobulated by fame that she was unconsciously taking refuge in a childlike state? Was she, in fact, going slightly crazy? Or all of these things at the same time? Clearly a combination of exhaustion, illness, her doctor's drug regimen, sudden fame, and the desire to be seen as both a sex symbol and an intellectual at one and the same time, added up to a heavy load to carry. Something had to give.

Eartha's first mentor, the redoubtable Miss D—Katherine Dunham.

Eartha's musical Svengali and longtime lover, the very suave Josh White, here in conversation with Symphony Sid.

Eartha with her fellow Dunham Company dancers, Lawaune Ingram, Lucille Ellis, and Richardena Jackson. She was always a little apart from the rest.

Left: Eartha in London. "She just came in and did her show and left, didn't talk to us at all, but stars have to be a bit like that, a bit aloof."

Below: Eartha and Orson Welles in Berlin. "That was one reason why he thought I was the most exciting woman in the world: I kept my mouth shut, and so he thought I was very intelligent."

Left: Her arranger Henri Rene told the press that "Eartha's very expressive physically when she sings. The musicians can't watch her and the music at the same time." So that explains the dark glasses.

Eartha's great friend and publicist Virginia Wicks in her modeling days.

Eartha getting changed backstage at the Blue Angel, New York.

Eartha with her great lost love, Arthur Loew, Jr., photographed together in public for the first and only time.

Beatnik Eartha, with the actor she called Jamie Dean.

Eartha does her homework prior to meeting Albert Einstein: "We talked about knowledge, and he said it was a surface thing."

Eartha and Hollywood friends (Heston, C., Garland, J., and Brando, M.) plan to attend Martin Luther King's great March on Washington for Jobs and Freedom.

Eartha at the Milk Fund Dinner with Mr. and Mrs. Arthur Miller (the fund provided free milk to the poor of New York City).

Eartha as Catwoman, fueling the sexual fantasies of a generation. Cesar Romero is the Joker.

Eartha with her *St. Louis Blues* costar Nat King Cole: not the first man she had to deny being romantically involved with.

Eartha meets Prince Philip: "He's not like a duke at all—he's all man. And so witty too."

Eartha and her "dear little husband," Bill McDonald, arriving in London.

Confidential magazine shows its customary sensitivity in its coverage of Eartha's marriage.

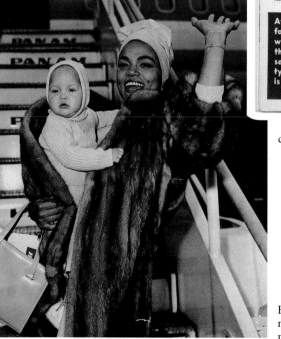

Eartha with baby Kitt, later a model and then her mother's manager.

Eartha at the White House with Lady Bird Johnson, prior to speaking her mind.

Eartha's bid to join the rock generation.

Eartha in exile.

Eartha in her prime.

EIGHTEEN

Mrs. Patterson Regrets

By the summer of 1954 the strain of Eartha's success was starting to become obvious. Matters came to a head when she reached Chicago. She was booked for two weeks at the Chicago Theater, where her audience included a young Jesse Jackson. She was completely exhausted by this point and *Jet* revealed that one night a "distraught, disoriented, edgy" Eartha had fainted upon coming off stage. On being brought around she had called for the services of a hypnotist she had previously visited. He succeeded in putting her to sleep for a little while or rather, as *Jet* put it, "he granted her a sweet 15 minute release from the myriad of tensions that consume her in a complex, jet-propelled world of stage and nightclub appearances, radio and TV shows, public appearances and recording dates, interviews, beggars, borrowers, false protectors and hecklers."

It's clearly not a good sign when it takes a hypnotist to get you through your stage show. *Billboard*'s review of the Chicago show was no more than lukewarm in its enthusiasm. Eartha needed a refuge and she hoped her next engagement, back at the Mocambo in Los Angeles, would provide it. She would be reunited with Arthur Loew, who would give her some protection from the outside world.

That was the idea at least but, unfortunately for Eartha, her relationship with Loew was starting to attract attention. *Variety* included a pointed little reference to his turning up alone to Eartha's opening at the Mocambo. A week or so later, when Eartha's stint at the club came to an end, the lovers' cover was finally blown. On August 3 the two of them went out to see Billy Daniels's show at the Mocambo and were photographed together for the first time. In the photo she looks nervous but happy; he looks pale and intense.

A few days later Eartha was back in New York to sign her contract to star in *Mrs. Patterson*, with rehearsals to start almost immediately, and appear on the first ever *Ed Sullivan Show* to be broadcast in color.

This show was a big deal. CBS was using it to try to sell their latest invention—color TV sets. These were fairly crude machines, and the color hardly corresponded to anything you might see in reality, but they were still something of a breakthrough, and this episode of the *Ed Sullivan Show* was lavishly produced to show them off to the best effect. Eartha was the headline attraction—a clear indication of just how much of a draw she had become over the past year. She sang two songs: first "Monotonous" and then her new single, "Mink, Shmink." For this number the Sullivan people built Eartha an acrylic stairway and had a whole parade of models come down it, all wearing mink coats and fabulous jewelry.[1]

Then Eartha herself descended the stairs, gradually divesting herself of her own furs and jewels as she went, while singing the lyrics "*Mink shmink, money shmoney/Think you're hot now, don't you honey?/What have you got if you haven't got love?*" It was a bravura performance and made for great TV. *Billboard's* review declared that "Miss Kitt was the showstopper," while Ed Sullivan himself told the press that "When this girl drops her head and walks straight at you, staring straight at you, it's like getting hit with a blackjack. When most singers walk, they walk. When Kitt walks, it becomes a personal proposition."

It's telling, though, that even this high-profile performance didn't make "Mink, Shmink" a hit. Partly that was due to the song itself—written under a pseudonym by the conductor Victor Young, it's no more than a sex-kitten-by-numbers ditty with a saccharine twist and no discernible tune—but it may also have been a sign that, although the American public was still fascinated by Eartha in person, it was starting to think it might have all the records by her that it needed. There's a thin line between being a unique act and a novelty act, and RCA was in danger of nudging Eartha toward the wrong side of that line.

Eartha herself wasn't too worried. Her next engagement would be in the legitimate theater. *Mrs. Patterson* was to be the vehicle that would establish her as an actress and not just a singer.

Mrs. Patterson was mostly written by Charles Sebree. Sebree, better known as a painter, was a gay black man who'd spent his early years in Madisonville, rural Kentucky, before moving to Chicago at age ten. By fourteen he was living on his own and running numbers for local gamblers. By eighteen he was studying at the Art Institute, and was a member of the Chicago Repertory Group alongside an extraordinary roster of talent including the writers Richard Wright and Nelson Algren, the radio broadcaster Studs Terkel, and Katherine Dunham. Before long he was designing sets for the fledgling Dunham Company. He served in the Second World War then came to Harlem, where he was a part of Billy Strayhorn's circle, and turned his hand to playwriting. For *Mrs. Patterson* he was helped by a Broadway pro named Greer Johnson, while the songs were composed by *New Faces* alumnus Jimmy Shelton, a friend of Eartha's.

The play is set in rural Kentucky. Its heroine is a fifteen-year-old black girl named Teddy Hicks, whose mother works as a maid for a rich white family called the Pattersons. Mrs. Patterson has become the embodiment of all the young girl's dreams of a better life.

It was a bold choice of play for Eartha, casting her firmly against apparent type as an innocent young girl from the Deep South. Sillman's next move was to secure a director. He decided to aim high and contacted Guthrie McClintic. McClintic had been a successful theater director for three decades, working mostly with his wife

Katharine Cornell, one of the great American theater stars over that same period. Leonard Sillman recalled the first meeting between star and putative director in his memoirs:

> When I signed her to do *Mrs. Patterson* I wanted Guthrie McClintic to direct her. I sent him a script. He called me to say, "You don't know it but I've been interested in this play for a long time. I'd love to direct it. But I've never seen Eartha Kitt." I told him she was opening that week in a club called La Vie en Rose and asked him to come to the opening with me. He agreed. I asked if Mrs. McClintic, the lady sometimes known as Katharine Cornell, would like to come. He said he'd ask her.
>
> She did come. We had a long table down front so that Guthrie could get a good look at the lady I'd signed to play a 15-year-old virgin in the Deep South. Eartha came out in about a million dollars of slinky dress and dazzling jewels . . . The whole performance was as far removed from the role in *Mrs. Patterson* as night from day, and I had my doubts as to whether Guthrie would see in her what I wanted him to see.
>
> He did. After she left the stage he said to me, "She'll be wonderful in the role. This girl isn't sexy—she's only a little girl playing at being sexy."[2]

Casting for *Mrs. Patterson* started in August in New York. The costarring part of Willie, the local boy with whom Teddy Hicks shares her dreams of a better life, was won by a young actor called Terry Carter. Carter would go on to have a very successful career; particularly in television, where he blazed a trail for integrated casting in everything from *The Phil Silvers Show* (known popularly as *Sergeant Bilko*), in the fifties, to the space opera *Battlestar Galactica* in the seventies, while the highlight of his film career was probably playing opposite Pam Grier in blaxploitation classic *Foxy Brown*. Back in the summer of 1954, though, he was still a young actor, and *Mrs. Patterson* looked like his big break, his first Broadway appearance.

He well remembers the main characters involved behind the scenes in *Mrs. Patterson*: Sebree, Sillman, and McClintic.

Sebree was the first black playwright to have a show on Broadway. He was a very pleasant fellow, smooth and funny, and he was around while we were doing the show; he was there for whatever changes needed to be made. Leonard Sillman's motto was "Ping!" He would come backstage and say "Ping! Ping!" I knew what he meant—he wanted things to be at their apex, to be on top of every moment—but it was more appropriate for one of his revue shows. He was a good guy though, and if there was any friction with Eartha I didn't see it. Guthrie McClintic was very pleasant but I frankly didn't get to know him. He was kind of an odd choice for the play in retrospect.

As for Eartha herself, Carter says:

We knew from the start that the play was to be a vehicle for her. It was quite evident to me that she was in command of everything around her. She acted like the star she was—even though she hadn't been one for very long—she was very self-assertive. She had a good sense of humor, but you had to be on the good side of her. Eartha was very determined to make it work. I think she did a great job. It was easy working with her, the show brought out the kid in both of us.

This was actually something of a mixed blessing for Eartha: she had her childlike side, of course, but having to imagine herself back in the South was more than a little traumatic. Over the past twenty years she had done a good job of appearing to come from everywhere and nowhere, and to be reminded, night after night, that she was actually rooted in the poor rural South was one further strain on her already overstressed mind. Night after night she was being dragged back to a place she thought she'd escaped forever.

The show opened in Detroit in early October before moving on to Chicago for a seven-week run. The Detroit critics were kind; the Chicago ones less so, with the *Chicago's American*'s Roger Dettmer commenting that Eartha possessed "enormous vitality and commensurate discipline, but not the physical person or personality to suggest pre-adulthood for three recognizably long acts." This lack of critical enthusiasm didn't stop the public from coming in considerable numbers to see Eartha playing a fifteen-year-old in a pigtail wig.

For Chicago's African-American community in particular the play was a big deal: a major theatrical show focusing unapologetically on black life. Sillman made the first night a benefit for the Chicago Urban League, a long-established African-American charity, and this ensured the attendance of an array of black celebrities, including the boxer Joe Louis. Meanwhile Sebree and Johnson worked on cutting and sharpening the script, to get it ready for New York.

Behind the scenes, however, Eartha's life was starting to unravel. Missing Loew, she began flying out to Los Angeles on her days off—Sundays—just to have some time with him. A week or two into the Chicago run, she went to see Sammy Davis, Jr. appear at the Regal Theater, accompanied by Terry Carter, with whom she'd now become quite friendly. They went backstage to talk to Sammy and, according to the subsequent newspaper reports, they were closeted together for a while before Eartha stormed out and Sammy gave orders that she was to be turned away if she ever reappeared. Most of the press assumed this was to do with the alleged romance between the two stars, but Sammy himself suggested that it was actually an argument over racial matters. And a leading black newspaper, the *Pittsburgh Courier*, reported that "They differed violently over their respective allegiances and loyalties to members of their own race. It began with a hassle over whether she should play Harlem's Apollo Theater and ended with her eviction."

Terry Carter doesn't remember it being quite such a heated debate and offers his impression of what actually happened, which suggests it was more a clash between two very strong egos:

> I remember the night we went to see him perform, and afterward when we went to talk to him. He teased her. He was the one person who could get the better of her. Not many people could tease her—I certainly couldn't! But Sammy was able to. You see Eartha at that time, well she

was a domineering person but she couldn't dominate Sammy—and I can't remember exactly what it was he said, but he upset her.

Two weeks later Sammy was driving from Las Vegas to Los Angeles when he had a terrible car accident which resulted in the loss of one eye. This news, following as it did after their argument, hit Eartha hard, but not as hard as what happened next. Late that November the new issue of *Confidential* magazine hit the news-stands, and among its cover stories was one entitled "Eartha Kitt and her Santa Baby, Arthur Loew Jr." Her secret love was now right out in the open.

NINETEEN

Hush-Hush and Strictly Confidential

Confidential was the original showbiz scandal magazine and an American phenomenon of the time.[1] Its house style, a weird mix of unlikely slang and innuendo, was memorably celebrated in James Ellroy's *L.A. Confidential.* The magazine's exposé of Eartha and Arthur's relationship is entirely typical:

> When Eartha Kitt, the sly sepia singer, croons, "Santa Baby, I want a diamond ring, yachts and things . . . so hurry down my chimney tonight," she's not thinking of any gent in a red suit and whiskers. She's got her cute, ambitious mind on a real-life Santa with a million bucks in his jeans. When she sings, those songs are for one guy in the audience who sits staring at Eartha as if he'd been bonged on the bean . . . He is Arthur Loew Jr., Eartha's real-life "Santa Baby"—a true, dyed-in-the-wool millionaire from two of the wealthiest, most respected and famous first families in Hollywood.
>
> [His family] quivered and quaked when Junior started dating the bronze baby, but hoped for the best. Their shock was far worse when cultured members of the family began getting a strange and husky voice on the telephone when they called Art. It sounded as though Arthur

and Eartha had taken up light and dark housekeeping. The family demanded an immediate check-up of Eartha's background, the results of which satisfied practically no one.[2]

This was precisely the sort of publicity that Eartha had dreaded. Her relationship with John Barry Ryan had been derailed by his family. She'd tried hard to keep her relationship with Arthur out of the press, hoping that, given time, it would become strong enough to withstand whatever the press or his unimpressed family could throw at it. She'd surely known that *Confidential* would take an interest in her, but she'd fobbed the magazine off a few months earlier by feeding them a rehash of her dealings with Orson Welles which they bought: "The colored canary from a cotton farm in Carolina and the butterball from Broadway really had the hots for one another."

Now though, with their relationship not just out in the open but the subject of general gossip, Eartha would find out whether her connection with Arthur really was strong enough to survive the inevitable pressure from his family to find a less controversial partner.

The answer was quick in coming. After the piece appeared Arthur rang her at 4:00 a.m. one night and told her he loved her. Then, a full three days later, he called again to add the all-important proviso: "I've never been in this situation before. I love you but I'll never be able to marry you."

It was Bayeux Baker and John Barry Ryan all over again. This time, however, it wasn't a straightforward breakup. Instead, Arthur, in so many words, was proposing to continue their relationship but without the possibility of marriage.

This was a terrible betrayal. Eartha must have believed Arthur Loew was going to ask her to marry him. Instead, just like the others before him, he was asking her to be his mistress and nothing more.

It's a sign of just how besotted she was with Arthur that, rather than telling him to get lost, she forced herself to consider this shaming compromise. After all, she knew by now how the world worked. The Loew family's reaction was painful all right, but hardly unexpected. And while she had angrily rejected similar proposals in the past—from Maury Yaffé, from Bayeux Baker—Eartha cared enough for Arthur actually to countenance the suggestion that they carry on their relationship without the prospect of marriage. She decided that she wouldn't go so far as to actually live with him, but she was prepared to find a place of her own in Los Angeles and carry on their affair discreetly.

What must have made the situation all the more painful was that interracial marriages, while rare, were not unknown in the fifties, especially not in the entertainment world. There was Pearl Bailey, who had recently married white jazz drummer Louie Bellson; Lena Horne, the biggest black female star of the past decade, had been married for years to her white bandleader and arranger Lennie Hayton. And, while neither Hayton nor Bellson were as rich as Arthur, the Loews, too, were a family with a background in entertainment.

Arthur Loew's world was that of Jewish-dominated showbiz, not WASP-dominated Wall Street. If he had wanted to face up to his family and marry Eartha he could have done so: he had already come into a huge inheritance. Though she tried hard to put a brave face on things, this rejection was more than Eartha could take, debilitated as she already was. A few days later she ended a matinée performance of *Mrs. Patterson* in uncontrollable tears and unable to take her curtain calls.

Terry Carter was aware that something was very wrong with the show's star. He's clear that it was her relationship with Loew that was at the root of her distress:

> Yes, I was very aware of it, we were very close. I certainly recall the night
> we went on stage and she just stood there for what seemed like an eter-
> nity in the middle of a scene and they just had to bring the curtain down
> I can recall being in her hotel suite when she was on very long phone
> calls with Arthur Loew. They were kind of emotional! I think at that
> point he was trying to let her down easy. There was no way there could

be a happy ending. She told me his family said it could never happen. They were ready to disown him and I don't think he was ready for that. And I know she was very committed to the relationship; it meant a great deal to her, so that was the end of the world for her.

Nevertheless the show had to go on. In December they opened on Broadway with a tightened-up version of the play. This attracted rather more positive reviews than they'd had in Chicago. John Chapman of the *New York Daily News* hailed it as "the most exciting piece of theater I have encountered so far this season." That said, most of the enthusiasm was for Eartha herself rather than the play as a whole. The *New York Times*'s Brooks Atkinson, the man whose rave for *New Faces* had kick-started its success, was still a fan. He describes her as "an incandescent young woman with lively intelligence, a darting style of movement, keen eyes and an instinct for the theater."[3] Louis Sheaffer, later the Pulitzer Prize–winning biographer of Eugene O'Neill, offered a more detailed account in his review.

> This Eartha Kitt is also a mighty ingratiating little actress. She carries quite a load with commendable skill and great personal appeal in *Mrs. Patterson*. She is on stage almost continuously, playing a restless, imaginative fifteen-year-old in a small town down South . . . From the moment she first races on barefoot, wraps herself in a tired old black feather boa and grins shyly from beneath a ridiculous, floppy hat as she playacts at being grown up, Miss Kitt provides an unwavering center of interest in this wayward, uneven comedy-fantasy. Occasionally you catch glimpses of the highly stylized personality which brought Eartha Kitt fame as an incendiary singer, but she is a performer of integrity and most of the time entirely convincing as a raggedy Negro country girl who dreams of growing into a "rich white lady" like Mrs. Patterson, her mother's employer.[4]

To those who knew Eartha well, the surprise wasn't that she might empathize with a young country girl, but rather how well she was able to act the part on stage. One old friend who was particularly struck by Eartha's performance was Van Aikens, who had just arrived in New York after a long tour with the Dunham Company. "When I came back from Argentina I saw her in *Mrs. Patterson* and it was the greatest surprise of my life. For the first time I realized just how very talented she was."

Ticket sales were strong, the show broke the house record at the National Theater, grossing $36,000 in its second week, and was booked up for three months in advance. After that, Sillman planned to take it on tour. Eartha, however, was visibly weakening as the run went on.

Her fragile state can't have been helped by an *Ebony* cover story, in the December issue, headlined "Why Negroes Don't Like Eartha Kitt." The coverage inside was actually very favorable, arguing that Eartha was not a snob, just a highly strung artist, but most people would only see the cover, with its deliberately controversial tagline. This must have added to her sense of the unfairness of her situation, a sense that she was being exploited on all sides and appreciated on none.

Arthur Loew was proving ever harder to reach on the phone, and anyway had made it clear that he only wanted her as his mistress. She felt as though Leonard Sillman saw her only as a cash cow, and sent her back for more so-called vitamin shots when she complained of exhaustion. And now she was being accused by the black press of being an uppity star who didn't want to have anything to do with "her own people." This was a patently unfair charge. Eartha might have preferred to live in the world of the beautiful people, but she certainly didn't forget where she came from, and right from the start of her success she had been involved in a whole range of charitable activities.

This charitable work ranged from the regular good causes that any black celebrity might contribute to, like benefits for the Urban League, to the more small-scale and specific, like her financial support for ex-Dunham dancer Syvilla Fort's new studio in Manhattan, which was struggling to keep the Dunham flame alive now that Miss D. was spending most of her time in Europe. Eartha herself would go to the studio from time to time, on occasion with a friend of Arthur's, an up-and-coming young actor named James Dean.

Her favorite charity, however, was the Northside Center For Child Development in Harlem. During 1954 Eartha had donated $18,500 to this pioneering outfit, led by Kenneth B. Clark, the black educational psychiatrist whose research had been pivotal to the *Brown v. Board of Education* case. Its mission was to treat the psychological effects of racism and poverty, as experienced by Harlem's youth. It was a cause Eartha clearly felt close to her heart and the size of her donations (tax deductible though they might have been) clearly demonstrated her commitment to antiracist causes.

Moreover, the idea that any African American could really forget their color in the America of 1954 was absurd. While *Mrs. Patterson* was playing in Chicago, Eartha and Terry Carter had been subjected to a familiar humiliation: "I remember that Eartha and I, when we were in Chicago, wanted to go out to dinner. We saw a restaurant, looked kind of nice, so we went in. The guy said sorry we are only taking reservations, yet the place was half empty . . . Eartha was indignant, but what could we do?"

Inwardly devastated by Arthur Loew's ever colder shoulder, Eartha did her best to carry on as normal. In January, as well as appearing in *Mrs. Patterson*, she also had to make time to get back to her recording career. She cut eight new songs over two sessions. Again they were a mixed bag. On the upside, there were a couple of dramatic numbers that suited her stage persona perfectly: a three-minute melodrama called "The Day that the Circus Came to Town" and the delightful "Dinner for One Please, James" (which remained unreleased until the 1990s). And on the downside were a couple of perky novelty throwaways: the infantile "I've Got that Lovin' Bug Itch" and a new composition from Jimmy Kennedy (the man responsible for the execrable "Sandy's Tune"), who once again showed off his ineffable ability to besmirch the musical cultures of faraway places with his "Mambo de Paree."

Two further tracks were chosen as Eartha's next single release. The A-side, "My Heart's Delight,"[5] is fascinating inasmuch as it was Eartha's first attempt at recording in a straight rhythm and blues style. Eartha sounds absolutely at home, though very little at all like "Eartha Kitt": there's hardly any vibrato and no mannered asides, just a confident R&B swagger. The B-side meanwhile was absolutely Eartha. Called "The Heel," it's an English translation of a song written by the great French chansonnier Léo Ferré, and its tale of a woman locked to a faithless lover could hardly have been more appropriate to Eartha's situation.

The week after these recording sessions, Eartha headed off for one of her more unlikely assignations—tea with Albert Einstein. This was Eartha's idea. Einstein was the popular epitome of pure intellect at the time, and he was attached to Princeton University, just a short drive from New York. So Eartha told Virginia Wicks that she wanted to meet him. It was a typical star's whim, if the star was of the sort who liked to flaunt her intellectual side—and Eartha most certainly was.

As it happened Virginia Wicks was able to figure out a route to Einstein. It transpired that one of the Northside Center's staff was a friend of Einstein's secretary, and following a series of letters between Eartha and the Professor, a meeting was finally arranged for Sunday, January 16. Most likely Einstein agreed to the rendez-vous for the simple novelty of taking tea with a vibrant young star. That said, he was also known to be an outspoken antiracist, who had joined the NAACP on arrival in the United States, corresponded with civil rights activist W.E.B. Du Bois, and referred to racism as America's "worst disease."

Virginia Wicks drove Eartha down to Princeton and waited for her down the hill from Einstein's house, where she stayed for an hour or so. What transpired there was meant to be private, as Virginia remembers. "That trip was arranged by my office. We promised Einstein's secretary that there would be no publicity, and I meant it.

But someone in my office leaked it to the showbiz columnist Doro-thy Kilgallen." One can't help suspecting that that someone might have been Eartha Kitt. This was far too good a story to keep to her-self. Her fellow cast members were greatly amused by the news, as Terry Carter remembers: "We were just wondering what they had to talk about!"

The answer to that question, according to Dorothy Kilgallen and an interview Eartha gave to Associated Press, was that they touched on a whole range of subjects and Einstein himself was "warm and very affectionate." "I saw him upstairs in his study. He wore an old pair of pants and a real sloppy joe sweater. The first thing he said to me was 'My dear you are so young.'"[6]

They discussed the theater and agreed that it was in a shoddy state. American critics, according to Einstein, lacked an aware-ness of tradition. As for his opinion of her own role in the theater, he admitted that he didn't have a clue who she was. His taste in music was for Beethoven. In general Eartha seems to have asked a series of naïvely general questions and Einstein seems to have been faultlessly polite in his responses. She asked what the earth was like "in the beginning," and Einstein replied: "My dear, I don't know. I wasn't around then!" Then, presumably having been asked if he believed in reincarnation, he described it as "an illusion." Finally, according to Eartha, "we talked about knowledge, and he said it is a surface thing. He said he had been privileged to get deeper into some studies than other people, but even this was still a surface study."[7]

Eartha's visit to Einstein was an example of her trying to wrest back some control of her life, to present herself as an independent and original person, for whom the restrictions of race were petty absurdities and not the kind of thing that a thinking person would take seriously. It was this sense of herself, as Terry Carter points out, that was being so badly damaged by her treatment at Arthur Loew's hands: "It was a big blow in so many ways; to her ego aside from everything else. She was certainly very intent on having things go the way she wanted. She wanted to build her own reality."

This desire to change the way people thought about her is most apparent in a revealing interview Eartha gave to the London *Evening Standard*, whose reporter was intrigued by stories of her meeting with Einstein:

It turns out that this temperamental brown spitfire of a girl has other unexpected ways of spending her days off. "I often go to the United Nations," she said. "The other week I met the man I admire most there, Dr. Ralph Bunche.[8] I lunched with a Korean delegate to talk over the Far East situation. Nightclubs? Don't be silly. I haven't time. There's nothing unusual about it," she snaps. "I wanted to meet Einstein because he means so much to any thinking person." On her visiting list for the future are Prime Minister Kwame Nkrumah of the Gold Coast and the Aga Khan.

Negroes say she ignores them and cultivates whites. To this Eartha answers, "It's true that I have been a lot of places that other Negroes have not, but this has been because of my lack of inhibitions and because I do not carry my race on my shoulders."

There was silence while she jabbed bobby pins into her short urchin hair, cut for her stage part as a poverty-stricken child of fifteen living in a Negro shack and dreaming of life as a great lady.

"I hate to wear the glamorous dresses actresses are supposed to wear. I like to wear slacks and read and read and read. Try to learn as much as I can. I read the life of Einstein, I read James Joyce and Jacques Prévert. Just now I am reading Emerson because he writes about nature and that is calm and simple. When I am in the mood I paint—not well, just still-life studies I like doing. I write too, when I feel like it. The other night I started to write when I got home from the theater and when I looked at the time it was nine in the morning. I'm about halfway through my autobiography. No ghost-writer for me. That's horrible, it's dishonest."[9]

Unfortunately much of this was simply bravado. Eartha loved the idea of herself spending her days painting and reading James

Joyce before popping over to the UN for coffee with one of the great men of the age, but the reality was that she was on a show-business treadmill, while the man she loved was treating her badly. The strain of trying to look on the bright side meant that her sense of reality was growing more fragile every day.

The situation was all too evident to everyone involved in the show. Leonard Sillman sent her to the doctor for more "vitamin" shots, and announced that the show would be closing at the end of February and heading off on a three-month tour. Preparations were made, the cast had their bags packed, and Terry Carter had sublet his apartment. And then, one Thursday evening, February 10, just eight minutes into the performance, everything went to hell. Eartha walked out on to the stage and just stood there, completely mute. She heard the stage manager prompting from the wings, but it wasn't a matter of having forgotten her lines, she was simply incapable of making herself say them. After a few agonizing minutes of this, the curtain came down and Eartha was rushed to her dressing room.

Terry Carter remembers the occasion vividly: "It was a disaster waiting to happen. So when she 'went up' as they say on stage . . . well, that was that."

Eartha spent a few days in the Doctors Hospital on the Upper East Side. The remainder of the New York run was canceled, as was the tour. Leonard Sillman was furious. As far as he was concerned this was a deliberate move by Eartha to get out of her contract and rejoin her boyfriend in Los Angeles. Yet it was also clear that whatever ailed Eartha went well beyond playacting. Sillman told the press that "If two doctors and two psychiatrists can't decide about it, then who knows?" On Eartha's behalf, Virginia Wicks discarded speculation that she was suffering from "boyfriend problems" and assured the press that she had a kidney infection. In the end it scarcely mattered what the precise problem was. The fact was that Eartha was in no state to carry on. The rest of the company was given its notice. Sillman lost $60,000, he told the press. The cast responded to the situation philosophically. It had been clear to all of them that Eartha had been under intolerable strain. Terry Carter:

> We were certainly disappointed, but not angry, we could see what was happening. As for Eartha herself, she certainly didn't have anything more to do with the rest of the cast after that moment onstage—I don't remember that I had a chance to speak to her again, or that anyone else did, other than Sillman.

As to whether Eartha's collapse was essentially mental or physical, Carter simply says, "It was both, simultaneously."

TWENTY

Back to Black

Leonard Sillman's suspicion that Eartha's illness was partly caused by her desire to get back to Los Angeles ASAP was quickly confirmed. By the beginning of March she was out of the hospital and had decided that the best place to convalesce would be in sunny California. She booked herself into a suite at the Sunset Tower Hotel, a deco landmark on the Sunset Strip, along the way from the Mocambo. And just around the corner from Arthur Loew's place on Miller Drive.

But if she was hoping for a romantic reconciliation she was sadly disappointed. She phoned Arthur, and he didn't take her calls. She went to the Mocambo in the hope of seeing him. That didn't work either. So she hung out with their mutual friend, James Dean, hoping for news. Dean encouraged her to be patient and wait for Arthur to see sense and break free of his mother's influence.

In the meantime Eartha became closer to Dean. Dean, too, was struggling to deal with the experience of sudden fame. He'd recently finished filming *East of Eden*, and had followed that up with some TV work in New York, where he'd first met Eartha. He'd come back to LA just a few weeks before her. He was preparing for his next role: the lead in a film called *Rebel Without a Cause*. At the beginning of March he bought and raced a Porsche Super Speedster, and ducked out of going to the premiere of *East of Eden*. The following week there was a glowing profile in *Life*, while the reviews for *East of Eden* immediately established him as the hottest new star in American cinema. The only trouble was that the whole experience seemed to bewilder and frighten him. For the next few weeks James Dean and Eartha Kitt, both ostensibly at the top of their fields, spent time together. The two of them, despite their fame, were a kindred pair of lost souls.

Together they talked and went on nighttime motorbike rides. It was a friendship conducted well away from the gossip columnists' haunts. However, the LA writer John Gilmore did see them together one night:

> We met out of the blue. Eartha was on the back of his bike. We went to Googie's diner, then went for a ride, then headed back to Googie's. I remember Eartha had on a belt like one weightlifters wear, but made in leopard-skin! I asked her about it and she said she had it made in Paris—of course! She seemed very young, she was very young-acting.[1]

It's an account that matches Eartha's own memories of her nights spent riding around with James Dean. He'd phone her in the middle of the night and suggest going out for a ride. She'd get dressed, put on a helmet, and jump on the back of his bike. Together they'd cruise Sunset Boulevard before stopping off at a coffee shop to talk.

Occasionally these talks would turn serious, mostly in connection with their romantic problems. Dean would also complain about his difficulties with the studios, but, according to Eartha, he didn't want advice, he was sure of his own mind.

After a couple of weeks in LA with no sign of interest from Arthur Loew, Eartha had had enough. She decided to head up to Las Vegas for a few days. Before she left, however, she showed up at the Mocambo one night to support fellow Virginia Wicks client Ella

Fitzgerald, who was making her debut at the club. This was quite a big deal as Ella was emphatically a jazz singer, rather than a cabaret star, and the Mocambo didn't generally do jazz. Marilyn Monroe had lobbied hard to persuade Charlie Morrison to make the booking. At the end of the show, however, it was not Marilyn herself but her friend Eartha who came out on stage and handed Ella a dozen red roses. This was a nice gesture that helped to smooth an uneasy relationship. For, as Virginia Wicks remembers, Ella and Eartha admired each other, but could hardly have been more different:

> I don't remember any female singer Eartha wanted to emulate or was particularly close to. Maybe Ella, though they weren't that close. See Ella was a family person, a down-home personality, and she was impressed by Eartha, but she was also a little afraid of her, her sophistication and her sharp tongue. She felt inferior, I think.

Eartha Kitt spent a week trying to relax at El Rancho in Las Vegas, then returned to LA where the Katherine Dunham Company was making its first appearance in years. They put on the nightclub version of their show at Ciro's and Eartha was there every night. Clearly any bad feeling was out of the way, at least between Eartha and the regular members of the company. The antagonism between Eartha and Miss D. would take a little longer to die down. Eartha's presence at the shows was also very likely motivated by her knowledge that Arthur Loew was a big fan of the Dunhams.

No doubt she saw him there, at one or another of the shows, but at the end of the run Arthur threw a party for the company and pointedly failed to invite Eartha. It was a calculated snub and sent her a very clear message. The relationship was absolutely over. Not only did Arthur not want to marry her, he was no longer even interested in having her as his mistress. She had humbled herself and still been rejected. Before long Arthur would be seen around town in the company of a new British starlet named Joan Collins.

No wonder that the following week's *Variety* announced that Eartha would not be returning to the West Coast till October, when she would appear at El Rancho. In the meantime she was back on the treadmill, her heart well and truly broken.

Eartha began her tour back home in New York with her first appearance at Jules Podell's Copacabana. While there she also became a godmother for the first time: to Virginia Wicks's daughter Christina.[2] In the runup to her opening night Eartha fell out with her proposed pianist, an English expat called Ronnie Selby, over a "temperamental difference of opinion" and was reportedly in a foul mood come showtime.

Billboard was distinctly unimpressed with the show, comparing her unfavorably to her predecessor at the club, Sammy Davis, Jr. Following the Copacabana, Eartha headed off for a run at the Latin Casino club in Philadelphia. She was in no shape to perform though. On her first night in Philly she collapsed onstage for the second time that year. This time she was diagnosed with a throat problem and she returned to New York and the Doctors Hospital for a throat operation and a period of enforced rest: her first in years.

While she was laid up, Eartha pondered which way her career should go. If the high-society types at the Copacabana, et al., were starting to provoke her to anger, then perhaps she should try something different. Sammy Davis, Jr. had conquered the Copa, but he was also able to appeal to a black audience. Their famous argument in Chicago had partly been over whether they should make an effort to attract "their own people." At the time she had felt that she had no responsibility to anyone but herself. Now though, she must have wondered whether Sammy hadn't been right after all. Perhaps it wasn't a question of the black audience needing her, so much as one of her needing them. Perhaps it was time she went back to her roots.

To that end she recorded a couple of songs with the very popular Pérez Prado and his Latin orchestra—"Freddy" and "Sweet and Gentle"—and got herself a booking at the Apollo in Harlem, then the epicenter of the black American entertainment world. Before she braved the Apollo, however, she decided to go out on a charm offensive into some less-intimidating black venues. After all, it wasn't going to be easy to dissuade black Americans from the received wisdom that Eartha was nothing but a snob.

Her first port of call was the Loendi Club in Pittsburgh. The Loendi was no nightclub but rather a private and exclusive African-American social and literary club whose membership included Pittsburgh's African-American crème de la crème: doctors, lawyers, business owners, and celebrities, with a distinct bias in favor of the lighter-skinned. Local journalist Hazel Garland described Eartha's appearance there for the long-established black newspaper the *Pittsburgh Courier*:

> Take it from me, folks. Don't ever make preconceived notions about anyone until you've actually met the person. Like a whole lot of folks I had a whole lot of preconceived ideas about Eartha Kitt which were not at all favorable. You see I too had seen Kitt on television, had heard her various recordings, but wasn't impressed with what I had seen and heard. A lot of the stuff that I had read set me against the star; especially those stories about her not caring too much for our folks. But now I'm convinced those stories were false.
>
> I got my first opportunity to meet Eartha at the lavish press party given by the Loendi club last Thursday night. Before the evening was over—and along with everyone else there—I was completely captivated by her charm. By the time we finished dinner, and the men had left the room, we had a good old-fashioned hen party. We learned that she was a "meat and potato girl," meaning she liked plain food, preferably the kind referred to as "down-home" meals. I really warmed to her when I discovered that she, too, loved what we call "ruffles." You know what "ruffles" are. Just plain chitterlins.[3][4]

By the time Eartha came to give her show the next night Garland was a starstruck fan, noting that the live Eartha experience was not simply about the voice, but rather the whole of her. "She is an artist and an actress. She dramatizes a song. Her rich brown coloring is brought out in the lighting. And she doesn't use any pasty make-up to disguise her unusual features." The only negative note in the piece is struck when she bemoans the fact that more people didn't come out to experience Eartha Kitt for themselves. But that was the reality of the situation. Eartha might now have the black press on her side but the black public simply wasn't all that interested. She might have wanted, even needed, a black audience, but the black audience itself, in the middle of 1955, was spoiled for choice. A look at that week's *Billboard* R&B chart shows Fats Domino, Ray Charles, and Bo Diddley in the top three positions. Eartha was never going to beat any of those at their own game. Like it or not, she was always destined to be the odd one out.

Still, she practiced hard for the show at the Apollo, introducing some dance routines into her act, realizing that she had to project rather further in a big theater than in a nightclub. It was all to little avail though. The show didn't attract much in the way of a new black audience, and *Variety* simply commented that she was better suited to the "class nitery groove."

This was no more than the truth and, indeed, her next live appearances were due to be in the class niteries of Las Vegas and Los Angeles. Before she opened at El Rancho she spent a couple of days in LA. While there, still unable to accept that the relationship was over, she went to Arthur Loew's house. Arthur wasn't there, but James Dean was. Dean and Eartha went for one last drive together, this time in his Porsche rather than on his motorbike. Looking back later, Eartha claimed that she sensed his spirit was somehow absent. A week later she was in Las Vegas and James Dean was dead in a car crash.

As for Eartha, she had to keep on working. It was soon clear that *Variety* was right—Las Vegas's cabaret rooms really were her natural habitat. She was as popular as ever at El Rancho, and the magazine called her new show "one of the most exciting acts ever displayed along the Strip." The club's owner, Beldon Katleman, was so pleased he gifted her all the gowns he'd bought for her show. Then, when Eartha arrived back at the Mocambo, *Variety* declared that "she remains the darling of the denizens of the better boites."

Her fate was sealed. She might be a chitlins-and-collard-greens girl in private, but in public she would have to make do with beluga caviar and champagne in the better boites of Las Vegas, New York, and Los Angeles: a gilded cage if ever there was one.

Eartha was caught between worlds. The great irony was that white society was reluctant to embrace her offstage, while black society showed little interest in her onstage. There was nowhere she could be fully at home. Here surely are the roots of her claim that she was rejected on all sides because of her notionally light skin color, an idea that was first expressed by her in the autobiography she was starting to write at around this time. Yet it was less her actual skin tone that was to blame for this perceived rejection than her utter independence of mind as reflected in her personality and in her music.

While Eartha was wowing Las Vegas, news started to come in that she had after all found a new audience; not in black America, but back across the Atlantic, where the British were starting to get the Eartha Kitt bug.

That summer HMV had released a compilation LP, drawn from her first two US albums and titled "*That Bad Eartha*." The *Sunday Telegraph*'s Francis King, who remembered Eartha from her Churchill's stint, gave it a rave: "Her syllables smolder or zing like bullets," he wrote, "and if you don't like all this very much then maybe you'll hate it quite a lot."[5]

The Eartha Kitt cult started to gain members fast. Even the cinema distributors who had initially passed on the film of *New Faces*, due to its lack of big-name stars, started to think again. The film was given a limited release in the provinces and was starting to prove a sleeper hit. London's leading cabaret venue, the Café de Paris, contacted Eartha to see if she might be willing to accept a booking early in the new year.

For the moment Eartha refused. There were exciting developments in the United States too. She had been booked to play the part of Salome in a TV adaptation of the Oscar Wilde play of that name. This was the first time the part had been given to a black woman in the United States, and provided belated recognition that, for all its problems, *Mrs. Patterson* had at least demonstrated that Eartha could act. That she got the part was entirely down to Eartha herself. Her screen agent at William Morris hadn't thought it worth bothering to try for it—"After all, Kitty, you're a Negro" was his excuse—so she'd called up the producer herself and persuaded him to give her a shot. After the Mocambo stint she would be heading back to New York to prepare for that. Meanwhile she had also been offered a starring role in a new Broadway production, a show called *Jazz Getaway*, a revue-style history of jazz, which was due to open in late January. London would have to wait.

Back in New York she made plans for her life, post Arthur Loew. She had been intending to buy a place near him in Los Angeles. Instead she bought her first home of her own in New York, a brownstone on East 92nd Street. Next she gave interviews to the newspaper telling them that she would be retiring from nightclubs for a while—"I don't want to become stagnant"—to concentrate on her acting and writing her autobiography, which she was due to deliver to her publishers early in the new year.

While she waited for her new house to be renovated she went to live with Virginia Wicks and her two children: "She stayed at my house for quite a while, in between apartments, and I got to know her habits. She was like a little child, a very little child, needing love and appreciation. We'd stay in and drink coffee and talk." The two of them were undoubtedly very close. Virginia likens their relationship to mother and daughter. Terry Carter, after recalling how beautiful Virginia was, was happier to think of them as sisters. Either way, the time Virginia and Eartha spent living together gave Virginia a chance to take stock of her protégée:

> Eartha didn't get along with many people, she didn't suffer fools gladly, she was very proud. At times she was several people, she was a star and she was a poor little black girl at the same time. She wasn't a regular black person but she didn't necessarily want to be a white American

either, she wanted European high society—London or Paris. She was on Ed Sullivan, did all the big shows. And even if they didn't like her personally—because she could be very snarly—they knew she was a good act. You see, she took to people or she didn't take to people. She was very definite about who she trusted in life, whether they were interviewers or whatever. I think she had good instincts, I don't think she should have acted the way she did sometimes, but I think she was basically right.

And as for Arthur Loew Jr., Virginia just sighs as she recalls the relationship and its ending: "I knew all about Arthur Loew from what she told me. I think he was the only man she really cared about: she was quite crazy about him. And she was always afraid that she was going to leave her and, of course, he did."

There were signs, though, that Eartha was starting to come out of her grief at losing Arthur. Buying the house in New York was one. Another was a flurry of recording work. Since the breakup with Arthur she'd been in the studio four times. The first time, back in May, was the Pérez Prado session, and she had sounded strained and uncomfortable, lacking all her usual spirit. In August in New York she'd recorded two more songs, a bizarre mock-Japanese novelty called "Sho-Jo-Ji (The Hungry Raccoon)" and a number called "Nobody Taught Me," written for her by Virginia's friend Leonard Feather, which seemed to address the Arthur Loew split directly but still found her at less than full power. A forgettable Christmas single followed in October.

But come December Eartha recorded two more songs that were the best things she'd done in ages. "If I Can't Take It with Me" saw her as breezily flirtatious as she'd been on "C'est Si Bon." The other song was called "Just an Old Fashioned Girl" and it was reminiscent of Noël Coward, with a marimba standing in for a harpsichord as Eartha tells the world that she's just a sweet and simple girl who longs for nothing more than an old-fashioned house and oh yes, of course, an old-fashioned millionaire. It played well with her public image and it would become another of her signature songs.

Strangely, though, it was never released as a single in the United States, and, indeed, had to wait for more than a year before it was released at all, as a track on Eartha's next album.

Nevertheless it was one more indication that Eartha was on the mend, and so too was her appearance in *Salome*. This went very well indeed. Part of the *Omnibus* series of classic dramas performed live on TV, it was presented by the great British expat journalist, Alistair Cooke, and costarred Martin Landau. Music was courtesy of Leonard Bernstein, no less. The critics praised Eartha's reinterpretation of Salome in her own image, as a very modern, deceptively childlike, minx.

This latest success should have left Eartha well set for her return to Broadway, but then, at the very last minute, the plans for *Jazz Getaway* fell through, and Eartha made a spur-of-the-moment decision to head over to London after all. She was not able to fix up a Café de Paris date at such short notice, but Churchill's had a slot for her. Better still, Britain's fledgling commercial TV channel ITV agreed to feature her in a show called *Chance of a Lifetime*. She flew out immediately after Christmas.

TWENTY-ONE

Literary Eartha

Eartha arrived in London on December 27, weighed down with bags, telling the press that they were Christmas presents for Sir Winston Churchill from his daughter Sarah, a wayward spirit and acquaintance of Eartha's.[1] She was very happy to return to Europe. After the last few years in the United States she was pining for the particular glamour of the old world.

The British media were likewise excited by the arrival of Eartha Kitt, this exotic creature they'd heard so much about. She immediately started giving them interviews. First was a brief one with ITV news, notable for her new and fantastically upper-class European accent. At the end of the interview she obviously realized that sex kittens aren't supposed to sound quite so refined, so she threw in a quick purr and a knowing smile to finish things off.

She gave a longer interview to the future TV producer Desmond Wilcox in her hotel suite. It's a classic Eartha performance. She's wearing a gold lamé sheath, the room is festooned with flowers, and after telling Wilcox that she "brings out the beast in men," she suddenly proclaims herself to be just a simple girl. She then makes the entirely spurious claim that she sews her own clothes, as "the fashion designers just aren't simple enough." She finishes off by tell-ing him that she earns the oddly specific amount of $230,000 a year. Perhaps she had just submitted her tax return.

By the time Thomas Wiseman of the *Evening Standard* turned up she was on a roll. She told Wiseman that "I am reading the great Rus-sian novelists at the moment. I think the only way to know whether the Russians are as bad as they are painted is to read about them. So I read Dostoyevsky, Chekhov, and Tolstoy." Wiseman had the nerve to ask her what she thought about sex. Eartha, clearly enjoying her-self, replied, "On the whole I am in favor of it. But I don't agree with Freud that everything has to do with sex, I mean when you look at a picture; that has nothing to do with sex. Or has it?"[2]

A few days later Eartha appeared live on British TV for the first time. The *NME* reviewer was thoroughly impressed:

> So Eartha Kitt finally came back to England as a star! This American girl, who was here as an unknown six years ago, was the heralded star guest on *Chance of a Lifetime* on Wednesday evening. How she scin-tillated! The subtle gestures, the vibration, the control over voice and movement were fascinating. She half-snarled, half-laughed her way through "I Want to Be Evil." A woman couldn't possibly be as evil as this woman seems.[3]

The *NME*'s rival music paper, *Melody Maker*, memorably described Eartha as "the Buddha-faced girl." The *Daily Sketch*'s Herbert Kretzmer, however, was unable to ignore the famously poor production values of the early ITV shows, noting that at the moment Eartha started singing "the scene shifters decided to get busy behind her. Up went one scene, down went another. Eartha raised her voice, glared like an angry Peke. Of course her voice had its old fascination but it was a case of first-rate talent battling with clumsy production right down the line!"[4]

ITV was clearly happy, however, as it signed her to make a short telefilm to be called *Twenty-Four Hours in London*, which would feature Eartha performing at various locations around London—an ambitious project for the times. Some of this was filmed during this visit, with Eartha doing her best to pretend that she wasn't freezing as she sang and danced in front of assorted London tourist hotspots.

This New Year visit was a brief and exhausting trip—by the end of her stay Eartha was telling the *News Chronicle* that "I'm so tired, I've had so little sleep since I got here, and the smog is getting right down inside me." However, it was also an extremely worthwhile one. Just before she left the *Daily Telegraph* declared her one of their women of the year, for "adding lemon to the honey of love songs." She was scheduled to return in three months' time to appear at the Café de Paris.

On the surface, at least, Eartha was getting over her failed love affair with Arthur Loew. What kept her going, though it was also wearing her out, was the ceaseless round of work. Before she returned to England, she appeared for the first time in Cuba, paid a small fortune by the gangster Meyer Lansky to perform at the opening of his new casino in Havana. She worked on her book and even made time to get back to the recording studio. Both RCA and Eartha herself were still hoping for a revival in her fortunes as a recording artist. What neither party could decide was which musical direction she should take.

Eartha herself had been getting back into the Latin music that inspired her as a teenager in Spanish Harlem. In her live shows her regular accompanist was the great Puerto Rican percussionist Lil' Ray Romero. She took this new sound into a New York studio and cut three songs including the driving "Mademoiselle Kitt" (sung, despite the title, in Spanish). RCA, however, wasn't convinced and commissioned further sessions in Hollywood, with material that was much more in the classic Kitt mold. The one exception was a slight but fun novelty number called "Honolulu Rock and Roll," which saw Eartha making an unlikely bid for the new rock and roll market that RCA was starting to do rather well out of, thanks to their brand-new signing, Elvis Presley.[5] It was released as a single and died a quick death. Rock and roll was here to stay, but Eartha was never really going to be a part of it. The label decided to wait for the publication of Eartha's book before releasing any more new material.

Eartha arrived back in London toward the end of April. During her previous visit she had signed a contract with the British publisher Cassell to put out her autobiography in the UK. So she was delighted to accept an invitation to a lunch for Cassell authors at the Royal College of Surgeons on April 23. The reason for the lunch was to celebrate the publication of a new book by Cassell's most famous author: Sir Winston Churchill.

The book in question was the first volume of his *A History of the English-Speaking Peoples*, which would eventually win him the Nobel Prize for Literature. Eartha showed up wearing a beige lace dress, a beige lace hat, and a mink tippet. "Thank goodness I wore my hat," she said to the *Daily Express*'s interviewer Nancy Spain. She sat next to two of her fellow Cassell authors: Pat Smythe, the show jumper turned writer, and Neville Duke, the pilot and then holder of the world air speed record. They ate roast beef and drank champagne and Pouilly-Fuissé 1953, which may have helped embolden Eartha to go and talk to Lady Churchill at the end of the lunch and then to introduce herself to Sir Winston himself: "I hadn't the courage to approach him direct, I spoke first to Lady Churchill. I don't think he'd ever heard of me before. I still doubt whether he knows what I do. But he said goodbye to me three times!"[6]

A week later she opened at the Café de Paris, and despite her professed love of simplicity, her show was a complex, sophisticated operation. She later recalled the setup in minute detail. Pierre Balmain made her an aquamarine silk satin dress, with a train of chiffon that she could remove as she descended one of the club's dramatic staircases. Then she persuaded the Café's flamboyant impresario, Major Donald Neville-Willing, to build a special walkway for her. Turkish-style poufes were placed in strategic positions. She had catlike makeup and her hair combed into bangs. She made a dramatic entrance with just a single bastard-amber[7] spotlight following her.

All the planning paid off. London society came along in droves, led by the fashionable couple of the moment, Princess Margaret and her new boyfriend, the photographer Tony Armstrong-Jones. The critics were unanimous in their rave reviews, none more so than the great theater critic Kenneth Tynan, writing in the *Observer*:

> Miss Kitt combines three epochs of womanhood. Her plaintive furry vibrato is that of an injured child, her face bears the scowl of a discarded mistress; and her words are those of a mistress-to-be. Beginning in a state of extravagant repose (no one in show business can hold a pause longer) she rises slowly to ecstasy, always seeming—and this is true of many stars—to be communing more with herself than with her audience. After a dozen numbers she curls up on the stairs, a silver cicatrice against the purple carpet and sings a song about the day, long ago, when the circus left town; the tenderness of this item, and its hunger for lost paradises, make one forget for a moment the arrogance with which her act began; the moment when, icy and insolent, she sauntered down to the microphone and bade one grovel at her feet. Miss Kitt is the vocal soul of every Siamese cat who ever lived.[8]

Once again there seemed to be no limit as to what Eartha might achieve. A week or so into her Café de Paris run she started rehearsing for her starring role in a play called *The Valiant* to be filmed live by the BBC the following week. Sadly this is lost to posterity. Eartha played a convicted murderess. The play started with her shooting a man and ended with her being led to her execution. The *Express* interviewed her during rehearsals and wondered if she might be interested in quitting the world of cabaret in favor of the legitimate theater. Eartha replied with delicate understatement, "I suppose if I went into theater my living would be fairly comfortable but not as comfortable as it is now."

Two days later, clearly inspired by her Churchill lunch, Eartha showed up at the House of Commons, invited for lunch by two dashing young Tory MPs: Anthony Eden's nephew John and Hugh Fraser, a war hero who would shortly marry Antonia Pakenham, daughter of Lord Longford, and the future Lady Antonia Fraser. Eartha told the *Daily Mail* that "I think your PM is just marvelous. Such a sense of humor."

Eartha took to the British aristocracy and they to her. She was seen around town with a series of eligible young men. The one she was keenest on, however, was a typical Eartha boyfriend, an Anglo-American called Columbus O'Donnell, a scion of the immensely wealthy Hartford family. His mother had remarried an Englishman named Ivar Bryce—a close friend of Ian Fleming from their days in intelligence work. Eartha and O'Donnell met at the Café de Paris, one night when the film director Otto Preminger was also at the club. Preminger, who had auditioned Eartha for *Carmen Jones*, was trying his luck with her. She decided she preferred this young millionaire, with his Lotus parked outside. Their romance lasted until she left London to go on tour at the beginning of July.

As before, it was following a visit to her latest lover's family that Eartha started to suspect that things weren't right. This time, however, O'Donnell's mother wasn't the problem. Instead it was O'Donnell himself who clearly couldn't reconcile Eartha with his background. She wasn't too surprised when he took up with an Italian countess as soon as she was out of the country.

Eartha's penchant for the high life began to attract some sniping, just as it had in the States. In Britain, though, it was motivated less by an idea that she was getting above her station than a feeling, from those on the left, that a black American should take more interest in political issues, the nascent civil rights movement in particular. It was a point made forcefully by the writer and activist Jill Craigie (wife of the Labor politician Michael Foot) in the *News Chronicle*, in a piece about the bitter battles against segregation that were being fought in Alabama. "Many people are fighting racial discrimination at great personal sacrifice," wrote Craigie. "All that is required from Eartha Kitt and her colleagues is recognition that the fight is on."[9]

This obviously had an effect on Eartha. As her change of heart over playing the Apollo had shown, Eartha did listen to criticism—over political matters at least—and genuinely wanted to do the right thing. So the following month she gave the *News Chronicle* an interview in which she discarded the frivolous tone of her early engagements with the British press in favor of a more serious approach. The interviewer, Patricia Lewis, found Eartha in her Mayfair hotel suite, surrounded by her two kittens and a selection of books on philosophy and history. To further emphasize her seriousness Eartha is wearing glasses and appearing to read a Turkish newspaper. She tells Lewis that she speaks seven languages.[10]

She then gave Lewis her views on segregation, starting with a frankly sugarcoated version of her own experience: "I go where I want, I do what I want and I meet the people I want. I've never had anything barred to me. But this has caused resentment only among my own people, maybe it's envy . . ." She then used her upcoming visit to Israel to muse on whether such a state would work for black Americans (the dream then beginning to be expounded by the Nation of Islam, back in the States). Eartha thinks not. Finally she sounds a note of rather casual militancy with her conclusion that "the only way to teach people to live together is to make them live together."[11]

That same week, this newly serious Eartha attended a T. S. Eliot play and a Foyles literary lunch, this time for Edith Summerskill's *The Ignoble Art*, an anti-boxing tract. The *News Chronicle* was there too and was pleased to report that "Dr. Edith grasped Eartha's hand. 'Are you a feminist?' she asked. 'Yes,' whispered Eartha."

Over the next few months Eartha's schedule was more punishing than ever. If she was trying to distract herself from her recent heartbreak by hard work, she was in danger of overdoing it. She was at the Café de Paris six nights a week. On Sundays she played two shows a day at different theaters around town. She found time on June 18 to film a second play for the BBC, a cut-down version of *Mrs. Patterson*, which was the first play to be filmed at the BBC's new Riverside studios in Hammersmith. Once again Eartha's personal reviews outshone those for the play as a whole. *The Times* was impressed: "Sebree and Johnson have written a part that does not diminish Miss Eartha Kitt . . . Miss Kitt has a dozen faces and can become at will a native of Virginia or of ancient Greece." "Why not let her play St. Joan?" asked the now-devoted *News Chronicle.*

Her fellow cast members—among them most of the leading black actors based in Britain at the time—were less impressed by the star who had landed among them, as the fine singer-actress Elisabeth Welch told her biographer, Stephen Bourne. She bemoaned, in particular, Eartha's treatment of the veteran actor Connie Smith:

> Eartha Kitt was a strange creature. During rehearsals she didn't socialize with any of the cast and one day she upset me. Connie was beginning to lose her sight and had trouble remembering her lines. She needed the job. She didn't have many opportunities to work at her age, but Madam had her thrown off *Mrs. Patterson*. I never forgave Eartha Kitt for that.[12]

From Eartha's point of view, of course, it's worth keeping in mind that a TV play is not a charitable undertaking and actors have to be able to do the job they've been hired to do. Otherwise they let down everyone else involved. Also Eartha's own fearsome work rate may well have led her to be particularly hard on anyone who couldn't keep up. After all, the same day she filmed *Mrs. Patterson* she also managed to record an episode of *Desert Island Discs*, with a nicely varied choice of music.[13]

Even Eartha couldn't keep up this kind of work rate indefinitely and by the time of her final British engagement—a week at the notoriously tough Glasgow Empire—she was once again close to exhaustion. Her first set on her first night was cut short and left the audience thoroughly disappointed.

And still there was no respite. From London Eartha went to Stockholm for another successful club stint. Sweden was another country which took to Eartha in a big way. While there she recorded two songs in yet another unlikely language—Swedish—for an album recorded there by her pianist, Sanford Gold.

Next stop was Israel, where she was able to show off the Hebrew material she'd learned for the Ed Sullivan show. And then back, at last, to New York.

Eartha was hoping that her autobiography would turn the momentum of her career around. It was another of her dreams, that she would have a whole new career as an author. Then surely she would receive more respect. Then perhaps the white world that had rejected her so painfully would accept her as an equal and not just as an entertainer, a glorified courtesan. That at least was the hope.

Thursday's Child was published on October 21 by Duel, Pierce & Sloan. Unusually for a show business autobiography it was plainly all her own work (she had written it by hand on whatever paper was around, and Virginia Wicks had typed it all up). However, it's a frustrating book, an impressionistic affair that leaves much unanswered. Perhaps the most telling things about it are the omissions. Thus the fact of her mixed-race parentage is glossed over. Similarly, as we've seen, most of her love affairs are airbrushed into insignificance. The great exception is her affair with Arthur Loew, whom she refers to coyly as "Paleface," which she goes into in some detail. Even then there's one huge omission: Eartha ends *Thursday's Child* with the New York opening of *Mrs. Patterson* and her relationship with Loew still in the balance. Clearly she was not yet ready to admit in print that her great love affair was over.

When it came to launching the book Eartha did her best to have things both ways. On the day of publication she opened at the Persian Room, an exclusive New York cabaret joint which had never before booked a black artist. This hardly helped the popular perception that Eartha Kitt had more time for the high life than "her own people." So she also had a book launch up in Harlem at Lewis Michaux's National Memorial bookstore on 125th Street. Appearing alongside her was her great champion in the black press, Langston Hughes.[14] Overall though, the occasion worked better in terms of Eartha's star power helping Langston Hughes than vice versa.

Despite all this promotion *Thursday's Child* made very little impression on the literary world. It didn't help that it received a slating in America's most important literary forum, the *New York Times Book Review*. The critic Gilbert Millstein was unequivocal in his disdain for both book and author: "This autobiography of a moderately talented night club and musical-comedy performer named Eartha Kitt is an indubitably earnest demonstration of large, gamy pretensions in gummy alliance with small, amorphous ideas."[15]

Even in quarters where there was more sympathy for Eartha herself, like the NAACP's house magazine, the *Crisis*, their critic found it hard to work up much enthusiasm for the book, commenting accurately enough that "This reviewer does not know any more about her character now than he did before he read her life story."

Thus Eartha's dream of literary respectability, in her homeland at least, was stillborn. Neither did her new album, released by RCA to coincide with her book launch, excite much interest. For the first time in Eartha's hitherto meteoric career, doors were closing rather than opening. Her only consolation was that the book would be coming out in England soon, and perhaps it would fare better there.

TWENTY-TWO

International Eartha

What Eartha really needed was a break. As she'd told an AP reporter at her book launch, she hadn't had a vacation in five years and she desperately needed a rest: "More than anything else in the world I want time off for a little privacy. Now that I'm no longer hungry I want to just be myself for a while again, and get reacquainted with me. Who am I? I've been so busy I no longer am sure."[1]

Relief from the treadmill finally came from an unexpected source. Before leaving for England she received a firm offer to make a new film; her first in a dramatic role. It was to be called *The Mark of the Hawk* and was set in an emerging African country, just on the cusp of independence. She would play the wife of an African leader and be given top billing, along with the hottest young black actor in America, Sidney Poitier. Filming would take place at the Associated British Picture Corporation studios at Elstree, outside London, and on location in Nigeria.

The director was a man named Lloyd Young, up until then a music editor on an assortment of Hollywood films including *Sweet Smell of Success*. *The Mark of the Hawk* could hardly be further from *Sweet Smell*'s cynicism. Young was writing the script but the funding for the movie came from the missionary arm of the US Presbyterian Church. This was to be a movie with a very clear message.

Eartha doesn't seem to have been too concerned about the source of the film finance. She went out for Japanese food with Young and his wife. He explained that she needn't even visit Africa: all her scenes would be shot in the studio in London. Eartha said that, on the contrary, she would only make the film if she was allowed to come to Africa for the filming, whether or not her scenes were to be filmed there. Lloyd agreed and the deal was done. Eartha's filming would start in London in the New Year, but first she would get her long-dreamed-of vacation.

Africa was a blast, exactly the kind of break that Eartha needed. She wasn't actually appearing in any of the scenes filmed on location, so while Sidney Poitier and the rest went on filming she was able to do as she pleased.

The location shooting took place in Enugu, the city in eastern Nigeria that would later become the capital of breakaway Biafra. The cast was staying at a government-run hotel, the Catering Rest House. Eartha met her costar there. Sidney Poitier was emerging as a new kind of black film star—not an apologetic Uncle Tom or a light-skinned charmer, but a dignified, personable, dark-skinned man.

The relationship between the two stars seems to have been cordial more than anything else. Eartha recalls that one evening they went out for a walk and everything was set for romance, except "he was the wrong man, a married man." Anyway if Eartha had wanted a romance with an American film star she had plenty of opportunities back home. Instead she wanted to get away from the film set and see something of the real Nigeria.

It was a time of upheaval in West Africa, as its newly emergent nations were on the verge of independence. Eartha was aware of the political developments and eager to find out about them for herself. To that end she started to explore the town of Enugu by bicycle, clad only in a bikini much of the time on account of the heat, which must have made her something of a local sensation. Before long she took up with a local newspaperman and persuaded him to take her off on a tour of the locality. They spent several days traveling around together, including a stay in an Igbo village, where she became oddly fascinated by the bat population and the role of the bat in the local culture.

Eartha being Eartha she neglected to tell anyone connected to the movie about her explorations, and when her absence was discovered there was a general alarm, as Poitier remembered: "We were panicked. We thought she had been kidnapped or something, [then] she just reappeared as if nothing had happened. She is the freest spirit you have ever met."[2]

While in Enugu, Eartha also struck up a friendship with Nnamdi Azikiwe, the writer and politician who was the premier of the Eastern Region and, post-independence, would become the country's first president. Azikiwe visited the cast's hotel regularly, and must have been happy with the film itself, at least in terms of its message.

However, as it turned out, *The Mark of the Hawk* was no classic. Instead it was a ridiculously dialogue-heavy movie in which an African politician, played by Poitier, navigates his country's way toward independence. For its time, though, it offered a commendably thoughtful take on the anti-colonial struggle. And while the critics were mostly unimpressed, the support of the Presbyterian and Methodist churches back in the United States led to regular showings at their Sunday schools. Within a couple of years of the film's release, the Church was claiming that it had been seen by some five million people.

As Poitier's wife, Eartha herself had very little to do in the film other than wear implausibly glamorous frocks and sing a wholly unnecessary song. Still it was the experience of visiting the new Africa, as it moved toward independence, that she had longed for, and that she certainly got For a politically conscious African American like Eartha it was a profoundly encouraging trip. She came back to Britain to complete the filming with her energy apparently restored.

She arrived in London just in time for the launch of the British edition of her book. This time the reviews were rather more friendly, but hardly the raves she had been hoping for. And though in future years she would occasionally claim to be working on a novel, she seems to have accepted that her dream of being a successful author was over.

Unsure as to where her career should be headed, Eartha decided not to go back to the States right away. Instead, inspired by her Nigerian trip, she resolved to see some more of the world. She plotted a leisurely route back to New York, traveling east rather than west. Along the way she stopped in Karachi, Delhi, Burma, Hong Kong, and Hawaii. The most interesting of these stops was the Indian one. Eartha had gotten the notion that she would like to meet Jawaharlal Nehru, India's leader through the first years of independence. She later explained her reasoning to the *News Chronicle*: "When I was a child Gandhi was ruler of India[3] and I remember I had the same warm feeling for him that I had for President Roosevelt. I wanted to meet Nehru because I was looking for another Gandhi."

She raised the subject at the American consulate, which thought she was crazy but passed the request on anyway. To their amazement they had a reply saying that Nehru would be delighted to dine with Eartha on her arrival in Delhi.

On arrival at Nehru's imposing official residence, Teen Murti House, Eartha, wearing a gold silk-print Dior dress, was ushered in to an anteroom where she waited for her host, surrounded by a mix of antiques and ceremonial gifts from other world leaders. After a considerable delay the doors opened. Two dogs entered, followed by a middle-aged English lady. She was all the more taken aback when the woman introduced herself as Lady Edwina Mountbatten. By the time Nehru himself arrived Eartha was thoroughly bewildered.

It's hardly surprising that Eartha was confused by this turn of events. Lord Mountbatten had been the last Viceroy of India, responsible for the handover of power, and now his wife was giving a dinner with Nehru, seemingly in the role of consort. In fact it was an open secret—of the sort that the press were quite happy to collude in suppressing back in the fifties, when it was understood that the aristocracy lived by different rules to the common man—that Lady Mountbatten was Nehru's mistress. Their affair had begun soon after independence and lasted till she died in 1960. Her daughters claim that it was a spiritual rather than physical relationship, but it certainly went well beyond the bounds of an ordinary friendship. Eartha recalls seeing them holding hands together, and even Lord Mountbatten himself wrote to his daughter Patricia to say that "She and Jawaharlal [Nehru] are so sweet together, they really dote on each other."[4]

It may well be that it was Edwina Mountbatten, then, rather than Nehru himself, who was the more curious to meet Eartha. That's borne out by Eartha's account of their dinner, in which she complains both about Lady Mountbatten's incessant small talk and her own inability to find anything to talk to Nehru himself about, other than "African art and American income taxes." In later years she would frequently refer to this meeting and always complain about the food—she was served "chicken à la king" rather than the Indian delicacies she was hoping for. The topic she never touched on was the way that she had been welcomed by Nehru and his mistress. Or that the mistress in question was a woman of the highest social class.

This must have been a revelation to Eartha. All this while she had been seeking the respectability of a "good" marriage to confirm her admission into high society. Now it turned out that high-society folk were happy to carry on with a shameless disregard for the sanctity of marriage. Perhaps she had had the wrong end of the stick. Perhaps, after all, there was no shame in being a mistress, if the man involved was rich or powerful enough. Perhaps she should forget all about being respectable and just act as she damn well pleased.

TWENTY-THREE

Integrated Eartha

After her world tour, Eartha returned home to New York in good spirits. Her relationship with Loew was no longer in the forefront of her mind. Furthermore she was immediately offered a starring role in a new Broadway show. Not only that but it was an integrated show in which her costar would be a white man. It looked as if America might at last be relaxing its racial divisions.

This show in question was a Broadway musical based on Don Marquis's offbeat short tales featuring a cockroach named archy and his friend, a cat called mehitabel. It looked like a perfect project for Eartha. She'd regularly been compared to felines of one sort or another, but, by now, as her career had gathered its failures alongside its successes, the role of a New York alley cat seemed both poignant and fitting.

The archy and mehitabel stories were originally published as newspaper columns between 1916 and Marquis's death in 1937. They were the literary equivalent of George Herriman's great *Krazy Kat* cartoon strip: satirical and poignant. Appropriately enough Herriman himself provided the illustrations for the three book-length compilations of the strip which proved to be enduringly popular, and provided the basis for the stage show, which was the brain-child of writer Joe Darion and composer George Kleinsinger. They turned the original stories and poems, ostensibly typed with con-siderably difficulty by archy the cockroach (their names are always in lower case because archy couldn't operate the shift key) into a mix of dialogue and songs. When it came to giving the show more structure they called in their friend Mel Brooks, who much enjoyed both the task and the reunion with Eartha, his old friend from *New Faces* days. Brooks takes up the story:

> Joe asked me to join in writing the book. I knew archy and mehita-bel because of Don Marquis's column and I thought it was brilliant casting. The only thing that was wrong with the show—the book was very good and the songs were wonderful—the only thing wrong was that it played on Broadway to a theater with 3000 seats and it should have played in the Village at somewhere with 300 seats. Some-where intimate for this lovely funny emotional portrait of this alley cat that falls in love too easily.

The casting was smart: Eddie Bracken, a Broadway regular with a fine line in looking put-upon, was archy. Eartha was an obvious choice as mehitabel, though a brave one too, given the general taboo against interracial casting that was still in place.

The show was given the name *Shinbone Alley*. It opened on April 13 and ran for a little over a month. The reviews were broadly positive. Eartha's friend Langston Hughes was particularly enthusiastic:

> Eartha Kitt is one of America's tiniest stars, but she is every inch a star. In her latest musical *Shinbone Alley* she shines very brightly indeed. And the whole show, for my money, is one of the best shows on Broad-way. It is a most original, melodic, and delightful evening of story, song, and dance, with some of the funniest comedy sequences of the year, and the prettiest dancing girls I have laid eyes on for a long time. On the way out of the theater, I ran into George S. Schuyler[i] in the lobby,

and that sage of Negro journalism agreed with me in my enthusiasm. Adding to all its other excellent features is the fact that *Shinbone Alley* is the most thoroughly integrated Broadway show I have ever seen—with a completely mixed cast of colored and white principals, singers, and dancing girls and boys. Nobody is human in *Shinbone Alley* and so, in its wonderful world of make-believe, pretty blond kittens leap into the arms of big dark tom cats, and cute little brown pussy cats dance with white toms as happily as can be.[2]

All of which makes it a real shame that *Shinbone Alley* didn't attract sufficient audiences to run for longer than a month. Most likely it was, as Mel Brooks suggests, down to the mismatch between show and venue, but there may also have been other forces at work. George Irving, who appeared in the play, later recalled that the show attracted its fair share of hate mail from bigots outraged by the interracial casting: "Eddie Bracken would get these disgusting letters. 'How can you kiss that . . .'"

So even if Broadway producers were ready to present racial integration on stage, the sorry truth was that, even in liberal New York, the audiences were less enthusiastic, and as for the wider American public . . . well, suffice it to say that *Shinbone Alley* was a long way ahead of its time.

Eartha didn't let the closing of *Shinbone Alley* get to her. It was clear that the amount of time she'd spent abroad had lowered her profile at home, but she didn't mope around. Instead she spent her suddenly free summer doing pretty much whatever she liked. First up, she decided to revive *Mrs. Patterson* and tour it around New York's hinterlands.[3] It wasn't the major theater tour that the cast had previously anticipated, but it was still work, and most of the original cast were happy to take part, among them Terry Carter.

We came back and took the show on tour in '57. Ruth Attaway was there, I was there. We went on a New England tour—a bus and truck tour! I had a VW minibus at the time and carried the cast from city to

city. By that time I had a few more credits under my belt, so my relationship with Eartha was more even. It was fun.

The tour visited such hotspots as the Westport Country Play-
house in Connecticut and the Country Playhouse in Fayetteville,
New York. On the other hand, for once the pressure was off and
Eartha was able to enjoy herself. The summer stock tour was
indeed fun and so too was her visit to the Newport Jazz Festival in
Rhode Island.

Then in its fourth year, the festival had become a highlight of
the jazz calendar. That year's lineup included everyone from Louis
Armstrong to Dave Brubeck to Ella Fitzgerald. Eartha showed
up on the first day, July 6, to make a guest appearance with the
Dizzy Gillespie Big Band, not as a singer but as a dancer. This was
most likely Virginia Wicks's idea: Gillespie was another of her clients and she was always encouraging Eartha to dance more in her
shows. For the occasion Eartha brought along a teenage percussionist named Don Alias. Eartha had discovered Alias accompanying the dancers at the dance class she had set up at the YMCA in
Harlem, for the local kids. Years later Don Alias recalled the show
in an interview:

> She got to go up to Newport to dance with Dizzy Gillespie's big band.
> This was 1957. All these great musicians were in the band. I was seven-
> teen years old. She decided that she would take me along to accompany
> her. Dizzy Gillespie would play behind her while she was dancing. "Oh,
> my god, I'm going to be playing with Dizzy Gillespie!" He had all these
> Latin-oriented tunes really suited for the conga drum. So she danced,
> and I played with Dizzy Gillespie, which was my first professional,
> union-card-carrying job. I was still going to high school![4]

The tune Don played on, and Eartha danced to, was "Manteca,"
written by Gillespie with Gil Fuller and the great Cuban conga
player Chano Pozo. It was part of a remarkable set that also saw
Mary Lou Williams come out of self-imposed retirement to lead the

band through a performance of her *Zodiac Suite*, which Eartha—to whom it was in part dedicated—may have danced to as well.

The remainder of Eartha's summer was spent in the cabaret joints. Again it was clear that her career was on the wane: she appeared at such second-tier venues as the Elmwood in Windsor, Ontario, and the Diamond Beach Lodge in Wildwood, New Jersey (where she shared the billing with ex-stripper Gypsy Rose Lee). In between times, she hit the headlines following a contretemps at a jungle-themed nightclub called the African Room on Third Avenue.

This venue, which featured a bawdy New York calypsonian called Johnny Barracuda as host and boasted a motorized gorilla as part of the decor, was a regular haunt of Eartha's. One night, after turning up with friends at 1:00 a.m. and ordering champagne all around, she flew into a temper when presented with a bill totaling $137. She refused to pay, and the club, which was run by an ex-homicide detective named Harold Kanter, responded by suing her, alleging that she "shattered glassware near and about tables occupied by other patrons, disported herself upon the stage in a lewd and suggestive manner, poured champagne and liquids on the table and made herself generally offensive to other patrons," and when presented with the bill shouted "This is a clip joint, you are nothing but a bunch of thieves." Asked for her side of the story, Eartha claimed that she didn't drink and that the bill was preposterous.

Outside observers might have been forgiven for suspecting that Eartha's career, in America at least, was about to go into free fall. Her record company had lost interest, her Broadway career looked to be over, and the cabaret work was in decline. But then, just in the nick of time, Hollywood came riding to the rescue.

Eartha had been talked about for various parts in the wake of *New Faces*, but none had ever materialized apart from her supporting role in *The Mark of the Hawk*, which was not a Hollywood production. This all changed in August, when Paramount approached her in connection with a forthcoming biopic of pioneering jazz composer W. C. Handy. The film was to be called *St. Louis Blues* and would star Nat King Cole, the pianist and singer. At the time Cole was the most popular black artist in America, and had recently begun hosting his own weekly TV show. On August 26 it was announced that Eartha had landed a major part in the film, that of the femme fatale, a singer called Gogo Germaine. Other stars appearing in the film were a cross-section of major black musical talent of the period, including Pearl Bailey, Ella Fitzgerald, the gospel singer Mahalia Jackson, and bandleader Cab Calloway. Rehearsals were set to commence at the end of September. This was great news for Eartha, precisely the break she'd been looking for: a chance to act and sing alongside an all-star black cast.

TWENTY-FOUR

St. Louis Blues

So just at the moment when Eartha had started to adapt to reduced circumstances she was catapulted up toward the top of the showbiz ladder. Her dream of film stardom, which looked to have gone the way of becoming a successful author or marrying a millionaire, was back in play. Now she was heading back to Hollywood, the American dream factory.

But just as Eartha arrived in Los Angeles, ready to start rehearsing for Tinseltown's first high-profile black film in ages, events in the outside world conspired to change the whole context within which she—and every other black artist—was working. Quite simply the fall of 1957 was the moment at which black America decided it had finally had enough.

Ever since the end of the Civil War black Americans had hoped that integration would come gradually and peacefully. The black intelligentsia, including writers such as Langston Hughes and artists such as Eartha, had hoped that shows such as *Shinbone Alley* would be a part of that process. Now it was clear that this vision simply wasn't going to happen. If change was happening at all then it was happening far too slowly, and black America was impatient and angry. During September 1957, as rehearsals for *St. Louis Blues* began, the major racial confrontation that had always been inevitable, ever since *Brown v. The Board of Education* signaled the end of segregated schooling, finally came to pass. It took place in Arkansas, in the city of Little Rock.

It had been agreed that educational integration in Little Rock, the state capital, would begin at the start of the school year. The NAACP selected nine of the brightest and best black students to attend the previously all-white Little Rock Central High School. When the date approached the segregationists threatened demonstrations. The Arkansas governor, Orval Faubus, called in the Arkansas National Guard to prevent the nine students from entering the school. What happened next made national headlines and the TV news. The sight of soldiers stopping black children from going to school, while a white mob hurled abuse at them, was one of the pivotal moments in elevating the civil rights struggle to national prominence. The crisis carried on for most of the month of September, with the president, Dwight Eisenhower, notably dragging his feet when it came to intervening.

The black population of America was incensed and mobilized by this as never before. Black celebrities joined the cause too: Louis Armstrong, the grand old man of them all—and one of the most popular with white audiences—was one of the first to make his feelings plain. He'd previously been invited by the government to visit Russia on a cultural propaganda mission. Now he pulled out, telling the press that "the way they are treating my people down South, the government can go to hell. It's getting so bad a colored man hasn't got any country." He went on to say that Eisenhower had no guts, and that Faubus was "an uneducated plow-boy."

This was a rallying cry. The press interviewed other black celebrities to see who else was prepared to stand up and be counted. Lena Horne said mildly that "I think people of all colors should be concerned about what's happening down South." The baseball star Jackie Robinson was more forthright: "I congratulate Louis Armstrong," he said. "This is a feeling that is becoming rampant among Negroes. I am very pleased. It shows a unanimity that has been lacking in the past."

Next in line was Eartha, and she was as militant as anyone: "Armstrong is absolutely right," she said. "We shouldn't go to Russia preaching things we are not." As for Eisenhower, Eartha called him "a man without a soul," before adding, "I don't see how President Eisenhower can have any pride or any respect for his position when he lets someone like Faubus get away with this."[1]

After their pronouncements, Armstrong, Horne, and Kitt all received their share of abuse from the segregationists. A Mississippi radio station banned their records. Tempers cooled a little at the end of the month when Eisenhower reluctantly moved into action, sending the 101st Airborne to escort the children into school and taking the Arkansas National Guard out of Faubus's control. Armstrong sent the president a congratulatory telegram and this particular fire died down for the moment (though not for the nine black students who endured all manner of abuse with extraordinary dignity over the following years).

This then was the context within which work began on *St. Louis Blues*. Filming took place during October and early November of 1957. Eartha managed to combine being on set with another stint at the El Rancho in Las Vegas. Her costar, Nat King Cole, was also keeping up his weekly TV show, and on October 7 he invited Eartha on as his special guest.

The show remains one of the best surviving records of Eartha in her prime, and one that clearly shows her at her most relaxed, with no signs left of the angst that had followed her breakup with Loew. She performs two songs on her own and then two with Cole. The songs are linked together by brief skits, with the amusing conceit of having Cole act as a psychoanalyst and Eartha as his patient, lying, inevitably, on a couch. Thus she sings "My Heart Belongs to Daddy," then asks Cole what he thinks it might possibly mean. He replies by asking about her dreams. A quick dissolve and she's singing "The Sheik of Araby" to Cole, who has added a burnoose to his psychoanalyst getup. Soon it becomes a duet, sung while Eartha drapes herself over Cole. Both of them look to be enjoying themselves—at one point Eartha can't repress a giggle. Finally, they sing another duet in which they swap places on the couch and ultimately declare that what is missing from their lives is each other.

The whole performance is funny, sweet, and beautifully nuanced. There was such obvious chemistry between Cole and Kitt that it fueled rumors of a relationship between them. Certainly that's what Nat King Cole's wife, Maria, suspected. Nat had given her plenty of reasons to be jealous over the years, and she was sure that here was another one, never mind the fact that he'd called immediately after the show went out live, to reassure her that they were just playing around and she shouldn't read anything into it.

Years later Eartha gave her version of events. According to her, Nat enjoyed working with her so much that at the end of the filming he sent her a huge bouquet of red roses and a note saying "Handy misses Gogo" (these being the names of the parts they were playing in the film). Eartha returned the note saying she missed him too. Maria intercepted the note and sent Eartha a furious note of her own, telling her to stay away from her husband.

By Eartha's account, of course, there was nothing between her and Cole, but then her denials of such matters are hardly definitive. Nevertheless she wrote back to Maria telling her that "I feel sorry for someone who obviously has never had a relationship of love without sex, and I feel sorry for someone whose love of her husband is trustless."

Meanwhile the making of *St. Louis Blues* continued. Early on, *Variety* reported that Eartha wanted it to be a closed set as she was so nervous. This seems uncharacteristic, but could have been a response to appearing alongside such a wealth of musical talent including three women—Pearl Bailey, Ella Fitzgerald, and Mahalia Jackson—whose voices were stronger, in conventional terms, than her own.

The film itself is at once the best of Eartha's early films as an actress and something of a disappointment. Musically it's great; Cole is as relaxed and charismatic as ever. Ella and Mahalia are both as impressive as you'd expect; Pearl Bailey sounds effortless. But as a vocalist, Eartha is the real surprise package. She was hardly known as a straight jazz or blues singer, yet her versions of Handy classics like "Careless Love" and "Yellow Dog Blues" show her raising her game with apparent ease, no doubt spurred on by the talent surrounding her.

Dramatically, however, the film is less than enthralling. There's a rudimentary dilemma: should Handy marry his adoring fiancée, played by Ruby Dee, and live a straight-arrow life, or should he play the devil's music in nightclubs alongside the glamorous Gogo Germaine? In the end he keeps everyone happy by writing spirituals as well as jazz and, above all, by making plenty of money. Cole is adequate as an actor while Eartha and Pearl Bailey are both very good. However, there's only so much for them to do, given the weakness of the script.

The production values were also weak. There's a clear sense that the studio, Paramount, had decided that they weren't going to spend a cent more than they had to on an all-black movie. The most obvious piece of cost-cutting was the decision to film in black and white despite the fact that the popular musicals of the day were always in color. It's evident that as far as the studio was concerned this was just a cheap movie for black people, who were so rarely catered to by Hollywood that they'd probably accept whatever they were given.

After finishing work on the film Eartha went back to cabaret in Las Vegas where she soon had a flow of visitors from Hollywood. The film's director, Allen Reisner, came up to Vegas the day after finishing work on the film. A few months later the gossip columnists were listing him as a possible husband for Eartha: he certainly fit the profile of a typical Eartha Kitt boyfriend much better than Nat King Cole.

Eartha was in her element in Vegas. It was now the place where whitebread America came to let its hair down. Especially whitebread American men. The salesmen and junior executives of Eisenhower's America would wink and reassure each other that "What happens in Vegas, stays in Vegas." The newspapers called it "Sin City": commercial sex was readily on offer, and the cabaret acts that went down the best were those that spoke the language of sex.

It was an ideal audience for Eartha of course. She might not find a husband there—indeed she must have been starting to wonder if she was ever going to find the old-fashioned millionaire of her dreams—but she could certainly have some fun with the suckers who came to see her at the El Rancho.

It became a feature of her stage act—and would remain so right up until the end—that she would pick out a man in the audience and direct all her formidable powers of flirtation at him for the duration of a song, or longer if she found a victim she liked. A new friend of hers from Hollywood, a club owner called Roy Sannella, whose nightspot, the Royal Room on Hollywood Boulevard, had been used as a setting for *St. Louis Blues*, got the full treatment when he came up to El Rancho to see her:

> A movie featuring Eartha Kitt was made in my club. We got along very well. After the movie, she was to appear in Las Vegas. She invited me, and when Barbara and I arrived, we went straight to the hotel floorshow. Eartha had arranged front-row seating for us, and when she appeared on the stage, she was lying down on a love seat. She sang a very sexy number, never taking her eyes off me. Barbara was so upset that she walked out and didn't talk to me for a week.[2]

Eartha was well aware of her sexual power, and if it hadn't yet netted her a suitable husband she certainly didn't mind playing around with it, teasing men and enraging other women. It was a playfully effective way of getting a little of her own back on the white world that treated her just as capriciously as she treated the men in her audience.

The early word on *St. Louis Blues* was positive, and Eartha was hot again. In December RCA got her back into the studio to make a whole album of W. C. Handy songs to be released alongside the movie. Backing was by a jazz group, Shorty Rogers and his Giants, rather than the usual studio players, and the result was Eartha's most stylistically homogenous and consistently well-sung album to date, at least as far as the secular material goes—its two spirituals are really a reach too far.

The same month it was announced that Eartha was to appear in another movie. It was called *Anna Lucasta*. It would be shot in April and she would receive top billing right above Sammy Davis, Jr., who would be making his movie debut. Allen Reisner was to be billed as the director.

It was just as well that the contract had been signed before *St. Louis Blues* came out. When the film was released that April the reviews were lukewarm and business slow. In these turbulent times Black America had no interest in looking back to the pre-war era. The point was underlined when the man whose life was celebrated in the films, W. C. Handy, died in the same week as the premiere. *St. Louis Blues*, for all its strengths, couldn't help seeming like a film out of time. Eartha's album also failed to sell. It was her last release on RCA and her career as a major recording artist was effectively over.

Just like *St. Louis Blues*, *Anna Lucasta* had plenty of potential. A project with a tangled history, it was originally written for the stage by Philip Yordan, who would go on to become a remarkably prolific screenwriter.[3] The original stage play bore an obvious resemblance to Eugene O'Neill's *Anna Christie*—even the title is a giveaway—and was initially set in an immigrant Polish community. When Broadway failed to show an interest, Yordan made the central family black instead, with the help of an uncredited black playwright.[4]

In its new incarnation *Anna Lucasta* was a big Broadway hit in the mid-forties. As was usual with Broadway hits, a Hollywood studio bought the rights. But when it came to the actual filming they went back to the original version of the play and gave it an all-white cast.

Yordan was angry about this and persisted in his efforts to have the black version filmed as well. Finally, in 1958, with the civil rights movement on the rise, it seemed that the time was right. Hollywood could see that it needed to make at least a token effort toward desegregating itself, and *Anna Lucasta* got the green light. However, it was to be another low-budget affair, its stage origins obvious, and once again shot in black and white.

On the upside the film showcases a whole cast of talented black actors, most of whom had either been ignored or underused by Hollywood. And, alongside the more experienced actors, the marquee names, Eartha and Sammy, are both vibrant screen presences. It is refreshing to see a fifties film with an all-black cast that isn't set in a cotton field or in a ghetto, but in middle-class suburbia, and in which the central drama isn't to do with race but with family.

Unfortunately these positives are outweighed by the fact that the film is largely incoherent. The script hints at dark themes then ducks away from them. Also problematic is that much of the cast was taken from the original Broadway version of the play. And while that means we get to see great stage actors like Frederick O'Neal in action, it also means that they're all fifteen years or so too old for the parts they're playing, which makes the whole thing rather unconvincing.

Eartha does her best with her part, but again the casting doesn't help. She's meant to be torn between two lovers. One of these is nice guy Rudolph, played by an unknown called Henry Scott, and he's just too bland for any sparks to fly. The other is a sailor called Danny, played by Sammy Davis, Jr. The scenes with Eartha and Sammy provide the film's highlights; there's a crackling energy between then and, even if it isn't really the energy of sexual attraction, but rather that of professional competition, it doesn't matter too much. They are still fascinating to watch, these two diminutive black stars, with their unusual features and their dancers' moves, each struggling to best the other. Yordan certainly saw their relationship as a battle, with Eartha trying to dominate and Sammy fighting back. "He carried his role and she couldn't tower over him. He stood up to her."

Anna Lucasta did not get a good reception on release. First the Motion Picture Association of America complained about the ads for the film. They were upset that Eartha's character was clearly portrayed as a prostitute, that Eartha's dress was too tight, etc., etc. All of which might have made for good publicity, but the critics were contemptuous, none more so than the *New York Times*:

> This incredibly artless film . . . directed by Arnold Laven as if he were looking out of the window most of the time, and . . . played with surprising amateurishness by a big-name Negro cast. Eartha Kitt in the role of Anna, the girl who is driven into a life of shame by a bewilderingly chuckleheaded father, slinks all over the place (and all over Sammy Davis, Jr.) as if she had been tutored by a snake. And when it comes time to act decent and win the good farm boy (Henry Scott), she smoothes herself out into the primmest, most benign little trick you ever saw. It is pure, unadulterated posturing, without concept or conviction that Miss Kitt does.[5]

It's the kind of review that might have been laughed off if the film had been a public success, but it wasn't. Eartha blamed this failure on the undoubted reluctance of Southern cinemas to show it. At the time the film's stars resorted to writing personal letters to Southern cinema owners in an attempt to persuade them to consider running an all-black film, but to no avail. Later Eartha would also claim that this was another example of her being picked on because of the supposed lightness of her skin: that the Southern people had objected to the film on the grounds that Eartha looked too white on screen.[6]

This is obvious nonsense. For one thing Eartha doesn't look remotely white on screen. There are several other members of the cast—like Isabelle Cooley, who played her sister—who are light-skinned with Caucasian features, but Eartha looked as dark as she ever had. Perhaps the sentiment was borrowed from Lena Horne who continually told interviewers that this was the reason for her lack of real Hollywood success, that audiences were confused by the lightness of her skin. In Lena Horne's case this had a kernel of truth—she really was light-skinned—but it still ignored such unfortunate factors as her lack of acting ability.

None of which is to deny that racism had its effect on Eartha's acting career. This was very quickly confirmed when it came to her next role. On November 6 Eartha filmed a TV version of Joseph Conrad's *Heart of Darkness*, playing an African queen. Her unlikely costars were Roddy McDowall and Boris Karloff. Roddy and Eartha rehearsed together in her new house. They worked on the love scene only to have it cut by the director, who proceeded to explain the TV facts of life, summarized by Eartha as follows: "No white man could kiss a black woman on screen. He could throw her about a bit, but not make love to her."

Eartha had given screen acting her best shot, but a lethal combination of racism and bad luck was making it very clear that this aspect of her career was going nowhere. There was absolutely no future in Hollywood for an overtly sexy, black leading lady.

Despite all this, Eartha was having still having fun. Gradually the focus of her life was moving from the East Coast to the West, from New York to Los Angeles. The Mocambo was there, with Las Vegas only a drive away. While making *Anna Lucasta* on location in San Diego, a two-hour drive south of Los Angeles, she rented a house overlooking the ocean in nearby La Jolla. All she needed now was an LA-based personal assistant. She found a young woman called Joyce King, who would go on to become a noted Hollywood script supervisor working on all manner of movies over the next few decades. King told a film journalist how she first met Eartha:

James Edwards was working with Eartha Kitt on *Anna Lucasta*. He took me and his girlfriend to Tijuana to the bullfights, and when we came out and were inching our way toward the gate, this convertible pulls up next to us. Eartha says hello to Jimmy, and Jimmy says hello to Eartha, and Eartha says to the guy she's with, "Screw it!" She jumps out, jumps in our car in the back seat with me. By the time we got to Hollywood, she hired me.

The job itself turned out to involve a lot of improvisation and an ability to read her unpredictable employer's mind. Joyce did her best to outline her duties: "Well, secretary-slash-gopher-slash-try to avoid anything that you can. On your toes. It worked sometimes."

While in La Jolla, Eartha met Aldous Huxley, among other artistic types, and appeared in a play, Thornton Wilder's *The Skin of Our Teeth*, at the La Jolla Playhouse, alongside Cloris Leachman[7] and a young Dennis Hopper. Eartha enjoyed the show and found Hopper an entertaining costar. She was amused at his devotion to method acting, particularly his habit of running around the block several times just before his entrance, just so he could appear authentically tired. Offstage Hopper flirted wildly with both Eartha and her new secretary.

But if Eartha was having a good time and still managing to earn a very decent living, she was all too well aware that she was the lucky one. One of Joyce King's tasks was to deal with Eartha's mail, which would inevitably include begging letters from former friends going through hard times or simply hoping for a share of Eartha's wealth. Eartha was typically unpredictable in her dealings with old friends. Some would complain that she ignored them. At other times, though, she could be very generous—for instance she set Roxie Foster up with a dress shop in Harlem. During the summer of 1958, however, she was contacted by the last person she would ever have expected to be asking her for favors: her former mentor Katherine Dunham.

By then things were not going well for Miss D. The Dunham Company was struggling to survive. In the previous two years there had been only a tour of Australia and another of the Far East, plus a little bit of freelance choreography. Not enough to sustain a whole company, or to fund the ambitious property development plan she had begun in Haiti. There was nothing in the way of the state support that such a company might hope to receive these days. In a series of anguished letters, written while on tour in Japan and sent to her lawyer, Lee Moselle, Miss Dunham is close to the end of her tether. She asks Moselle to try various avenues to raise some finance. Maybe he could secure her a book deal, maybe he could arrange to sell some of the jewelry given to her by various admirers? Finally, and obviously with great reluctance, she suggests he contact her old protégée. Perhaps Eartha might be interested in giving Miss Dunham some work.

> I hear that Eartha Kitt has started a Scholarship fund and will send you a letter to get to her personally if possible on a plan whereby a school operated by me may train these people to whom she is offering scholarships. I am sure that this move of Miss Kitt's is as much a tax-evading one as it is philanthropic or even identification with me which is one of her strongest drives as far as culture pattern goes.[8]

It is unfair of Dunham to suggest that Eartha's charitable work was merely a matter of tax avoidance. However, there's more than a little truth in her suggestion that she had been Eartha's role model through the years. A week later Miss D. had refined her putative approach to Eartha.

> I see that Eartha Kitt is establishing a dance foundation. Is there any way for you to reach her personally through Nat Kalcheim [a senior figure at the William Morris Agency] or otherwise, asking if she would donate a sum of money (too bad you can't tell her to just pay back some of her scholarship money) for the establishment of a school in Mexico. I suppose that the tax exemption of the former school is still in effect. Having in mind the possibility of funding for a Mexican school, I have had revised and reprinted a school certificate, several copies of which I am herewith enclosing for your use. I do not know whether you should show one of these to Eartha Kitt or not, as she is apt to go ahead and set up her own school. I doubt, however, that she would have the time

or acumen to do so, but how on earth can she set up a foundation for people to study primitive dance, as I don't know anybody else who teaches it unless they are abortive cast-offs of our outfit.

If someone could convince her to try and support the matrix, it might give me an opportunity to start the school on a good basis, and Mexico would cost a great deal less than anywhere else. I am thinking of writing her myself but have strong belief in an approach that you would make personally and feel that Nat Kalcheim might be of some help if you could have a talk with him, as to some degree I believe they guide the placement of her income, insofar as anyone could guide her.[9]

Eartha's response to this is not recorded. She certainly didn't set Miss D. up with a school in Mexico, but she may well have helped out financially, as the subsequent correspondence from Miss Dunham to Eartha has a much friendlier tone, but generally involves a request to borrow more money. It's clear that Eartha, a naturally generous woman, did her best to help out her old mentor rather than bearing a grudge.

In truth Miss D.'s career had been on the wane almost from the moment Eartha left the company. However Eartha didn't crow over the reversal of their fortunes. Rather it must have been sobering for her to see the woman she'd learned so much from having to struggle so hard just to get by.[10] If her own career wasn't going to follow the same downward path, she was going to have to make some decisions, in both her professional life and her personal life.

PART THREE

The End of the Affair

TWENTY-FIVE

What's a Woman to Do?

Ever since Arthur Loew had rejected her, Eartha had confined herself to strictly casual affairs. Part of her had still believed that they might have a future together, had been waiting and hoping that Loew might come back to her and finally ask her to marry him. That forlorn hope explained why she hadn't included their breakup in her book. But now, over three years after the split, she had to take on the reality of the situation. She was beginning to accept that she might have to look elsewhere when it came to finding a man to marry. After all there was still no shortage of men taking an interest in her. One such was an actor called Robert Dix, whom she ran into in San Francisco.

Bob Dix was second-generation Hollywood.[1] His father, Richard Dix, had been a big star of the early Westerns. Bob, clean-cut and six foot four, was a B-movie leading man with a new wife and baby when he was called up for Army Reserve training in the summer of 1958. He was sent to Camp Roberts in central California. A weekend pass saw Bob and a couple of his buddies head for San Francisco where they found themselves passing the Fairmont and saw a poster advertising Eartha's show. Bob had already met her once before and decided to see if he could use this slight acquaintance to impress his friends.

Bob tells the whole story of how he got to know Eartha with the practiced ease of a professional raconteur:

> We ended up at the Fairmont Hotel because I had seen a sign out front that said Eartha Kitt was performing. I had met her once before through a friend, Tom Tannenbaum, who was in the talent department at MGM and knew her. We'd met on a plane flying back from Las Vegas but Tom had monopolized the conversation as he was trying to pick her up. He was the son of the mayor of Beverly Hills. So I wasn't sure that Miss Kitt was going to remember me, but I took a chance.
>
> So I pick up the house phone and get her secretary and say, "Hello, this is Bob Dix from Hollywood," and then Kitty gets on the phone and says, "Hey, come on up." So my buddies are impressed and we go on up and not only does she come to the door, she's very dramatically dressed in a thin blue flowing dressing gown and she comes and jumps onto my arms and I caught her and these guys are "Oh boy!" And she invited us to the show that night, but by the time we'd done bar-hopping I was there by myself, my friends had found other young ladies and were busy. So there I am, they put me in the front row, at her request I guess.
>
> The maître d' gave me a note after the show saying Miss Kitt would like to see me in the Circus Room, that was a kind of revolving bar, so I went there and sure enough she came out and we had a very friendly conversation and I had the bright idea maybe she could come sing to the regiment at the regimental party the following Sunday. So I said, "Would you like to come to a party with me?" She said, "What kind of party?" I said, "An army party!" and she said, "OK."[2]

Bob went back to camp and told his captain that he had arranged for Eartha Kitt to entertain the troops.

> He said, "You're kidding." I said, "I'm not!" and I got a private to rehearse some of her songs on the piano and I borrowed a car from a 101st Airborne guy and on Sunday morning I drove the two hundred

miles to San Francisco. I got there just as she was coming back from walking her dog, Snowball. She said "How far is this party?" I said, "Oh, not far." I counted on the fact she'd been up really late performing the night before. And so here I am in this new Plymouth driving along and sure enough she says, "I'm sleepy, you mind if I take a little nap?" and I said, "Sure," and then I just put my foot down.

We came outside of King City and the sheriff pulled out in front of me and put the siren on and escorted me into the camp and all the guys are really excited and Eartha wakes up and says, "What's going on?" And she got very upset with me, but what's she going to do? She's right in the middle of a regimental party, there's the general there, the captain puffed up like a peacock. So she sings "C'est Si Bon" and "Santa Baby" and another one and the guys threw their hats in the air and it was wonderful.

So far, so good. But all the while Bob was wondering just how Eartha was going to respond to his deception.

We were driven back to the local airport and I could feel the vibes, I mean really! So there are only two seats left on the flight—I'm meant to be escorting her back to San Francisco. Fortunately she's in the front of the plane and I'm in the back, so we get off the airplane in San Francisco and in the airport, she comes over. I was ready to be lambasted, but instead she says, "What are you going to do now?" in this low sexy voice. I say, "I'm going back to the base." She says, "How about coming back to the hotel with me?" I knew what she was suggesting and I was completely surprised. I said "I have to go back." She says "Don't worry, I'll take care of the army." So that's what she did, she called them and we went back to the Fairmont and . . . Fade out baby.

Eartha and Bob's relationship didn't turn into a full-blown affair immediately. Both had business to attend to before that could happen. Bob had a failing marriage to extricate himself from and Eartha, as ever, had travel and work commitments. Also she still lived in New York and Bob was in Los Angeles.

Not for long though. Soon after meeting Bob, Eartha bought herself a house in Los Angeles. She'd been looking around for a place for a little while but had come up against a color bar: neither of the two neighborhoods she liked living in, Bel Air and Beverly Hills, welcomed African-American home owners. But then she got a call from a realtor who claimed to have the perfect house for her on La Collina, off Sunset Boulevard. It was part of the old Doheny estate which lay precisely on the dividing line between Beverly Hills and West Hollywood. The house Eartha was shown was formerly the stable block. It cost $87,000 and it came with two acres of land. It was exactly what Eartha wanted: a rambling house covered in bougainvillea vines, with a huge garden and a swimming pool complete with a pool house for guests. She bought it at once.

Her friend Beldon Katleman, from El Rancho, paid for the house to be redecorated as a favor in return for all the business she'd brought him. Eartha moved in right away, along with Snowball, and set to work on clearing the grounds and planting her very own vegetable gardens, a little piece of South Carolina in Beverly Hills.

It was a brief respite from the treadmill and a rare chance to take stock of where her life was going. She was now in her early thirties and the blissful certainties of her youth—that she would be a huge star married to an old-fashioned millionaire—were steadily being replaced by a more workaday reality. She was a highly paid cabaret artist who could invite pretty much any man she wanted up to her hotel room. But was that enough? The security she longed for was as elusive as ever. She was smitten with Bob Dix, but he was still a married man.

Before Eartha could come to any real decisions, however, she had work to do. In November she flew off to Britain, where the highlight of her visit was an appearance on the *Royal Variety Performance*, at which she was presented to the Queen and Prince Philip. Blasé as she may have been by now, this was definitely a thrill, as she gushed to the *Daily Mirror*: "She is so simpatico. I mean she is so warm and vibrant and so very much younger looking than I ever imagined, I felt like Alice just after she stepped through the looking glass. And he's not like a duke at all—he's all man. And so witty too."[3] Actually, the Duke of Edinburgh's wit seems to have consisted of telling the assembled TV performers how awful television was, but no doubt it was all in the delivery.

She also found time to give a revealing interview in the *Sunday Graphic*, in which she held forth on the subject of being a woman, something that was clearly much on her mind, especially when it came to the matter of finding a mate:

> It's dangerous to be too feminine—too much a woman. And it's more dangerous to be an intelligent woman . . . if she has reputation for being intelligent the man is fearful of her and feels he cannot compete. If she is feminine and has the reputation of being sought after by other men, the man usually feels that she has so many men in her life that he doesn't want to compete . . . ambition is frightening to men . . . Most nice women don't like other women because they know what women are capable of doing as a woman—of using their femininity to achieve a goal no matter what that goal is.[4]

Back in Los Angeles before Christmas, she called Bob Dix's answering service and discovered that the actor had separated from his wife and was living with friends in Malibu. The two of them took up where they had left off at the Fairmont, but, as ever, Eartha's ability to really commit to a relationship was constrained by her relentless touring schedule. After a week or two in LA it was back to New York for a week at the Waldorf Astoria over New Year, and then the following week at the Apollo Theater, where the audiences were finally starting to warm to her.

Not many acts could possibly have played both those venues, and the culture shock was considerable, as Joyce King remembered:

> We were in the Waldorf Astoria and the phone rang. It was Joseph Papp, the guy that produced Shakespeare in the Park in New York. He said he'd like to speak to her, and I didn't put my hand over the mouthpiece,

and she yells out, "Tell him to go fuck himself!" So I never got to meet him! I don't know what she was mad about, and then she was mad at me because I hadn't been smart enough to get my hand over the mouthpiece. It was a lesson learned. I don't think it ever happened again. But it was all an education, you know. Think about this for a second. You're in a top-floor suite at the Waldorf Astoria on Christmas night. The next night you're in the Apollo Theater. And I have to tell you that my sensibilities were jarred a few times. The drink backstage at the Apollo was 150-proof rum![5]

After the Apollo, Eartha was off to the Eden Roc in Miami, then the Latin Quarter in Philadelphia. By the time she wound up at Blinstrub's Village in Boston, in the last week of February, she had had enough. She was exhausted and her throat was giving way once again. She canceled the Friday night show at the last moment, much to the displeasure of owner Stanley Blinstrub, who put up a sign reading: "Due to difficulties beyond our control, Miss Eartha Kitt has taken it upon herself to cancel her engagement and will not be heard tonight."

Eartha's temperament was becoming ever more erratic, not helped by life on the road or her uncertainty as to whether her new relationship with Bob Dix had any future. He was an undeniably attractive man and had started coming out to see her when she was in New York. They had a good time together, but he had no money to speak off and had only just left his marriage. He wasn't an obvious prospect for the long term. And her financial future was very much on her mind.

She headed back to her New York house, pursued by threats of legal action from Blinstrub, and gave an interview to the ever-loyal *Jet* magazine in which she talked frankly about everything that was bothering her—her throat, her exhaustion and, most of all, her money troubles. These she went into in exhaustive detail, in an effort to persuade *Jet*'s readers, black and unlikely to be particularly well off, that someone earning up to $300,000 a year had money problems. She assured *Jet* that for all the money she'd earned, she only had $4.80 in her bank account:

Maybe it's hard to believe, but it's still true. My lawyers allow me $200 a week for hotel bills, food, taxicabs and incidentals, but I usually have to borrow from my secretary to make ends meet. I'm rich, yet I'm a pauper. My income taxes are so high that if I stop working I'll go bankrupt. If I continue to work at these $4,000–$5,000-a-week jobs my tax bill just keeps on climbing. There's no way out. I'm so poor now I have to cook my own meals in a hotel room to cut my expenses. I can't even go to the hairdresser anymore. And, except for the gowns I use in my act, I haven't had a new dress in three years. Just can't afford it.[6]

She went on to detail her outgoings—a $28,000 tax bill, $100,000 in wages for her staff of two to four musicians, a maid, and a secretary—and to explain that even well-paid work at the Waldorf Astoria didn't necessarily make money for her: "It costs me over $1,000 a week just to live there. With musicians, a maid, a secretary, and all of the expensive arrangements, I came out on the short end. After my agency gets its percentage (off the top) and all other expenses are paid, there's nothing left."[7] Neither had her investments worked out as well as she might have hoped. The dress shop she financed for Roxie Foster lost her $15,000. As for her property investments like the Manhattan brownstone, that was just a money pit: "It cost me $30,000 to buy the building and another $30,000 to put it in good enough condition to rent."

She makes the reasonable point that the government might introduce special provision for entertainers: "Congress should allow people like me, who have only a few productive years, to spread out our tax bill. We pay out nearly all of our current income during the peak years, then we have nothing left."

Finally she bemoans the implacable, impossible logic of her situation: "I've got to play anywhere my agency books me. My lawyers tell me that if I don't work 52 weeks a year I'll be bankrupt. On the other hand, doctors advise me that if I don't give my voice a much-needed rest I'll lose it for keeps."[8]

* * *

Meanwhile, her affair with Bob Dix carried on, both in Los Angeles and in New York, where she went back into the recording studio for the first time in eighteen months. Dave Kapp, the man who
signed her to RCA six years earlier, had given her a deal with his
new label, Kapp Records. Stylistically the new recordings harked
back to the Eartha of old: a hodgepodge of songs from around the
world, but overall it seemed as if all concerned were going through
the motions.

Eartha at least was starting to take her relationship with Bob seriously. In June she leaked the news of her new romance to friendly
gossip columnist Dorothy Kilgallen, who duly informed her readers
that Eartha and Bob had been seen together three nights running at
an East Side club called Goldie's, popular with show business folk.

Come July, however, Eartha was back on the road again, launching a full-scale concert tour of what *Jet* referred to as "the Negro
Circuit." She was backed by the Apollo's resident bandleader, Reu-
ben Phillips, and his combo. The tour started in Buffalo and ended
up back at the Apollo at the end of August. From there she headed
back to Las Vegas, where she met up with Bob again.

This time Bob brought a buddy along for the ride. Bill McDonald was a childhood friend of Bob's from LA, the oldest son of a
wealthy family. He'd been invalided out of the army, having been
seriously wounded in action in Korea. Bob had made it his mission
to cheer Bill up:

> I had told my friend Bill about this adventure I'd had with Kitty. I was
> going to Las Vegas to visit her and I said, "Can I bring my friend Bill?"
> and we went up there and soon we were like the three musketeers—
> I was the date boyfriend, but Bill was a friend too—he was dating a girl
> called Sandy at the time.

The foursome's friendship continued once they were all back in
Los Angeles. Eartha had really fallen for Bob now. She wanted to
marry him, money or no money. Bob, however, had just got out of
one marriage and was in no mood to commit to another. He was

happy for his affair with Eartha to carry on just the way it was, but if she wanted more, then that wasn't going to happen.

Eartha put up with this not-unfamiliar situation but, in her early thirties now, she was not at all happy about it. Bob got an acting job and Eartha started spending more time with Bill McDonald, who was in the middle of breaking up with his girlfriend. Before long they were pouring their hearts out to each other.

At the end of September Eartha left Bill and Bob back in Los Angeles and headed back to New York. She had been cast in a new Broadway play called *Jolly's Progress*, a Southern take on the Pygmalion theme, with Eartha, now thirty-three years old, in the part of a naive sixteen-year-old. Curiously, the play's producer was Arthur Loew, Sr. This can hardly have been coincidental, as Loew, Sr. would surely have had a say in casting the play, so why would he choose his son's ex-girlfriend? Eartha herself was baffled, wondering if perhaps Loew, Sr. was bankrolling the show out of some sense of guilt over what had happened between her and Arthur, Jr. Conceivably Loew, Sr. had his own designs on Eartha.

Then, to make matters much worse, just before rehearsals for the new play got going, Eartha had some bad news. While having dinner with Virginia Wicks's ex-husband Jack Dunaway, Eartha discovered that Arthur Loew, Jr. had gotten married to Tyrone Power's widow Deborah.[9] Coming as it did on top of her latest knock-back from Bob Dix, this was devastating. All the hurt from all the rejections she'd suffered at the hands of men, at the hands of Arthur Loew most of all, came back in a terrible rush.

In the immediate aftermath of this news Eartha was a mess. Rehearsals for *Jolly's Progress* did not go well. Franchot Tone quit the show, allegedly over a billing dispute, and soon Dorothy Kilgallen was reporting in her column that "Eartha Kitt's temperamental outbursts and fits of depression are giving her managers reason to buy headache pills in large quantities."

Wendell Corey replaced Tone and during November the show went on tour along the eastern seaboard as they waited for a

Broadway theater to become free. Whether Eartha's mind was really on the show is debatable. Instead she was taking a long hard look at her romantic options.

Once she'd got over the initial shock of it, the fact of Arthur Loew's marriage was also a kind of liberation. She could finally rid herself of the lingering hope that he would one day come back to her and take a more realistic attitude to planning her future. What she still hankered after the most was the security offered by a man with serious money. And she was starting to accept the previously abhorrent notion that such a man might not be prepared to go so far as to marry a woman like her, but might nevertheless keep her in the style to which she had become accustomed.

So while she was still having fun with Bob Dix, Eartha was keeping at least one eye open for a more affluent mate. She had spied a particularly attractive prospect during a recent booking at the Caribe Hilton in San Juan, Puerto Rico. During her stay she had been invited to a cocktail party given by a gentleman named Charles Revson, who had rented the entire top floor of the hotel.

Eartha claimed later not to have known who Revson was at first, but she must soon have discovered that he was the exceedingly wealthy founder and boss of Revlon cosmetics. The party was a lavish affair: rooms full of orchids, free-flowing Dom Perignon, buckets of beluga caviar, and so forth. As Eartha left, Charles Revson gave her his card and invited her to call him when she was in New York

After a decent interval she called the number. Revson was very happy to hear from her and promptly invited her to come for lunch in his office the next day. Later on Eartha did her best to pass off this lunch engagement as a very genteel sort of occasion, but even her own account of what transpired suggests a relationship between a rich and powerful man and a very high-class courtesan, rather than any conventional sort of romance.

Revson had a palatial office on the fortieth floor. There was a table in his office set for two with fine china and silver, Dom Perignon chilling and beluga caviar on ice waiting. Over steak and salad

Revson explained that he and his wife didn't get on, he wanted a divorce and so on. And after lunch, well, according to Eartha, "I had a wonderful afternoon laughing at his stories and enjoying his company." Revson enjoyed Eartha's company so much that the next day he had his aide deliver her a gold bracelet and a note saying, "Thank you for a happy afternoon."

And so the relationship began. By Eartha's own account they didn't go out in public but he showered her with ever more expensive gifts. It must have been clear that her role now was absolutely that of mistress rather than girlfriend.

Certainly Revson was the kind of man she liked. He was twenty years older than her, but he was smart and powerful, and of course very rich. And, unlike John Barry Ryan or Arthur Loew, Jr., he was a self-made man. The son of Jewish immigrants, he had grown up outside Boston and had started Revlon in his mid-twenties and developed it into an enormously successful company. He was a classic Ayn Rand–styled business leader. Talking to an employee he summed up his approach as follows: "Look, kiddie. I built this business by being a bastard. I run it by being a bastard. I'll always be a bastard, and don't you ever try to change me."[10]

One again though, as Eartha tells it, the insidious effects of racism undermined their relationship. Revson's estranged wife learned of his affair with Eartha and threatened to leak the news of his black mistress to the press if he didn't agree to her demands for their divorce settlement. Charles, powerful though he may have been, was still a man who put money first, and he wasn't prepared to risk the potential wrath of his shareholders if he started attracting sensational publicity, especially given that he was already nervous about a breaking scandal attached to the quiz show his company sponsored, *The $64,000 Question*, which was rightly suspected of being rigged. So he told Eartha that their relationship, already secretive, was going to have to become clandestine. He laid out his plan: he would buy her a house in Connecticut. She would live there in luxury with servants and a chauffeured car, and he would see her when he could.

Eartha affected, in her final autobiography, to have understood this as a possible prelude to marriage, and even children—"I wondered if we could ever have a child between us. I wanted a child by Charlie, a child by marriage."

It's hard to imagine that Eartha was really that naïve. She surely knew exactly what Revson was offering. Whether she really would have been happy to have been Charles Revson's kept woman seems unlikely. But, as it happened, matters were taken out of her hands. An anonymous caller told Charles Revson that Eartha was having an affair with Bob Dix's friend Bill McDonald. Revson checked up, decided that the anonymous caller was right, and ended the affair then and there.

Eartha later claimed to have been entirely innocent, just a little thoughtless: "Why did I allow Bob and Bill to be in my house when I was waiting for Charlie? Though I was never guilty of any wrongdoing, I suppose it looked suspicious."

Today Bob Dix offers a rather more convincing account. Bill was still miserable after his breakup with Sandy, and Bob decided to take him to New York, where they would stay with Eartha (who was keeping her involvement with Charles Revson secret from Bob). Bob would be sleeping with Eartha, and Bill would stay in the guest wing of her apartment. Once in New York the three of them took up where they had left off in Las Vegas, enjoying the city's nightlife. And then, one night, everything changed, as Bob recalls:

What happened was we went to see Tony Bennett and we had been to the Stork Club and a few other places. We'd been tipping a few and we got back at 3:30 or something in the morning. She owned a brownstone there, she lived in the lower apartment, so we get back and we come in through the door, it was a warm balmy summer's evening, Kitty had on one of her performance gowns with a zipper all the way down this side of it. She said, "Oh, I'm hot," and pulled the zipper down and just stepped out of it and Bill went "Woah!" I said goodnight and just kept walking toward the master bedroom. Out of the corner of my eye I saw Bill escort Kitty into the guest wing and that was the beginning. It was fine by me. Bill and I were really like brothers and I was just happy for him as he'd been going through a bad patch. I went to bed. From that day forward they were together romantically, and I was friend Bob.

Eartha's romantic options had suddenly changed dramatically. Charles Revson was out of the picture, Bob Dix was heading off to Hong Kong to make a movie. And that left Bill McDonald, her comforter turned lover. Bill headed back to Los Angeles and Eartha soon followed, as *Jolly's Progress*'s Broadway run lasted for only nine performances, closing in early December.

Yet again the critics mostly liked Eartha, but found the play itself woefully lacking. It was an odd-sounding affair. The writer, Lonnie Coleman, was a gay white Southerner who would later move to Brighton, England, and write a bestselling, and highly romanticized, novel of plantation life called *Beulah Land*, which he sold to the movies for a fortune. Langston Hughes summed up the story of *Jolly's Progress* as follows: "Set in the South, it concerned the adoption of a wild little colored girl in a bigoted community by a wealthy white liberal who is, incidentally, a bachelor." *Jolly's Progress* was intended as a liberal contribution to America's racial debate, but the time for white Southern gentlemen to set the agenda for race relations was slipping away. As 1959 turned into 1960, matters of race in America had moved beyond the fairy-tale stage.

Eartha, however, was looking set to have her own fairy-tale ending. In the first months of the new decade her relationship with Bill blossomed. It was a relatively quiet time thanks to the early closure of her show. Her only major engagement was a return trip to Puerto Rico to play a supporting part in a low-budget feature called *Saint of Devil's Island*, produced once again by Lloyd Young.

For the first time in her romantic life everything went smoothly. She wanted to marry Bill, Bill wanted to marry her, and his family, not plutocrats but solid Los Angeles business folk, were, if not exactly delighted, at least prepared to go along with it. So, in early

May, just as a young senator called John F. Kennedy was about to win the nomination to be the Democratic candidate in that year's presidential election, Eartha announced that she would shortly be marrying her own clean-cut, all-American war veteran from an Irish-American family: Bill McDonald.

TWENTY-SIX

My Dear Little Husband

Eartha announced her impending marriage on May 11, 1960. At the time the happy couple were at the El Rancho in Las Vegas, where Eartha was performing. They broke the news to an Associated Press reporter. "I'm terribly happy, now I'll have something I never had—a family of my own," said Eartha. Her fiancé, billed as "handsome, sandy-haired Bill McDonald, son of a wealthy Los Angeles business executive," named the date for their marriage as June 9. The AP went on to note the difference in their backgrounds—"She was born on a dilapidated farm outside of Columbia, S.C. McDonald, who is white, attended a prep school at Ojai, California, then the University of California"—but refrained from commenting explicitly on the racial question.

This was raised, however, when Eartha called the London *Evening Standard* to announce her news: "It's a problem you have to live with like any other problem. Some people aren't going to like the idea of a Negro marrying a white. But the world I live in is show business and the racial problem is not so great there. Why when Bill first told his parents we were getting married, his mother hugged and kissed me and said, 'My little sun-tanned daughter.'"[1]

As for Bill's view on this, he simply commented that "I don't know what to say. It never enters my mind."

The papers were intrigued by Eartha's new husband. He had no public life at all, so they were scrambling for information. All they came up with was that his family was fairly wealthy and he had fought in Korea. By the time of their marriage a few weeks later, the only new information was that he had a job in real estate. This was the way he wanted it. Throughout his marriage to Eartha, Bill kept his profile as low as possible.

Eartha's friends were every bit as mystified as the press by this turn of events. Virginia Wicks, still one of her closest confidantes, was unconvinced by Eartha's choice of husband. "I couldn't understand why she married him—he wasn't a person to marry Eartha Kitt, that was the main thing."

So who was Bill McDonald? Eartha herself barely describes him at all in her autobiographies. As a result it was tempting to assume that he was what appeared to be: a clean-cut all-American type. Bill McDonald, himself, died in the first decade of the twenty-first century and never gave interviews to the press.

Bob Dix, of course, knew him well, though not as well as his wife, Mary Ellen, who is also Bill's younger sister. Talking to the two of them about Bill, a rather different picture of Eartha's husband emerged. Mary Ellen started by filling in the basic details of his early years:

We grew up here in the Los Angeles area, Cheviot Hills. Our father was in manufacturing, the family had a company that made bathroom fixtures. Bill went to St. Paul the Apostle Elementary School, then he made the rounds of the high schools. Evidently he had some discussion with the authorities! He wasn't good with authority—except for mom and dad as he knew his life depended on that! So he was at Loyola, then Villanova, then Uni, then Beverly Hills High; he finished up there. He was very athletic, very much into track, a good runner, did a lot of hurdles, high jump, we had a setup for that in the front yard. Bill and Bob did a lot of partying. They were party boys and there were always very pretty girls around with both of them. Then he enlisted in the army.[2]

 It was this army experience, according to Mary Ellen, that changed Bill from the party boy of his youth. Bob agreed and took up the story:

Going into the army was the turning-point in Bill's life because he got injured in Korea, around 1954. The way he got there was he was being reprimanded by a captain in the army and he went over to the desk and punched the guy. They put him in the stockade and from there they sent him to Korea instead of Germany. The story of how he was wounded is a very dramatic one.

Bill had been out on what they call an LP—a listening post—at night. During the night the enemy came through and slit the throats of every one of his men except Bill who was out on the post. When the relief came he went to wake up his men and found all of them dead. After that he went to his commanding officer and said "Put me out on point, I don't want to do any more of this LP business."

So he went out on patrol one pitch-black night. The guy on his left bugged out and Bill didn't know it. And all of a sudden there was the enemy with a burp gun, and there was Bill with a Thompson, and they both fired simultaneously. Bill aimed for the guy's head and this guy aimed at Bill's body. Bill had a bulletproof vest on, but four slugs went through it, so as he was laying there and our guys started laying mortar rounds down, and one of them blew his finger off—that's where all the shrapnel came from that would trouble him later—and that motivated him to get up.

Damn, he said to himself, I won't be able to play pool again with Bob. So he got up with these four slugs in him and he started walking toward a UN unit, and he was stumbling through a plowed field. A Dutch patrol sent up a flare and he thought they would come get him, but they didn't. It turned out he walked right through a minefield, and then this Dutch sergeant threw him over his shoulder and he woke up two months later in an army hospital in Japan.

Even then, his convalescence was far from straightforward, as Mary Ellen remembers. "He spent two years in hospital; he must have had twenty-some surgeries on his gut, his hands. Bill had a rough time. Till the day he died, fifty years later, we were still picking shrapnel out of his head, out of his back, it was oozing out.[3] He was in pain every day of his life." And, as it turned out, it wasn't just his war wounds that had lasting effects, but the treatment he received for them. Mary Ellen again: "You see Bill had some problems, drug problems. The nurses out in Japan were being very helpful. Because of the amount of pain he was in, they were giving him extra morphine, and I don't think they knew how addictive it was."

The result was that Bill came back from Korea with a serious drug habit that would persist for much of his life to come. Bob, at least, is fairly sure that Bill wasn't using drugs during the period of his marriage to Eartha, but acknowledges that they would play a large part in his later life. He does accept, however, that the Bill McDonald who came back from Korea with a Purple Heart and a formal 100 percent disability was much changed from the previous model:

> I noticed a big change, mostly a kind of hard core that wasn't there before. Before, Bill was always a likable, lovable guy. He wasn't so much so after Korea. He wouldn't go out of his way to befriend anybody. If he liked someone he could be a good friend; that's how it started with Kitty, they were good friends.

When Bill met Eartha he was still studying accounting at the University of Southern California, but by the time of their marriage he had graduated and was working for a mortgage company. News of his impending marriage came as a complete shock to his sister.

> I was driving to my folks' house from the Valley and I heard it on the radio and I almost drove straight off the mountain—"The real estate

tycoon and Eartha Kitt!" I was very surprised, could hardly wait to get
to mom's! I didn't even know he was seeing her. I had a youngster at the
time, I was busy with my own life. I was astounded. Mother told me
about it—they had come talked to her beforehand and they had gone to
see dad, they had gone down to his office and told him.

Bob too was amazed to hear the news, but for rather different
reasons.

I had a negative reaction because—not too long before I got the
phone call from Bill asking me to be the best man—he had said to
me that Kitty had been in love with me and, before they got together,
she'd cried in his lap over me and all this stuff . . . I mean, I wasn't
looking to get married at the time. So I told him, "Man I can't do
that." It would be like corroborating a lie, either she was lying then or
she was lying now. "You want to marry the gal that's fine, but I don't
want to be a part of it." He was very upset and didn't talk to me for
several months.

The marriage itself was to be a fairly small and intimate affair
held at Eartha's house. Both the event itself and the few days leading
up to it were covered exclusively by *Ebony* magazine. *Ebony* sent
a photographer and a journalist to meet the couple in Las Vegas
on the Sunday before the wedding, which was to take place on the
following Thursday in Los Angeles. On the Sunday night Eartha
and Bill went out to an Italian restaurant with Mary Ellen. During
the meal Eartha mentioned the press's harping on the difference in
their races, while Bill stuck to his line. "I never think about Eartha
being any color."

Monday and Tuesday were the last two days of Eartha's run at
El Rancho. The Monday was cloudy and Eartha was tense. Tuesday
the sun came out and the couple posed for photos, clowning around
in the pool and lying down on a blanket while Eartha read extracts
from the journals of André Gide to Bill (not something you generally see in celebrity wedding photos).

The reporter managed to find out a little more about Bill. He was "a gay blade with a predilection for speedy cars, light airplanes and sky-diving." He knew nothing of Eartha before he met her: "I had never even seen her before. No pictures, no movies, no television appearances, nothing until we met." But since they had been together, he'd quit drinking, lost weight, and started working harder. Asked to say just when he fell in love with Eartha, he sounded a rather enigmatic note: "In a friendship such as ours, it's difficult to tell where friendship ends and love begins, and where romantic love starts."

As for Eartha, she told *Ebony* about the Three Musketeers: Bob, Bill, and herself: "The three of us were very close." How she'd made friends with Bill: "Sometimes he would scoot up to the house for lunch, or just walk around the house a while and leave. He was always saying he didn't want to get married, and I said I didn't want to either." And how that friendship had changed: "Sometimes he'd come for lunch then stay for dinner. He said I was the greatest thing that ever happened to him, because I taught him that there were other values besides a different girl every night, and he became aware of his own potentials." Whatever she would say later on, it's evident that there was a real closeness between Eartha and Bill at first.

They drove back to Los Angeles overnight, following Eartha's final show at El Rancho, and, at ten the next morning, Eartha was at Don Loper's for a final fitting of her wedding dress, described as a "calf-length, chiffon Bristol-blue outfit." In the afternoon she tramped around her two acres, cutting flowers and telling *Ebony* that "I always said that, when I got enough money, I was going to plant a cotton field, and make the people from my booking agency come out and pick it!"

The wedding took place on Thursday and, as promised, it was a small affair with just twenty or so guests. The role of best man was taken by Mary Ellen's then husband, Stan Kane, given Bob Dix's refusal to take on the role. The matron of honor was Eartha's new best friend Marjorie Meade, ironically enough a principal writer for *Confidential*,[4] the magazine that had helped derail her relationship with Arthur Loew, Jr. The bridesmaid was Virginia Wicks's young daughter Christine, who remembers what happened that day.

> Everybody was very happy. I was anxious to please her, I played "I Love You Truly" on the violin, very badly. And the pictures demonstrate that I was young, stringy-haired and I look pretty nervous. I remember Eartha being very happy. My mother probably had a lot to do with putting it together.[5]

Virginia was indeed involved in organizing the wedding, despite the fact that she had stopped working with Eartha the year before, when Eartha's finances had gone into meltdown: "She couldn't afford me anymore and I wasn't very expensive! She didn't pay me for a long time and then, instead of money, she gave me a necklace that Arthur Loew had given her."

The wedding's only showy feature was a song from one of Eartha's newer friends, Johnny Mathis, a young black singer of inordinate smoothness, who had quietly become one of the biggest stars in America.

Married life made no immediate difference to Eartha's busy schedule of live performances, which carried right on going. She had a string of dates across America through the end of June and July. After these, the new couple decided that they were running up such a phone bill that, in the future, they might as well travel together. Bill would give up his job with the mortgage company in favor of looking after his new wife's business affairs. He did this in connection with Eartha's new financial managers Jordan and Nancy Carlin, a pair of accountants who looked after a lot of show business people. Nancy Carlin, one of the first women to practice as an accountant in California, still works in the business, with an office in Thousand Oaks, northwest of Los Angeles. She remembers Bill McDonald well:

> Bill was a party guy; he liked the show-business life, though he was only really a gopher himself. He was the guy who told me you could drink as much as you like as long as you took three aspirin before you went to bed, then you wouldn't have a hangover! He was working for us and he was kind of managing Eartha's affairs. But he wasn't strictly an accountant, so we did that for him. We looked after her investments, managed her properties and so forth. She didn't have a manager separate to that.[6]

This combined manager-husband had often been a recipe for disaster for female entertainers, but Mary Ellen insists that Bill, who had, after all, studied accounting, was very well suited to the job.

> All of us McDonald children were numbers people. And Bill, you know, he had a genius IQ. We were really raised with understanding finance. I remember one of the first things I did with my dad when I was a child was on January 1st he'd get out all his receipts for the year and I'd read them out while he put them into an adding machine. Bill did very well for Kitty, sorted out her investments and stopped a lot of the bleeding that goes on from agents, managers, hangers-on, the unnecessary entourage . . .

Bill and Eartha's first trip together was a long one. They headed for Europe, to England and Sweden, the places where Eartha was still a major star. While they were away, Bob Dix would stay in the pool house and look after the estate.

The newlyweds traveled to Europe on the transatlantic liner SS *Liberté*. They landed at Plymouth on August 30 and took the boat train to Paddington, where they were greeted by a mass of fans, press, and photographers. The photos show Bill looking handsome and Eartha looking thrilled. As the crowd surged around them Eartha and Bill were separated. According to the *Daily Mirror*, Eartha yelled, "Hey, where's my dear little husband?"[7]

The dear little husband was getting his first taste of Eartha's remarkable British popularity. In the States she was a name all right, but one already starting to become tinged with nostalgia. Indeed, her latest album, her last for the Kapp label, was just a set of rere-cordings of her earlier hits. She was doing fine in Las Vegas and the cabaret joints, but people were hardly excited by her arrival in a city. Not so in London.

So Bill just stood there, shuffling his feet, while Eartha pushed through the fans, grasped his arm and told the onlookers, "He's not used to all this . . . he's shy." If that wasn't embarrassing enough, Eartha followed it up by telling the press that "I want to be a mother soon. In fact I'd like to become an expectant mother while I'm in London for the next two months." Bill, said the *Mirror*, was looking as if he wished the platform would swallow him up.

The main purpose of Eartha's visit was to headline a season at London's newest and biggest cabaret joint, the Talk of the Town, opening in a week's time. During rehearsals she carried on her media rounds. She was filmed doing her fitness routine in a brand-new exercise gym in Marylebone; this at a time when going to a gym was an exotic novelty if you weren't actually a professional boxer. She went to the Tate Gallery to see the Picasso exhibition: "I was enjoying it a lot till I came to cubism," she told the *Daily Tele-graph*, "which may be all right for those who understand it but not for me. The blue period really hits me."

And with the advance money coming in from the Talk of the Town, the newlyweds decided to treat themselves. Bill went up to Coventry, to the Jaguar factory, to choose a new car, while Eartha spent a thousand pounds on antique silverware. It was all a long way from the financial and racial stresses of her last year in the States.

Though perhaps not quite as far as all that. In Britain, too, racial attitudes were hardening. When Eartha had first come to London, with the Katherine Dunham Company, black people, especially show business black people, had been an exciting novelty; now, after a decade of mass immigration from the Commonwealth coun-tries, and an outbreak of so-called race riots in 1958, racism was becoming commonplace. Openly racist movements like Oswald Mosley's Union Movement and the new British National Party were starting to gather members. A few days after she arrived in London, Eartha received a letter from one Peter Dawson, a member of the West London branch of the Union movement, who had previously picketed Sammy Davis, Jr.'s show at the Pigalle. Dawson was outraged by Eartha's marriage to a white man and promised to make "some form of practical protest."

Eartha passed the letter on to the press and they inquired of Mr. Dawson as to what kind of protest he was thinking of. He wasn't quite sure. In a response that aptly demonstrates why postwar British fascism never amounted to much, he finally explained that "We would possibly follow up this letter with another one."[8]

Eartha opened at the Talk of the Town on September 8. Shirley Bassey, whom Eartha had befriended on a previous visit, was to open three days earlier at another new London cabaret joint, the Pigalle. It was billed as a battle of the chanteuses, but while the press were keen to find some sign of rivalry, the two women remained good friends. Shirley sent Eartha red roses for luck and duly showed up at her opening night to cheer her on.

Eartha's show was a huge success with critics and public alike. Her run was extended and extended. When she finally closed in November, the Talk of the Town put out a press release to announce that after thirteen weeks Eartha had performed to 52,000 patrons and sold 1,500 albums.

After five months away Eartha and Bill came back to Los Angeles. They finally had the chance to try to live like a regular married couple. Eartha entertained guests including Langston Hughes and Sarah Vaughan, for whom she cooked up ham hocks and greens. Radical black comic Dick Gregory got a rather more elaborate mix of downhome and Beverly Hills when he was served chitlins and champagne, mustard greens from Eartha's own garden, and licorice ice cream.

During this relatively relaxed time, Eartha became pregnant, though she didn't have the news confirmed until April, when she was in New York to appear in another TV play, Maxwell Anderson's *Wingless Victory*, for which she was recommended by Guthrie McClintic. It was a part that Katherine Dunham, who was back in touch with Eartha, had hoped to play.

For a while it looked as if Eartha and Miss D., now thoroughly reconciled, would collaborate again, for the first time in a decade. Katherine Dunham had come across an unproduced script for a play about the Voodoo Queen Marie Laveau, called *The Widow Paris*. Eartha liked the script and the two of them were hoping for a Broadway opening the following year, with Eartha starring, Miss D. choreographing, and John Pratt designing the costumes. Sadly it never came to be, due to lack of financing. Meanwhile Eartha lent Miss D. some more money and headlined another season at the Plaza Hotel, once again offset by a week at the Apollo.

After that there was another series of dates on the road. This time, however, she was on her own. Bill had quickly decided that the life of being the traveling Mr. Eartha Kitt was not really for him. Outsiders, at least, started to speculate that all might not be well between them.

Sadly, there was no letup in Eartha's schedule to return to Bill or, indeed, to accommodate her pregnancy. In August she was back in London for another appearance on *Sunday Night at the London Palladium*. Viewers were allegedly horrified when, part-way through her spot, Eartha had difficulty climbing on to a high stool and, once installed, patted her stomach and said, "Okay junior, this is the last engagement."

The following day she talked to the *Daily Mail* about her pregnancy and her marriage. She confided she had only seen Bill once in three months, and then only briefly, but she said,

"I'm not lonely. I am very independent and I am used to traveling and working. I have always done it. I don't consider pregnancy to be an illness. It's a perfectly normal function. I'm not the type to pretend I feel ill when I don't. It should arrive in November or early December, I shall be working by February."[9]

Nevertheless, a pregnant woman spending months apart from her new husband soon incited the gossipmongers and, on her return home, Eartha had to begin denying rumors that her marriage was in trouble. "The only problem we ever had was that I'm away so much," she told *Jet*, "but we're over that." Asked for his thoughts Bill contributed a pithy "Hogwash."

A few weeks later, on November 26, Eartha and Bill's baby daughter was born at the Cedars of Lebanon Hospital in Los Angeles, after a difficult labor. The parents named her Kitt. Eartha summed events up in a telegram to her friends at the Talk of the Town:

> Kitt McDonald, girl, November 26, 1961, 2:19 p.m. 7lb 9oz. Twenty inches. Rough voyage, but very well worth it. Looks like a Hindu princess. Love Eartha.

Another telegram went to Katherine Dunham, and Eartha added the information that baby Kitt was "born with a Dunham arch—dancer's feet," while she and Bill were "very content and grateful."

Whether or not there was any truth to the rumors of marital strife before Kitt's birth, they were now very content. Mary Ellen recalls that "when Kitt was born they were both thrilled with their beautiful baby. She had the typical long-legged McDonald look, a little towhead."

A month later Eartha told *Jet* how she felt about being a mother:

> . . . of course, the relationship between mother and child that I lacked as a child makes me want to do things I think are basically right for my child more strongly. That's why I'm taking time to nurse my baby, so it will have the basic fundamentals. I want to give my baby the strength it needs, mentally and physically, to adjust itself to the world it lives in. I think the basic relationship between mother and child is more important than anything else. I don't think any of the material things my husband and I may be able to obtain for it will be as important as the love and affection I intend to give it.[10]

It's a decent, thoughtful credo, and one Eartha would do her best to live by, but it certainly didn't prove easy. She was still the bread-winner in the family and by the end of January she was back on the road, appearing at the Chi Chi in Palm Springs and the Eden Roc in Miami. Not even motherhood could slow Eartha's schedule.

TWENTY-SEVEN

Five Rules for a Successful Marriage

Kitt was christened in early February 1962. Eartha was completely devoted to her daughter and would remain so for the rest of her life. Here finally was a love affair that would last. Here was the security she'd always been looking for. Here was the chance to put right the wrongs of her own childhood.

Kitt's godmother, unusually, was Eartha's mother-in-law, Nora McDonald, more generally known as Mrs. Mac. Mrs. Mac was another powerful character. It's noticeable in the photo of the christening that there's also a definite facial resemblance between the two women. Eartha became very close to Mrs. Mac and to Bill's other sister, Noreen. At one time or another both of them would travel with Eartha to help look after Kitt on foreign tours.

The first of these tours took place immediately after the christening. By February 9, Eartha was back in London at the Talk of the Town, with Shirley Bassey at ringside once again to tell the press that Eartha was "not great but fantastic!" Next day Eartha was telling the future film critic Barry Norman about the new baby she'd had to leave behind as the airlines wouldn't let her travel with an infant under three months old.

> The baby has done it. She's brought me something I always lacked: serenity. How can I explain? It came from the very feeling of mother-hood, the carrying of a child the knowledge that you are . . . borning a person. God, I wish men could know the experience, the joy and the pain and the agony and then the glorious moment when you realize you are not just one person but two. This is what has changed me, I don't suppose I'm any happier than before I had the baby but now, at least, I have the sense to know that I'm happy . . . I've thought a lot about what I want for little Kitt and the most important thing I shall teach her is how to get along with people. That's something I've not always been good at. I grew up knowing I was hated by the white people and my own race and not quite knowing why. Believe me that leaves quite a scar . . . But little Kitt will never have to be like that. She'll be brought up with all the love and affection that everyone needs, and which I never had.[1]

It would be easy to write this off as PR gush, the wishful think-ing of a star who would shortly be handing over her baby to a fleet of nannies and getting on with her fabulous life. In Eartha's case, however, it was absolutely genuine. From the moment of Kitt's birth Eartha would always put her first. If she'd been self-centered in the past, from now on it was clear that her priority was always her daughter.

Sister-in-law Noreen arrived with baby Kitt at the beginning of March and Eartha stayed on in the UK till the end of May, appearing at the Talk of the Town for another thirteen-week stint. She also turned up on a wild variety of TV shows: yet another *Sunday Night at the London Palladium*; a new BBC play called *Member of the Family*, written specially by Michael Voysey and concerning a poorly educated girl who marries into a family of bankers; on *Juke Box Jury* lamenting the standard of modern-day pop; on a Sunday religious show reading bible stories to children.

Shortly before she left England Eartha gave the *Daily Express* her five rules for a successful marriage:

Rule 1. A woman should not let her husband get out of hand so that she eventually becomes a maid and cook and bed-warmer.

Men are naturally messy. They scrunch up their newspapers. They asphyxiate you with their cigar smoke. Men should be taught to be considerate and tidy. When I saw the way my husband was I took him by the hand and led him around the house saying: This goes here. And that goes there. A man should have a room of his own where he can, if he wishes, be a pig in privacy.

Rule 2. A wife should have one day off a week. On that day the man should cook and clean and look after the kids.

My husband brings me a tray in bed in the mornings. On Saturdays and Sundays he takes care of me absolutely. Wives should be pampered occasionally. It leads to a healthy relationship. My husband even runs my bath and knows the right scents to put in it too. He can change the baby's diapers and powder her bottom. Gets a big kick out of it too. This helps a man to realize his wife's responsibilities.

Rule 3. Not only should she have a free day, she should have a vacation on her own too.

A separation by mutual consent. Paid for by the husband. A little time apart makes the two more appreciative of each other.

Rule 4. If a husband insists on going out with the boys, the wife should be free to go out with the boys too.

If he spends his Saturdays on sport she should find a sport of her own. Plain shopping will do. Spend his money. Always remembering, when it comes to money, that what is hers is hers and what is his is half hers.

Rule 5. If the wife wants to sleep alone on occasions the privilege should be exercised.

I have my bedroom and my husband has his.[2] A marriage should not make people slaves. It can't make them the same person whatever the marriage lines say about one flesh. They are two individuals. That is why I have insisted my husband retains his job and never becomes just Mr. Kitt.[3]

Missing from this list, of course, was "spending much of your time many thousands of miles apart." Even when she returned to the States in July, Eartha was back on the road, pausing briefly to record an album called *Bad but Beautiful* for MGM, a fairly straightforward collection of American show tunes. She finally met up with her husband in Chicago, where she was a big hit at Mother Kelly's. Come the autumn, however, she was back in Europe and accompanied by Kitt, but not Bill. It was becoming clear to all who the most important person in Eartha's life was, and it wasn't her husband. Eartha took her maternal duties very seriously. She didn't have a nurse and only used a babysitter for the times she was actually on stage, while taking care of all the domestic duties herself, even washing out Kitt's diapers each night in hotel bathtubs.

Eartha was a sellout hit at the Tivoli Gardens in Copenhagen, where two shows were recorded for her first live album *At the Tivoli*. It included one of the few songs Eartha ever wrote herself, "I Had a Hard Day Last Night." Intriguingly, it was released in the UK by EMI, whose most successful new pop act would shortly release a song with a rather similar title—"A Hard Day's Night."

Meanwhile the TV special, *Kaskad*, that Eartha had recorded on her previous visit to Stockholm, was a huge hit across the European TV networks, wining the Golden Rose of Montreux for the best light entertainment TV show of the year. The performance is as good as the *Nat King Cole Show*, and the superior picture quality makes it the best surviving live record of Eartha in her prime.

*   *   *

Eartha finally made it back home that November. She'd told the British press how to have a happy marriage, now she was going to see if that was something she could manage for herself. She posed for a family picture with Bill, as part of a big *Ebony* spread on her adventures taking her baby around Europe, but underneath all was not well at home. It was revealing that, after an unusually quiet couple of months in terms of press coverage, Eartha was back in the news in early January when she announced that she would be giving dance classes in Beverly Hills in order to raise money for a pioneering drug rehabilitation center called Synanon. She explained her reasoning to the AP as follows:

> It could have been me. I've been offered the stuff, but I've been strong enough to walk away. These are people who are rejected, the least likely to be helped. I've been rejected myself and needed very much to find someone who cares. These people found someone at Synanon. But the place needs everything—food, clothing, money. So I decided to give dancing lessons.[4]

* * *

Given that Eartha was already supporting a number of civil rights causes—and that struggle was growing in intensity with each passing month—it seems unlikely that Eartha was simply looking for a new charity to support. Rather it seems far more plausible that she had found out about Synanon through a personal connection, to wit her new husband's drug problems.

Bob Dix suggests that Bill was not taking drugs during the time of his marriage to Eartha, but this can't be much more than a hunch, as Bob saw very little of the couple around this time. But if, as Mary Ellen suggests, Bill's habit dated back to the morphine he was given to cope with his injuries in Korea, then it would fit a familiar pattern if he continued to use morphine or one of its street alternatives like heroin. It would also be typical if he was able to keep that use secret from everyone else for some while. His need for the drug might also explain why he stopped traveling with Eartha. So it's a reasonable hypothesis that, on her return to Los Angeles, Eartha discovered her husband's drug problem and then found out about the pioneering treatment available at Synanon House.

Synanon was an eccentric endeavor. It was founded by a former alcoholic named Chuck Dederich who had been through Alcoholics Anonymous and realized there was no such facility for narcotics addicts. Entirely self-educated, and something of a loudmouth boor, Dederich nevertheless had remarkable energy. He began the Synanon project in Santa Monica in 1956, and by 1962 it had expanded to take over a big former armory right on the Pacific Ocean in Santa Monica. Some of its members lived there, others just visited. Central to its method was "the Game," a form of group therapy in which a bunch of people sat around in a room and told each other exactly what they thought of them. Also popular were its Saturday night dances which featured Synanon's own form of line dancing, dreamed up by Chuck's new wife, a black former heroin addict named Betty Coleman.

By the time Eartha took an interest, the operation had received coverage in magazines and on TV. It became popular with addicted jazz musicians including Art Pepper and Joe Pass. Other people to lend their support to Synanon ranged from the utopian theorist Buckminster Fuller to the Chicano labor leader Cesar Chavez to the future governor of California, Jerry Brown.

Eartha can't have done too much fund-raising for Synanon, however, as by February she was back in London for a brief visit to film a *Royal Variety Performance*. She also found herself a new record label. Thanks to Shirley Bassey's advocacy, and her producer Norman Newell, EMI signed Eartha up to EMI and they recorded an album, mostly of standards, at Abbey Road studios with Tony Osborne arranging.

The album was good, but it was nothing Eartha couldn't have recorded a decade earlier. And that was no longer good enough to catch the public interest beyond her regular circuit of cabaret joints. While Eartha had been busy getting married and having a baby and working, the fifties had turned into the sixties and the world had started changing fast. This was powerfully brought home to Eartha at the final date of her next American tour, when she turned up at the Apollo in Harlem.

She was booed by a section of the audience. She was booed for reasons that were unclear but evidently extramusical. Perhaps because she had a white husband, perhaps because she was seen as insufficiently committed to the black struggle. For out in the world the civil rights struggle was building to fever pitch and it was no longer possible for black entertainers to rise above it. Their people demanded to know which side they were on.

Birmingham, Alabama, which had a reputation as the most segregated city in the United States, had become the epicenter of the struggle. On April 16, Martin Luther King was arrested and jailed there during antisegregation protests. While imprisoned he wrote his "Letter from Birmingham Jail," which argued that individuals had the moral duty to disobey unjust laws. On May 2, King's organization, the SCLC (Southern Christian Leadership Conference), decided to take things up a level. That day's demonstration would be led by children. Thousands of black children took the day off school. The hard-line segregationist police chief, Eugene "Bull" Connor, locked up as many as he could, but by the end of the day the jails were completely full. The next day the children led the way again, and this time Connor used fire hoses and attack dogs on them. He could hardly have given the movement better publicity had he tried. The photos of this went around the world causing outrage wherever they were seen. President Kennedy was at last moved to take civil rights seriously. Black Americans, unsurprisingly, were livid. No wonder that the crowd at the Apollo wanted Eartha to show them that she was too.

Once again Eartha responded quickly to criticism of her politics. A day or so later there was a Harlem rally in support of the Birmingham Freedom Riders. Eartha appeared, along with the black comedian Redd Foxx, and she told the crowd that:

After reading the newspaper accounts on the situation in Birmingham, I overflowed emotionally. I could no longer remain silent, but felt I had to find a way to speak out. I am donating my entire salary of $5,000, which you have helped to pay me this week at the Apollo Theater, to Dr. Martin Luther King, Jr., and his noble effort.'[5]

In fact she had already been in touch with Dr. King. He had sent her a telegram the year before, asking her to contact him. And she had responded by lending her support and giving money to the SCLC. In response he'd written her a fulsome letter of thanks. Following her latest donation from the Apollo he took time out of the bitter struggle to send her a telegram of thanks.

Nevertheless, Eartha was still unhappy and determined to keep her own counsel on racial matters, as on anything else. She set out her position in an interview with a British newspaper, starting with her thoughts on being booed:

> It's racialism in reverse. These people are angry with me because I'm married to a white man. But being married to a white man doesn't make me any less a Negro or a fighter for Civil Rights. The Negro must decide what he wants. Either he wants equality and he is willing to accept it, or he doesn't. I want equality. Too many Negroes get angry and just sit back and want something to come to them just because they are black.[6]

*   *   *

That summer found Eartha back in Beverly Hills, with the country in uproar and her controversial marriage coming apart. In fact their racial difference seems to have been the least of the problems in the Kitt-McDonald marriage, but it's hard to imagine that it didn't increase the tensions between them, as one seismic event followed another.

On June 12, just a few hours after President Kennedy had made his first major civil rights speech, another Southern black leader, Medgar Evers in Jackson, Mississippi, was shot dead by a Klansman named Byron De La Beckwith. Eartha responded to this latest horror by persuading some of her rich Hollywood friends to throw a benefit party, with Eartha providing the entertainment, to raise money for a fund to put Evers's children through college. They raised $23,500, with her old friend Marlon Brando contributing $5,000.

Eartha and Marlon were both involved in the preparations for the summer's climactic event, the March on Washington for Jobs and Freedom. There 300,000 marchers would watch Dr. King give his "I Have a Dream" speech, and listen to Joan Baez and Bob Dylan sing. It was a defining moment in the struggle, as far as the outside world was concerned. But while Marlon was there in person, Eartha was back on the road again.

Three days before the March she flew to Australia, along with her daughter and her mother-in-law. Just as she was leaving, she put out a press release announcing that she was divorcing her husband on grounds of "mental cruelty," a catchall term much used in the years before no-fault divorces were allowed. Eartha's own dream—of a stable, secure family life—was over.

Eartha had kept back her divorce announcement to coincide with her leaving the country, in the hope of minimizing the publicity. She had also kept the news back from her mother-in-law, who had traveled with her to Australia and was not best pleased to learn about the divorce from an Australian reporter on their arrival in Melbourne.

This provoked a huge blowup, but before long the two women managed to make their peace, for Kitt's sake. Meanwhile the press was calling. Eartha gave her fullest account of what had gone wrong to the *Daily Express*:

> When I found out that I kept extending my tours I knew something was wrong. There had to be a reason why I, who love my home so much, was not anxious to return to it. Then I began to analyze myself and my marriage. I found out that though I adored my husband, I could not live with him. The stresses and strains of marriage and show business are many . . . If the woman is earning the board and keep, she carries all the burden, making her feel more the head of the family than the wife. Once the woman reaches this stage she no longer has time for petty trivialities such as jealousies, mistrust and childish behavior. The more independent the woman is, the less independent the man becomes. He begins to feed on her in every way, especially emotionally.

Everything was fine in my marriage so long as we were not together. I found when I was at home I was no longer looked upon as attractive, nor was I wanted or loved, I was unhappy and that disturbed me because I am by nature a very happy person. A few outings, a few social visits, and I really began to notice my husband's behavior. He became moody and wouldn't talk to anyone and made others feel uncomfortable. Whenever I was able to discuss these things with him his answer was "I am extremely jealous. There is nothing I can do about it. I know I do these things that hurt you but I cannot help myself." Being away as much as I am calls for complete trust on both sides. Jealousy breeds contempt.

I had nothing but the school of hard knocks and responsibilities. I learned to love life and enjoy it fully. This being so, I don't want anyone pulling on my reins, preventing me from taking part in the excitement that is by nature mine. When you have done so much in one lifetime as I have—traveled as much, lived as much and learned as much—you can't settle down to a track-house kind of world with television and *Playboy* magazines. My husband is a successful man but just not worldly enough for me . . . Now after three years of marriage I find American men, adorable as they are, are just babies, and I am tired of being a mother. They know how to make money and carry out big deals, but they seem to have forgotten how to love.[7]

For his part, the ever-laconic Bill told *Jet* that their separation had begun six weeks before: "We just haven't been getting along so I'm not staying at the house right now."

Talking to Bill's sister Mary Ellen and friend Bob Dix, however, it seems that the divorce may not have been Eartha's idea after all. Bob, in particular, is adamant that it was Bill who really wanted the split:

I think they were happy together for a time but in the end the divorce, it was something he really wanted. He was tired of being "Mr. Kitt." He didn't want to do that anymore. 'Cause really that's how it was on a daily basis. Mary Ellen told me that Kitty thought he would come back to her, but I never got that impression from Bill.

Mary Ellen confirms all this and points out that even though it was Eartha who divorced Bill, rather than the other way around, that doesn't mean very much: "With divorce, back in those days, it was a courtesy thing. It was a real big deal if the man initiated the divorce. So out of courtesy the woman always divorced you. In California at the time you couldn't have a mutually agreed divorce. You had to have incompatibility."

So it's quite possible that the whole matter of Bill's jealousy was simply something they agreed between them to use as a reason for their divorce, something that would make Eartha look strong, rather than simply a cast-aside wife. Either way, the suggestion that subsequently Eartha wanted to get back with Bill, rather than vice versa, does have some plausibility.

But whether or not Eartha really did want Bill back, she did her best to show the opposite while she was in Australia for what became an extended stay. By the time she arrived back in the States, early in the New Year, the rumor mills were full of stories about Eartha's potential new husbands.

In Britain the focus was on a young Irish comedian named Dave Allen who was then a TV host in Australia, and would became one of the UK's biggest TV stars in the 1970s. Eartha and Dave were seen holding hands together in public but, on a visit home in early January, the comedian was somewhat taken aback to be asked if he was planning on marriage. Nevertheless he did tell the *Evening News* that he was planning to visit her on a forthcoming trip to the States:

> "I'm not going to marry her. We met in Australia last year. Sure we went around together but that doesn't mean I'm going to get married. I want to give her a Christmas present. I know I'm a bit late but I've got her some specially bound books on philosophy."[8]

The visit never took place. A few days later Dave met an actress called Judith Stott, and married her instead. Meanwhile the American media, and indeed Eartha herself, were more interested in an older man Eartha had met out there, a TV mogul called Sir Frank

Packer. "I met Sir Frank when I was in Australia recently on a singing tour," Eartha told *Jet*, "We saw a lot of each other and we have been in communication since."[9]

She claimed that Packer had proposed marriage. "But I have not made up my mind yet. Sir Frank comes over here in June. By that time I probably will have decided what to do."

This claim is a little undermined by the fact that she seems to know remarkably little about this putative husband. "I don't know his exact age, but he must be in his fifties. That's all right with me. I'm tired of the emotional insecurity of the young men that I meet." Whether or not the marriage proposal was real, however, nothing more was ever heard of this particular romance.

Eartha's divorce came through in April 1964. She was in her late thirties. She no longer had a husband, but she had a daughter whom she adored, a house in Beverly Hills, two investment properties in Los Angeles, and a career that was still very financially viable, not to mention in its second decade, which is more than can be said for most such careers.

In reality though Eartha's options were shrinking. She could go on playing the Persian Room and the El Rancho and the Talk of the Town for year after year, but eventually the audiences would start dwindling—and what then?

When Eartha had emerged as a solo performer in Paris and New York, a decade or more earlier, she had been new and extraordinary. Now she was familiar and in danger of becoming a self-parody. What was classy and sophisticated in 1954 looked anachronistic in 1964 America, especially if compared to the likes of Nina Simone, who had replaced her own supper-club material with self-penned songs of civil rights struggle like "Mississippi Goddamn." And meanwhile, out in the wider world, John F. Kennedy was dead, the Beatles had invaded and the sixties were in full effect. Her former husband Bill would soon find a new identity as part of the nascent counterculture; Eartha too needed to find some new challenges.

TWENTY-EIGHT

Guest Starring Eartha Kitt

Marriage had not after all, turned out to be the beginning of happily-ever-after. Instead life went on the way it always had, only more so. Eartha had to continue her extraordinary, wearying professional schedule, but was now forced to combine it with the role of a single mother.

The cabaret dates in the United States and abroad continued, along with regular appearances on American and British variety shows. Her most interesting work was, once again, as an actress on stage, and in films and TV. On stage she appeared in a couple of her most challenging starring parts to date, while on screen, although she was no longer seen as a leading lady, directors and producers started to see that her unique personality made her ideal for special-guest and cameo roles.

Immediately after her divorce she traveled to Yugoslavia to appear in an unlikely, and by all reports very poor, German-made version of *Uncle Tom's Cabin* with blacked-up Serbs playing the parts of slaves. Eartha had a cameo as a singer (though her voice was overdubbed by Ella Fitzgerald).[1] It went down well at the following year's Moscow International Film Festival, but was dismissed as unintentionally hilarious by *Variety*.

Back in Los Angeles she appeared on several episodes of a new panel show called *The Celebrity Game*, presented by the future film director Carl Reiner and also featuring Mel Brooks. She took another trip to Australia to record a TV special, accompanied by the fine Cuban percussionist Modesto Duran, who was to become a close friend during this period.

On her return she was offered her first American film part in years. It was only a supporting role, but the subject matter was close to Eartha's heart, as it was a feature film about the Synanon drug rehabilitation project. Unusually it was to be filmed at Synanon itself, and the filmmakers planned to use many of the house's actual residents. Eartha was obviously a natural choice for the role of Betty Coleman, the African-American wife of Synanon founder Chuck Dederich.[2]

The film was shot in September 1964, and foregrounded the story of three inmates—played by Chuck Connors, Stella Stevens, and Alex Cord—locked in a rather unlikely junkie love triangle. Edmond O'Brien took the role of Chuck Dederich and Eartha did a good job of playing the part of Synanon's den mother, opening the film up with a speech about her own journey. It's a little hammy, but gives a sense of the tensions of the time:

> I began my drug addiction for kicks. I was what you call a swinger. I paid for it by prostitution until I became a such a vegetable nobody wanted me and I didn't want myself and I was nothing, The day I walked into Synanon I wasn't alive except for my hate. I guess my hate is what made me want to go on. I wanted to be alive so I could hate some more.

It's nicely filmed in slightly anachronistic black and white, and sports an excellent jazzy score from Neal Hefti, of *Batman* theme fame. Jazz fans will spot the great bass player Charlie Haden appearing as one of the Synanon residents.

Synanon was no kind of commercial hit, but it was Eartha's first Hollywood movie in six years, and it reminded the industry that she was still alive. One immediate spinoff was a week spent cohosting a new talk show fronted by a young personality named Regis Philbin, who'd made his name down in San Diego. Then, after appearing at a Christmas benefit for the Mississippi poor organized by her friend Dick Gregory, she was off to the Caribbean. She appeared at the Hilton in Puerto Rico again and made a trip to Jamaica where she bought herself a rural estate, perhaps influenced by Katherine Dunham's ownership of an estate in Haiti.[3] Eartha's new home was a considerable drain on her finances, as Nancy Carlin remembers:

> She had a house in Jamaica, but the trouble was if you don't live in a house there it gets very damp, and she'd only be there for a few weeks every year so we'd have to go down and get it ready for her. Then she'd be there for three weeks and leave again for a year. Eartha was like that though. She had a fifties Cadillac, you know with fins, she wouldn't get rid of it even though she hardly ever drove it. She just wanted it to be there ready for her. She kept the house while she was in Europe later on and the upkeep was expensive.

Next stop was London and another three months at the Talk of the Town. If there was one thing that was keeping Eartha going through this endless showbiz routine it was her relationship with her daughter. Kitt was now three years old, but Eartha managed to keep her with her throughout these travels. There's hardly a photo taken of Eartha during the sixties and seventies that doesn't feature Kitt as well. However it was far from easy, looking after a child while living in hotels, so Eartha was grateful when Shirley Bassey offered to let them stay in her mews house in Belgravia. Highlights of her shows in Britain included an appearance on *Sunday Night at the London Palladium* wearing a dress made out of monkey fur—"It's really sexy. It will be a wow in the States!" said Eartha—and a turn on the record review show *Juke Box Jury* in which her imperious dismissing of everything she heard provoked fellow panelist, the eighteen-year-old Marianne Faithfull, to say, "If I were doing a *Juke Box Jury* on Eartha Kitt records I'd find all her songs sound the same—because I don't know anything about her records and I don't want to know." It was a clear sign that, as a musical act, Eartha was yesterday's news.

It was fortunate, then, that things were starting to look up on the acting front. Back in the States Eartha received an intriguing offer, to play a major guest role in an episode of a new TV spy series that NBC had commissioned. It was called *I Spy* and for the first time it featured a black actor as the co-lead. The heroes were two American secret agents foiling dastardly plots in scenic locations around the world. Both leads were relative unknowns: one was Robert Culp, a good-looking white actor who'd been on the verge of a big break for years and had finally caught one; the other was Bill Cosby, a young black comic with virtually no acting experience at all.

The backdrop to this enterprise was that the TV industry was making a concerted effort to make more roles available to African Americans. The CBS president, Frank Stanton, had made a keynote speech the previous year in which he said that "We of radio and television are at a phase of history in this century similar to that of the daily newspapers when slavery was a commanding issue." *I Spy* was NBC's answer to this call for integration.

All concerned realized this was a big deal. None more so that Bill Cosby, as he told *Playboy* a few years later:

> The important thing to me, man, was to get a black face on the screen and let him be a hero. I was very, very happy that a black man was able to be on an equal basis with the show's white hero . . . The first time I saw Bob [Culp] was the first day we read for the series; I walked in and we shook hands, but we didn't really have a chance to talk before they gave us scripts. Then it was the moment of truth for me. Although the producers were with me, they were really listening to see if I could act. Well, they listened, and I was embarrassed, because I was no good— really no good. I fumbled and mumbled and couldn't concentrate or do anything right.
>
> But afterward, Bob and I got together and talked and, at Bob's suggestion, we agreed to make the relationship between the white

character, Kelly Robinson, and the black man, Alexander Scott, a beautiful relationship, so that people could see what it would be like if two cats like that could get along. Bob's a fine actor and a fine human being . . . Bob, by the way, wrote the first *I Spy* script in which I was interested in a woman—who turned out to be Eartha Kitt.[4]

In this episode, which was called *The Loser*, Eartha played a heroin-addicted singer kept by a sleazy club owner in Hong Kong. Bill Cosby ends up handcuffed to a bed in her parlor by the club owner's heroin-dealing associates. The heart of the episode is found not in the conventional spy antics, but in the drama of whether Bill can persuade Eartha to give up the junk. He tries his best and ultimately fails. Eartha, no doubt drawing on her experience of the Synanon project, is excellent as a woman who's given up on any kind of hope and is happy with oblivion. The scene in which her character performs a desperate version of her own "Lilac Wine" is an extraordinarily bleak piece of prime-time TV, with Eartha discarding even the faintest vestige of glamour and looking every one of her thirty-eight years.

The part won her an Emmy nomination, but for all the talk of affirmative action it would be nearly two years till she was offered another decent TV role. In the same month that *I Spy* debuted on TV, September 1965, Los Angeles went up in flames, as the Watts riots raged for a week.

Eartha's response to the rioting was to set up free dance classes for the children of Watts. This project, which became known as Kittsville, was very successful, and would run for the next forty years. Eartha presided over it with a woman called Ella Mae Evans, who had brought her daughter all the way from Watts to Beverly Hills when Eartha had given dance classes there.[5]

In the absence of more TV or film work Eartha took a stage job, as costar in the touring version of a Broadway hit called *The Owl and the Pussycat*. This was something of a comedown—the Broadway version was of course the more prestigious gig—but Eartha liked to work and the part was appealing. A comedy with occasional poignancy, the play is a two-person show that involves a bookish type spying on one of his neighbors, who happens to be a part-time prostitute. He gets her evicted but then she turns up at his door and demands to be allowed to stay. On Broadway the parts were played by Alan Alda and a fine black actress named Diana Sands. On the tour Eartha was cast alongside a comic actor called Russell Nype. The two leads didn't like each other much but the reviews were enthusiastic—critics who had seen both versions tended to favor the Kitt one.[6]

The play ran on into the spring of 1966. Meanwhile Eartha found time to appear in a show for the prisoners in San Quentin State Prison, and to help out a Washington, DC black youth group called Rebels With a Cause. She took a keen interest in their work and lobbied on their behalf to get funding for a variety of youth facilities, focusing her charm offensive on local representative Roman Pucinski. While in Washington she also spent time with disabled black veterans from the Vietnam War.

What's striking about Eartha's political activities is that they weren't publicity stunts but straightforward responses to causes that engaged her emotionally. Her grander political pronouncements were often muddled, but when it came to actually putting in time and effort at a grassroots level, she consistently showed a hardworking commitment.

That autumn Eartha ventured into the recording studio after a long break. Luther Dixon, the New York songwriter and producer responsible for many of the Shirelles' biggest hits, signed her to his new label Musicor. Dixon must have noticed the influence of Eartha's singing on the new soul star Diana Ross, and decided to return the compliment. The single he cut with Eartha—"There Comes a Time," backed with "Any Way You Want it Baby"—is an obvious but likable knockoff of the classic Motown sound. And Eartha does indeed sound remarkably like Diana Ross. However, it sank without trace on release (though it would later find a measure of popularity on the dance floors of Britain's Northern Soul clubs). It was not a style Eartha would return to.

By this stage Eartha's career was clearly starting to lose any kind of focus. Still, she kept working: another cabaret tour saw her through to the spring of '67. Along the way there was a curious incident in Houston, Texas, where she was appearing at the Cork Club (and was photographed at Muhammad Ali's training camp, wishing him luck[7] before his fight with Ernie Terrell).[8] After her show she'd been visiting friends with Modesto Duran. On leaving an apartment block they came upon a middle-aged white man collapsed in the lobby and attended by police officers. The police assured Eartha that the man was dead and told her to move along. Eartha demanded to see if she could revive the body, claiming a knowledge of nursing. The police declined her offer, but Eartha insisted and ended up being arrested for failing to heed police orders. She spent a couple of hours in jail before being bailed out. Today it's hard to be sure what the full story was, but there's at least a suggestion that she was in a volatile frame of mind, perhaps because her career was going downhill.

Then TV came calling again. First a regular slot on the celebrity quiz show *The Hollywood Squares*, and then something more exciting, a new spy series called *Mission: Impossible*. The premise was a team of maverick intelligence agents taking on the jobs that the regular agents couldn't handle. It was another example of integrated casting, with Greg Morris playing the part of Barney, the team's electronics whiz. There were regular guest stars too.

Eartha appeared in an episode called *The Traitor*, in which the mission involved breaking into the Russian embassy. She played a contortionist called Tina Mara, small and lithe enough to crawl through the embassy's heating ducts and steal a codebook. It was a part that might have been played by a man or woman, black or white, and Eartha does a fine job: dressed in a full bodysuit with pulled-back hair she looks completely natural, no sign of the erstwhile glamour puss at all. Her appearance sent out a clear message: that "Eartha Kitt" was by now only one of the roles she could play, if given the chance.

TWENTY-NINE

Catwoman

Working in TV had the obvious benefit of allowing Eartha to spend more time at home. She loved her La Collina estate, was never happier than when working in its gardens. At home she was defiantly un-starry. Her goddaughter Christina Wicks remembers that "She had her vegetable garden and she was so happy to be there and pull up a carrot and wash it off." Her accountant Nancy Carlin elaborates:

> The first time I met Eartha was at her house. As we were coming up the driveway she was outside chopping down stuff with an ax. Not what you expected! She loved anything to do with the earth. Eartha loved to buy land: the way she was raised she always liked to be close to the land. The house was wonderful, the dining room still had the original stable doors with the names of the horses above them. With us she was always down to earth, it was only when there were other people around that she would change into the star, I guess that's what people expected. She never had many people working for her. I suppose she must have had help with Kitt, but she was very hands-on.

While at home she kept up the teaching schedule down in Watts, taking Kitt with her, and on occasion Christina too. "She would go into Los Angeles and lead groups of kids and that was fun. I'm afraid I didn't join in, which frustrated her intensely!"

Her social world was increasingly varied. The stereotype suggested that she disdained the company of her "own people" preferring to hang out with high-tone white folks (as *Jet* put it she is "considered 'seditty' [stuck-up] by many Negroes"). But, as ever, the reality was that Eartha was far more involved in helping with civil rights and black educational causes than people realized. In her private life, Nancy Carlin remembers that she had a wide circle of friends of all races. Her closest friend at the time was probably the Afro-Cuban drummer Modesto Duran. And if the black press wanted proof that she was still in touch with her roots, well Eartha was always happy to show them the only collard green patch in Beverly Hills.

Her love of the land was an anchor in what were dizzying times, and not just for Eartha. Her ex-husband Bill was also going through a lot of changes. After the divorce he had rapidly remarried and, just to add salt to the wound, his new wife, Jan, looked exactly like his previous one, as Mary Ellen remembers: "She was very similar to Kitty in appearance, almost uncanny!"

Bill and Jan had a child together, a son called Chad. But their lives soon began to disintegrate. Bill's drug problems became obvious and Jan divorced him, then committed suicide, which sent Bill into even more of a downward spiral. His sister Mary Ellen remembers Eartha doing her best to help with the resultant mess. "When Bill was falling into problems, after his second wife died, Eartha had offered to take Chad in and raise him as her son. I think it was another way of hoping Bill would come back. She had hoped when Bill and Jan got their divorce that he would come back to her."

Eartha herself never publicly expressed any regrets at the breakup of her marriage, or the remotest desire to get back with Bill. However it's quite possible that she did privately harbor such ambitions but never admitted to them for reasons of injured pride.

For, whatever Eartha wanted, it's quite clear that Bill had no intention of returning to domesticity.

Instead he headed further into the new world of hippiedom, where drug use was no longer something that had to be hidden away. Bob Dix remembers the transformation:

> I was a social drinker for many years and it was against my nature to hang out with druggies. For me I socialized with people who'd have a cocktail, so Bill and I drifted apart during that whole drug-scene time. Bill's mom had passed and Bill became the executor of the estate and that's when his whole life started going cuckoo. Not long after that his wife Jan committed suicide and the whole thing was downhill from then on, even though materially he was in a better position than he ever had been.
>
> He invited me to a party once he was throwing, down on 6th St., downtown. I went to this party and Bill showed up with a black cape on and there were these weird people there . . . I looked at myself in a mirror and thought "What are you doing here Bob?" So I left. Later on Bill had this thing where he called himself "the silver fox," that was the disco era. He eventually did get into recovery, but in the life of a druggie there are a lot of sad memories. If you're familiar with the lifestyle, it's very much do anything for the next hit or fix.

Unsurprisingly Eartha and Kitt saw very little of Bill throughout this period. Any hopes of reconciliation were long abandoned. The only time Eartha refers to Bill again in any of her writings is in an account of Kitt's first wedding. Bill showed up, and her enduring anger with him over his lack of emotional and financial support gave way to something like pity as she took in his reduced state. He looked frail and old and helpless. She concluded that his diminished condition was no more than he deserved, before wrapping up her reminiscence with the enigmatic line "If only you had played fair."

It's just those few words that suggests the depth of regret Eartha nursed at the breakup of her one and only marriage.

*   *   *

Back in the summer of 1967, the Summer of Love, Eartha was offered her highest-profile TV role yet. *Batman* was looking for a new Catwoman. Julie Newmar had played the part in the first two seasons, but she was busy filming a Western. *Batman* the TV series has been one of the enduring success of its era, endlessly recycled around the world. It was as much fun to film as it was to watch, as any amount of cartoonish overacting was positively encouraged. All manner of Hollywood legends appeared as guest stars at one time or another, so competition for the role of Catwoman was fierce.

In retrospect, of course, Eartha was an obvious piece of casting—her whole career had been trailed with feline comparisons and her purr was a trademark—but at the time it was a pioneering move by the network, putting a black actress in a role previously played by a white actress. Thirty-odd years later she reflected on the part:

> A cat! My goodness there's not a lot of research to do. Who knows what a cat is like. What kind of research can you do? Something is in you that says you are that character. That character to me was so much fun. I was in dire need of comfort at that time and as a starving cat I had to find a way to survive. And that was one of the most wonderful bones that was ever thrown to me. People still remember my name because of Catwoman.[1]

In the end she appeared in five episodes—*The Joke's on Cat-woman*, *The Funny Feline Felonies*, *The Ogg Couple*, *Catwoman's Dressed to Kill*, and *The Bloody Tower*. Most of her scenes were played in company with her good friend Cesar Romero, in his role as the Joker, and she much enjoyed the experience. The major technical challenge was learning to drive Catwoman's car with its manual gearshift.

The whole thing was, of course, profoundly silly. Eartha had little to work with. The previous Catwoman had a flirtatious relationship with Batman, but no way was a black Catwoman going to be allowed to do the same. Instead she's essentially a cartoon figure of menace, a playful presence in one of the first TV shows to intentionally camp things up.

And yet, she was also much more than that. Here, after all, was a black woman dressed up in a frankly fetishistic outfit, and having a whale of a time threatening to do all kinds of mischief to white-bread American heroes Batman and Robin. And all this in a prime-time family viewing slot, as America's parents and children settled down together around the TV screen. Eartha might not have been allowed to flirt with Batman the way Julie Newmar did, but she was still undoubtedly an erotically charged presence in a kids' TV show. Middle America couldn't help but be reminded how much it used to like Eartha, and junior America had its eyes opened.

For the rest of her life, Eartha's brief role as Catwoman became the single thing she was best remembered for.

THIRTY

Lady Bird's Blacklist

As ever in Eartha's life, each triumph seemed inevitably to presage a fall. Just as Middle America was starting to look fondly at her once again, something happened to put her firmly beyond the pale.

Eartha's episodes of *Batman* aired between December 1967 and January 1968. Two weeks after the last episode, she was invited to the White House for a luncheon with the president's wife, Lady Bird Johnson. Thanks to her youth work in Watts, and her association with Rebels With a Cause in DC, she was one of fifty women invited to discuss the problems of today's youth. What followed demonstrated that, for Eartha, there really was no such thing as a free lunch.

The luncheon was one of a series initiated by Lady Bird Johnson. Called the "Women Doers' Luncheons", they were intended to be a chance for women involved in social issues to talk about their experiences and hopefully have their views filtered back to the president. In practice they were generally fairly cozy events with the participants simply thrilled to be in the White House. Lady Bird herself was a Texan heiress who had bankrolled her husband's start in politics. She was a fundamentally decent individual, if a little naïve.

She campaigned hard for LBJ's Civil Rights Act, but her major contribution to the body politic was to start "beautification" programs,
first for Washington, DC, and then for the nation's highways. Her
philosophy could be summed up in her own words as "where flowers bloom, so does hope," an odd echo of the West Coast flower-
child ethos.

This particular Women Doers' Luncheon was to focus on issues
of crime and what was then known as "juvenile delinquency." It was
meant to be a sedate affair: a lunch, a brief appearance from the
president, Lyndon Baines Johnson, himself, and then speeches from
three of the guests. The remaining forty-seven women were meant
to talk nicely, network a little, and listen politely. Eartha went off
script from the start. After LBJ came in to give a brief bland speech
she called out, "What do we do about delinquent parents who have
to go to work and can't spend time with their children? What do
you do with the children?"

LBJ trotted out a line about all the money he was investing
in day-care centers, and made his exit. Eartha, however, was not
to be denied. Once the formal speeches were over, she jumped up to
confront Lady Bird from directly across the dining table. She began
by explaining where she was coming from—"One of the speakers
talked about walking through the gutters. I lived in the gutters. I am
here to say what is in my heart"—and then set out her thoughts on
why the youth of America were angry:

Because their parents are angry and their parents are angry because
they're so highly taxed and because there is a war going on and we do
not understand why . . . I know the feeling of a baby coming out of my
guts. No mother wants to work to educate her child only to have him
snatched away and sent off to Vietnam . . . A bad guy gets thrown into
jail. He gets a record and the government takes care of him and they
don't send him off to Vietnam to get shot up. It pays to be a bad guy. They
don't want to get sent off to get shot so they rebel in the streets. They
take pot—in case you don't know the expression that's marijuana—and
they smoke a joint and they get as high as they can.[1]

It was by any standard a pretty confused and confusing tirade and, unsurprisingly enough, at this point one of Eartha's fellow lady lunchers jumped in on the argument. This was Betty Hughes, the New Jersey governor's wife, who told Eartha that she had eight sons and they weren't smoking marijuana: "Anyone who takes pot because of the war in Vietnam is some kind of kook." Then the attention went back to an evidently shaken Lady Bird. Tearful rather than actually crying, the First Lady did her best to shut the argument down:

> I cannot understand as much as I should, I have not lived the back-
> ground you have, I cannot speak as passionately or as well, but we must
> keep our eyes, our hearts and our energies fixed on constructive aims to
> do something that will make this a happier, healthier, better-educated
> land . . . Just because there is a war on—and I pray there will come a just
> and honest peace—that still does not give us a free ticket not to work on
> bettering things in this country.[2]

Eartha left abruptly and, after being driven back to her hotel, decided to visit Rebels with a Cause. She spent the afternoon and evening with assorted black radicals and was dropped off at her hotel around 2:00 a.m. by Stokely Carmichael, then the public face of the black revolutionary movement. She flew back to LA the next morning, surrounded by newspapers reporting what was now a major controversy—"How Eartha Kitt Made Lady Bird Cry." On arrival she gave a press conference in her new role of black radical spokesperson. Over the next few days she received shoals of hate mail, plus a significant amount of support. Martin Luther King's secretary wrote to tell her that "We are proud of you. More power to you!" Gore Vidal sent a one-word telegram—"Bravissimo." Op-ed columns in the newspapers fired volleys for or against the brave/rude black woman and the out-of-touch/gracious first lady. Bob Hope added Eartha Kitt jokes to his routine—"I've been busy calling LBJ, trying to get Eartha Kitt a visa to Cuba"—which did no harm to her countercultural credibility.

It's tempting to see this incident as Eartha's political coming of age, the moment she decided to stand up and be counted, to speak truth to power about a war that had lately taken over from civil rights as the focus of young Americans' anger and discontent. But as ever with Eartha, things were not quite that simple.

For starters Eartha's actual speech/outburst was less than coherent, as she veered between speaking for herself and for the poverty-line mothers of DC. It seems unlikely that the primary worry of families in the projects was to do with iniquitous tax rates, as Eartha began by suggesting. Her meetings with the community activists of Watts and DC's Rebels had clearly made a powerful impression on her, but they certainly hadn't left her with a well-thought-out political viewpoint.

An interview she gave *Jet* a week or so later was intended to clarify her thoughts, but did rather the reverse, as she explained that as far as the war in Vietnam went: "The bomb dropped slowly may be worse than if you drop it quickly. You have drained the souls of your own people and confused and harassed them. Intellectually the soul is being destroyed. I'd rather be dead."[3]

Eartha then told *Jet* about the lunch itself, explaining that she had largely eschewed the food, apart from nibbling some watercress, and stuck to wine. "I wanted to be extremely aware of what was happening," she said. "I was not going to let any artificial or superficial things cloud my mind. When you eat, all of the faculties of the body go immediately to the stomach and begin to work there."

Presumably Eartha was following some sort of variation on *Cosmopolitan* magazine editor Helen Gurley Brown's celebrated "wine diet" which goes like this: "Breakfast: 1 egg any style, no butter, one glass white wine. Lunch: 2 eggs any style, two glasses white wine. Dinner: 1 steak, finish the bottle of white wine."[4]

If so, she clearly forgot Ms. Brown's covering advice—"I'd suggest the weekend for the crash. Sufficient nutrition is here, but you get fuzzy." The sorry truth is that drinking on an empty stomach isn't much of a recipe for coherence, and perhaps explains why many of those present found Eartha's remarks off-putting: more because of the tone in which they were delivered rather than because of their actual content. Bearing that in mind, this account by Lady Bird's press secretary, Liz Carpenter, does offer a plausible alternative view of Eartha's performance:

> Eartha Kitt was suggested by the committee on the Hill . . . I checked her out with two or three people at Justice and so forth, and asked if her name had ever showed up on any kind of ad protesting the President on Vietnam. It had not. It still has not. In fact, as far as Vietnam [goes] the day that she appeared at the White House luncheon, she had asked a congressman to make an appointment for her at the Pentagon to see about going to Vietnam to entertain the troops . . .
>
> I think that she was always looking for headlines . . . I have wondered if the militant blacks got hold of her before she came to the White House or afterward. She was seen with Stokely Carmichael leaving the Shoreham Hotel where she was staying. To the best of my information, and I did considerable checking, it happened in an impromptu way. She has a lot of problems. One of them was she was dieting and she didn't eat a bite at the lunch. She had had some drinks. The second thing is she is a declining actress looking for publicity, and she was determined she was going to get it. Her agent had called me and asked me if she could make a speech. I said, "No, we have speakers." And so she didn't. But it ended up that she got the headlines.[5]

And yet, for all that Carpenter has a point about Eartha's mixed motivation, and Eartha herself had no clear agenda, just a set of rather conflicting gut feelings, a clear message did come over. America was becoming deeply uneasy about its war and the fact that Eartha was not, in the end, speaking as a political radical, but as a typically confused citizen, gave her remarks surprising power. In subsequent weeks anti-Vietnam marches would see protesters carrying placards with slogans like EARTHA KITT FOR HEAD OF DEFENSE.

Eartha had heckled power and the world had taken notice. And that perhaps helped the struggle against the war in some small way.

However it didn't do much for Eartha's own struggle. In subsequent years she talked of being blacklisted for her remarks. This is something of an exaggeration, but one with a hard kernel of truth. In the weeks following her outburst President Johnson set the CIA on Eartha's case. They delved into her life for evidence of communist links or immoral behavior. In truth this so-called investigation seems to have gone little further than rehashing a bunch of old *Confidential* articles and adding in some bizarre pieces of tittle-tattle, including the following gem, taken straight from the CIA report: "A confidential source advises that her escapades overseas and her loose morals were said to be the talk of Paris. The source stated that the Subject had a lurid sex life in Paris, and described her as a sadistic nymphomaniac."

Of course, America had moved on from Joe McCarthy's blacklists of the early fifties and, in theory, Eartha was free to go about her business. But in practice the opportunities soon started to dry up and her career quickly went into a downward spiral. Her contract with *The Hollywood Squares* wasn't renewed once the hate mail started coming, following her next appearance. There were no more guest-star appearances offered in prime-time TV shows, and her new and promising career as a versatile TV actress was cut off just as it was gathering momentum. *Mission: Impossible*, for instance, never invited her back to reprise her role as a safecracker. No chances either to appear on *Ed Sullivan* or the daytime talk shows plugging her latest record. The cabaret rooms generally stayed loyal, but over the next year or so, Eartha would realize that her career had taken a severe hit.

America had been considering quietly renewing its love affair with Eartha Kitt, but now she was refusing to be discreet and upsetting everybody by making a scene. Best for all concerned if there were a cooling-off period.

The irony of the situation was that this new counterculture credibility was of little use to Eartha. She had sympathy for the Black Panthers, but she was far too much of a maverick to toe any party line and, in turn, they had little use for someone so closely allied to old-school show business. And, once the brouhaha died down, Eartha had to get on with the business of earning a living.

The week after the White House luncheon Eartha flew to Italy to take part in the Sanremo Song Festival, perhaps the least counter-cultural event you could imagine. Leading Italian songwriters put forward their latest material to be sung by a selection of, mostly Italian, balladeers, and one would be chosen as the winner. Shirley Bassey was also performing that year, and may have been respon-sible for Eartha's invitation. Things did not go well. After the first rehearsals Carlo Rossi, the writer of Eartha's song, "What's Good for Me," came up to her in her hotel and asked her to withdraw from the festival, as he was sure that if she sang the song it would lose. This hostility reduced Eartha to tears, and she was led off by her boyfriend of the moment, a self-described record producer named Dave Best (he clearly didn't stick around long: he was a lot younger than Eartha, at twenty-four, and made so little impression on her that she later referred to him as Doug rather than Dave). Eartha refused to withdraw, but she didn't win, and the whole business can't have helped her already fragile state of mind.

Nor did what happened back in the States, two months later. On April 4, 1968, Martin Luther King was assassinated: an event that profoundly traumatized the country. Black America rose up in rage and rioting broke out in more than a hundred different cities. Even white America took notice: the baseball season was postponed and the TV stations devoted themselves to in-depth coverage. President Lyndon B. Johnson declared April 7 a national day of mourning, and on April 9 150,000 people thronged the streets of Atlanta as the funeral took place.

President Johnson didn't attend for fear of causing unrest, but his vice president, Hubert Humphrey, and the president's most likely successor, Senator Robert Kennedy, did. So too, of course, did all the great names of the black entertainment world, including Harry Belafonte and Sidney Poitier. And, of course, Eartha. In the photos she's being comforted by Sammy Davis, Jr. It was a deeply somber occasion, as the nation strove to come to terms with the very un-American idea that maybe things weren't going to turn out right after all.

Two more months and Robert Kennedy was dead too, assassinated in Los Angeles. Eartha opened at the Persian Room in New York that night and offered a singularly ill-thought-out quote to *Jet*: "When will this country learn?" she asked. "If somebody tries to do something here, they get killed—or they get canceled dates." She went on to explain that a San Francisco club had canceled her booking following the White House affair. These were destabilizing times, for sure, but it's clear that Eartha's sense of proportion and mental balance were badly out of whack.

August saw her performing in Chicago, where she went to hear one of Dr. King's heirs, the Reverend Jesse Jackson, preach a sermon. Ten years earlier Jackson had gone to see her in concert in Chicago, and now she had returned the compliment. The photos once again found her in tears, perhaps at the state of America, perhaps at the state of her career, or, most likely, a mixture of both.

By the end of that year of assassination and riot everyone wanted a change. The American people opted for conservatism and voted in Richard Nixon as their new president. For Eartha it was becoming clear that her time in the American limelight was drawing to a close. The kind of polished entertainment that she offered was falling further and further out of fashion.

And so too were the values that she was seen as espousing. The new creed of Black is Beautiful had no time for the glamour and sophistication that Eartha represented. Black America was looking to Africa for inspiration. The talk was all of being "natural" and going back to your roots, and as far as the black public was concerned, Eartha, with her wigs and her gowns, was about as far from natural as you could get. Despite the White House incident, she had come to represent a dream of gradual integration that was finally over. These were revolutionary times and the popular perception of Eartha was that she was part of the old guard.

It was unfair, of course. Eartha had been celebrating the beauty of blackness and getting back to its roots for more than twenty years, since she'd started with the Dunham Company. She had consistently supported the civil rights movement since its inception, but no matter. Aretha Franklin and her afro were in. Unless she could somehow change, Eartha was well and truly out.

THIRTY-ONE

Paint Me Black Angels

As ever, Eartha did do her best to adapt to the new situation. After a long time away from the recording studio she got herself a deal to make a new album. The label was Spark, a subsidiary of the mighty Peer-Southern music publishing empire. The producer was a young man called Denny Diante, who had a rock-pop background. The plan was to showcase a new, up-to-the-moment Eartha.

The album was called *Sentimental Eartha* and it was recorded in Los Angeles early in 1970. The innocuous title gives little indication that this would turn out to be far and away Eartha's most experimental album, and one of her best. Diante, who has subsequently worked with a wide assortment of artists from B. B. King to Sheena Easton, has a clear recollection of how the album, one of his first production jobs, came together:

> First I worked with Eartha at her home, a wonderful place. She had her own vegetable garden there and the house was elegantly designed and beautifully furnished. She was such a lovely lady, very sexual in a come-on kind of way. I mean she drew you in very quickly, she had this sexuality about her as a person, even when having a coffee!

Then we put the session together. We went to United Western studio B, a great studio. I got some great players—Carol Kaye on bass, Jim Gordon on drums, Larry Carlton and Louie Shelton on guitars. It took about two days to get the tracking done: three songs in three hours times three sessions, and we had all the tracks. Eartha was a cruise: she was so easy, she walked in, she knew her songs, she sang them. She was a two-taker—two takes and that was it; any more than that, you went downhill.

Then I got Jimmie Haskell[1] in, a great arranger, and he wrote the string arrangements and we had the Sid Sharp Strings play them. Then myself and Spencer Proffer worked on the backing vocals, with Kim Carnes and Ginger Blake from the Honeys and Andra Willis. No overdubs and it took me two days to mix it. Bob Kingston came over and he was there with me in the studio as I was pretty green. But I'd watched guys like Phil Spector recording when I was younger and thought, "I could do that!"[2]

The material is all taken from the Peer-Southern catalog. Some of it is familiar enough fare: a couple of forgettable ballads, a decent stab at the recent Herman's Hermits song "My Sentimental Friend," a piece of Cuban-flavored fun called "The Way You Are," written by Eartha herself with Modesto Duran, but the heart of the album lies in her interpretation of three songs by Donovan. From the moment a fuzz guitar leads into "Wear Your Love Like Heaven" we are treated to an alternate-world Eartha Kitt, a smoky hippie chick replacing the urbane sophisticate. It works remarkably well and Eartha repeats the trick on two of Donovan's more famous songs, "Catch the Wind" and "Hurdy Gurdy Man," the latter of which would become the first single from the record.

Denny Diante confirms that Eartha thoroughly enjoyed the challenge of tackling unfamiliar material:

She was thrilled to death; she couldn't thank me enough for pushing the more contemporary stuff. She was very contemporary herself, very progressive in her thinking. I think the two best tracks are

"Catch the Wind" and "Wear Your Love Like Heaven." I understand that Donovan really liked what she did with them. I had suggested her and Donovan doing some promotion together, maybe even a duet, but it didn't come to be.

All that said, *Sentimental Eartha*'s real standout, ironically enough, is a new version of a song she had recorded nearly twenty years earlier. Back then she sang it in the original Spanish as "Angelitos Negros."[3] Now Eartha sang it in English as "Paint Me Black Angels." The translation is a little awkward, but there's no denying the passion with which Eartha delivers this plea for racial equality. She had lately been telling the press how much she liked Aretha Franklin's work. This is Eartha's response. Her voice had never sounded this powerful before, but there's none of the triumphant assertion of Aretha's "Respect" here. Eartha had lived too long and seen too much, and her reading of the song is suffused with longing and pain, rather than revolutionary fervor.

It also has a more private meaning. The song was originally written for a film. In the movie a father sings it to his mixed-race daughter to make her feel proud of her roots. By now, of course, Eartha had her own mixed-race daughter. So "Paint Me Black Angels" is also a song for Kitt, her constant companion through these trying times.

A little while later, on tour in Germany, Eartha recorded a TV special called *Festival* in which she showcased her new material, accompanied by a surprisingly empathetic studio band, and for the most part a new look too. Like the new album it was a showcase for an alternative Eartha. There are only a couple of nods to the past—the ballad "When the World Was Young" and a run-through of "C'est Si Bon"— but the rest is new material. Again the highlight is "Paint Me Black Angels": for that song Eartha is filmed in medium close-up wearing a black shirt buttoned to the neck with a Nehru collar, simple makeup, and the same black shaggy wig she sported for most of that year. As she sings, a couple of tears run slowly down her face.

It could, perhaps should, have been the start of a new era for Eartha. But life rarely works out quite so simply. *Sentimental Eartha* flopped on release in Britain and was never even issued in the States. Eartha spent an unhappy year or so trudging around the American cabaret circuit, but come the spring of 1970 she decided she had had enough. She could take America's hostility but not its indifference.

On March 13, Eartha and Kitt left for Europe, telling the press that she was heading off to perform for the people "who make me feel loved." She was heading into exile. America barely noticed. The love affair was well and truly over. Yesterday's mistress is rarely mourned.

Epilogue

THIRTY-TWO

I'm Still Here

After the affair is over, life goes on. In Eartha's case it went on for forty more years. At first she carried on looking for the kind of love you get from adoring crowds. She found it in Europe, especially in Britain, for a while. But after five years of slowly dwindling fortunes; five years which had seen her run the gamut from giving a recital of Brecht-Weill songs at the Royal Festival Hall to guest-starring in *Up the Chastity Belt* with Frankie Howerd. She found herself living in a cheap hotel on the south coast of Britain with her daughter Kitt, appearing in the role of an aging prostitute in a play nobody wanted to see.

There had been a few boyfriends along the way, but nothing serious, and gradually she had given up on romantic love. Bill McDonald would remain the only man she ever married or even lived with. Her one enduring love was for their daughter Kitt, who traveled with her everywhere, went to schools in Manchester and London, and provided a reason for her mother to keep on going.

When Eartha reached the end of the road in Britain, she looked for a new frontier to conquer. She picked South Africa, unfortunately. She did her best to play to integrated crowds and so forth, and persuaded herself that she was doing her bit to expose the lunacy of that country's racial attitudes, but in the end she couldn't escape the taint of taking the apartheid dollar.

And that was the end of the line. There was nothing for her to do but go home. She had always been a hard worker, and once more she pieced together a living from B-movies and cabaret joints. And slowly the world changed around her. America, by the late seventies, was a chastened, more forgiving country. And Eartha was no longer the troubling, confusing sexual presence she had been. She was ready to enter the final stage of any performer's life, when their appeal becomes essentially nostalgic.

In 1978 she caught a decent break, a guest-starring role in a new Broadway musical called *Timbuktu!*—an all-black take on *Kismet*. Some smart work by her new publicist Alan Eichler led to a whole slew of articles announcing that Eartha was back. She even returned to the White House for an official welcome from the new president, a Southern liberal named Jimmy Carter.

If it was a comeback though, it was more symbolic than commercial. *Timbuktu!* finally finished touring in the summer of 1979 but the anticipated offers failed to flood in. As far as Hollywood was concerned, a blacklist was rather less of a problem than being middle-aged.

Not long after that she decided to leave Los Angeles. She sold her Beverly Hills house and moved to New Milford, Connecticut, to be closer to Kitt, who had spread her wings and was launching a modeling career in New York City.

Meanwhile Eartha found a new audience for her live shows. The civil rights movement had had a wide-ranging legacy, not least in inspiring both women's liberation and gay liberation. And the new out-and-proud gay audience loved Eartha, loved her for her resilience and her dedication to glamour. She made a disco record, "Where Is My Man?" and they loved her all the more. She had steady work for a while, camping it up in the gay discos of Europe and the Americas.

She camped it up for the TV and film cameras too. Eventually they rediscovered Eartha, found some new stereotypes to fit her, now that she was older. They loved to cast her as either a voodoo priestess or a madam. She played one or the other in an episode of *Miami Vice*, a B-movie called *The Serpent Warriors*, and a couple of British *Mandingo* knockoffs, trashy tales of slavery days called *Dragonard* and *Master of Dragonard Hills*, with the occasional drunken cameo by Oliver Reed.

Eartha's stage show had always had an element of camp, so self-parody was easy enough for her, but it was hardly artistically satisfying, and the eighties were not the happiest of times for her. Worst of all was the moment in 1987, when Kitt announced that she was going to get married. Eartha knew she ought to be pleased, but instead she felt devastated, abandoned all over again.

Nevertheless she put her best foot forward, making sure Kitt had the most lavish of weddings. Kitt was in her mid-twenties and had recently signed with Elite Model Management. Her husband-to-be was a young lawyer named Charles Shapiro and Kitt was determined that their wedding should be an *event*. Eartha had to sell one of her two small apartment blocks in Los Angeles, which had provided her with some degree of financial security, in order to raise the money.

The wedding was a great success.[1] Afterward, however, Eartha felt completely empty, and was in less-than-perfect mental health for a while, suffering from strange absences. Also her drinking— either Courvoisier or champagne—had steadily crept up over the years and was now becoming something of a problem.

Partial salvation came in the shape of an invitation from the British theatrical producer Cameron Mackintosh to take over the role of Carlotta in Stephen Sondheim's *Follies*. And so London provided her with the setting for her latest comeback. She was a hit. She made the signature song, "I'm Still Here," her own. And, as ever, she kept on working: more bit parts in movies, even an unlikely one-woman show as Molly Bloom at the Edinburgh Festival.

Then Kitt took over her mother's management and made sure she cut down on her drinking. Under her daughter's supervision Eartha's career entered a steady upswing. She cut some new records and received a Grammy nomination for her *Back in Business* album.[3]

The gigs got better. Smaller but better. Sophisticated cabaret was enjoying a revival and it was clear to aficionados of the form that Eartha was among the greatest of all cabaret artists. Larger theaters had never suited her as well as intimate cabaret rooms. While the likes of Shirley Bassey could command a theater with her big voice and her exaggerated gestures, Eartha worked best on a smaller, more human, scale. She needed to seduce her audience, not overwhelm them. And so she was perfectly suited to the new breed of elegant cabaret rooms, such as the Café Carlyle in New York, which became a home from home for Eartha in the last two decades of her life.

She also developed a lucrative sideline in cartoon voice-overs, mostly for Disney. There's a generation for whom Eartha is best known as the voice of the wicked queen Yzma in *The Emperor's New Groove*. She appeared in an assortment of unsuccessful Broadway and off-Broadway shows—*The Wild Party, Mimi le Duck*, and so on. She played Billie Holiday in a one-woman show in Chicago. She wrote a book about keeping fit. She represented MAC Cosmetics. She voiced the safety announcements in New York taxicabs. And still she toured the clubs. She simply did not stop.

And then, in 2006, as she approached her eightieth birthday, she learned that she had cancer. She had gone to the doctor because she was suffering from pain in her hands which was preventing her from carrying on her hobby of needlepoint. The doctor took some blood tests and discovered that she was dangerously anemic. A colonoscopy confirmed that the underlying problem was cancer of the colon.

Even this terrible news failed to slow her down for long. She had surgery and chemotherapy, and the following year she told *Jet* magazine that she was in remission. "They said it is all clear. They will give me a clean bill of health when I go to the doctor in another week or so. But I feel as if nothing ever happened to me."[4]

Two years later, on April 28, 2008, she performed to a sold-out crowd in the Pittville Pump Room in Cheltenham, England. It wasn't a big room but it was full and appreciative and the show was recorded for Eartha's first-ever live DVD. She was backed by her regular live quartet, skilled jazz players under the direction of a fine pianist called Darryl Waters, who had been her musical director for the past twenty-two years.

Eartha performed for ninety minutes. She started with "I'm Still Here," now established as her theme tune. The rest of the set was a mixture of classic Eartha—her fifties hits "I Want to Be Evil," "C'est Si Bon," and "Just an Old-Fashioned Girl"—and cabaret classics—"Guess Who I Saw Today," "If You Go Away," "September Song"—some of which had been in her repertoire for half a century. She took liberties with them, the ad libs came thick and fast. She knew how to win an audience over, how to make fun of herself, of the person she used to be, the woman they remembered, this gray-topped crowd. They'd come to see an artist who'd remind them of when they were young. She did that all right, but she'd also reminded them that they were growing old, and that there was nothing to do but enjoy it.

She ended the show with a single encore: a song called "Alone." It's written by Eartha herself, with music by Darryl Waters. The lyrics attempt to tell the story of her life. It's not a particularly successful attempt, the words are mostly trite, but there's a refrain that stays with you, "And I stand here alone." It can't help but be resonant, coming as it does from this woman of eighty-one, standing there alone in the spotlight, connecting us for a moment to a turbulent past that's slipping out of living memory.

That summer she kept on performing, but in October the cancer came back, this time with a vengeance. Even so, Eartha only canceled one show.

On November 24, 2008, she went into the hospital in New York. Her daughter Kitt came with her and stayed close by her side for the next month. When the end was near Kitt took her mother back to her home in Weston, Connecticut. They remained there, just the two of them together, till Eartha died on Christmas Day.

Typical of Eartha to pick such an inconvenient day to die. News takes a while to get out at Christmas and only gradually did the world wake up to the fact that Eartha was dead. Even then she had to share the headlines with another great contrarian, the English playwright Harold Pinter, who died on the same day. Several commentators remarked on the similarities between the two. Both of them had been major figures in the cultural landscape of the fifties; both of them had helped reshape the way we see the world.

After the Cheltenham festival show, Eartha talked on camera about "Alone," the song she'd performed as an encore, the last song she ever sang in Britain. She said, "Even though the song says I'm alone, I know that I'm not standing there alone. Look at all those people out there."[5]

It's a deceptively simple observation. What she meant by it, perhaps, was that in her eighties she was finally at peace with herself. Many years earlier she had told a newspaper that "My greatest fear is people. They can make you or break you, particularly in show business. There is nothing you can do that doesn't depend on people. You can't be successful without them—and all my life I've wanted to stand alone."[6] But now, at last, she was able to accept that she was who she was, she did what she did, and she was loved for it.

Eartha Kitt was one of a kind, both blessed and doomed to be such. But she was not an aberration; she was not really alone; she had simply lived her life ahead of her time. She had been born on a cotton field in South Carolina, only a couple of generations away from slavery. She had grown up in real poverty; had lived through the Depression and a world war. She had found fame in a Europe that was barely recovering from that same war. She'd gone on to find even greater fame at home, in a country which could still legally refuse to serve her in restaurants or let her stay in decent hotels.

She'd had the strength of personality to turn every stereotype on its head, as well as play a part in the civil rights movement and the protests against Vietnam.

She'd lived at a time when it was illegal in some states, and disapproved of in all states, for a black person to make love to a white person. And she had tried to rise above it all. She had tried to demand the rights a white woman would have taken for granted, and she got closer than she might have expected, but, of course, not as close as she should have done. What she did do, what she managed triumphantly, was to make white America look at a black woman and see her as an individual, an extraordinary individual, with her own unique intelligence and sexuality, passion, and charm.

And if white America soon tired of her, it didn't really matter, she had opened a door for others to follow through and follow they did: from Nina Simone to Halle Berry, Belafonte to Beyoncé. But Eartha had showed them the way; she was the most feline of revolutionaries.

ENDNOTES

Chapter 1

1 From undated letter to the *Lexington County Chronicle*.

Chapter 2

1 This and all following quotes from Mildred Amaker come from an interview conducted by the author in North, S.C. in 2011.

Chapter 3

1 The *New York Herald Tribune* reporter Beverly Smith summed up the situation succinctly in his 1930 article on the neighborhood:

> The attitude of the average white New Yorker to Harlem is one of tolerant amusement. He thinks of it as a region of prosperous nightclubs: of happy-go-lucky Negroes dancing all night to jazz music and living during the day by taking in each other's policy numbers; of Negro artists and intellectuals wealthy on the royalties of novels or salaries from the "talkies," and of a group of "high-society" Negroes, most of them with foreign white servants living high in the fashion of some of the characters in Carl Van Vechten's *Nigger Heaven*. The fact is that this community of 220,000 Negroes is the poorest, the unhealthiest, the unhappiest and the most crowded single section of New York City.

However, as Smith points out, difficult as things might have been for Harlem's population, the problem needs to be put into context. In reality black people there were still a lot better off than they were in the South, or indeed in most other urban black communities in the North. Smith goes on to offer an analysis of Harlem's problems, much of which is sadly true of black American urban communities today, pointing out that the root of Harlem's problems was economic: its speakeasies and clubs may have been famous, but they were almost all owned by nonresidents, mostly Italian gangsters. The same went for the vast majority of the retail businesses in Harlem, as the black people who'd settled there tended to have neither the prior expertise nor the necessary capital to run their own businesses, while the banks were, if not simply prejudiced, then unwilling to lend to unskilled shopkeepers. Meanwhile, as Smith observes: "Nine-tenths of the work that white folks do is closed to Negroes. In the chief trades open they are only taken on when the supply of white labor is exhausted. They are in the true and depressing sense 'marginal labor.'"

2 The street's nickname with downtown white folks was "Jungle Alley," which doesn't ring too well these days, but, to put it into context, a contemporary quote from the leading black newspaper, the *Amsterdam News*, on the top new bandleader Duke Ellington, runs as follows: "Ellington is the ace of rhythm jazz leaders, and his barbaric style of music is backed by a jungle atmosphere that has made this type of music a sensation."

3 Du Bois had a point, because Harlem wasn't just about music. The period after the First World War had seen the phenomenon known as "the New Negro," which was to say a new generation of black intellectuals and activists, many of whom had traveled to Europe to fight for the US army, only to be stuck in segregated regiments, and had then returned to the United States only to find the same old racism everywhere and the Ku Klux Klan on the rise. In 1919 race riots had broken out across America. So now a newly radicalized black intelligentsia, based largely in Harlem, was setting out its stall with a display of political and cultural militancy.

On the cultural wing were the groups of writers and artists who would later become identified as members of the "Harlem Renaissance," among them the polymath Langston Hughes, the novelist Claude McKay and the anthropologist Zora Neale Hurston (who introduced the outrageous and self-mocking term "the niggerati" to describe her herself and her contemporaries). On the political side were the NAACP chief James Weldon Johnson, Charles S. Johnson, and the elder statesman Du Bois, not to mention a West Indian firebrand named Marcus Garvey. And if Garvey had far more of a popular following than the Harlem Renaissance intellectuals, so too did the new spiritual leaders, most notably a charismatic preacher called Father Divine.

Chapter 4

1 From an unpublished interview with Edith Bank, conducted by Sandra Bromberg.
2 Ibid.

Chapter 5

1 Dunham, K. (2005). "Early New York Collaborations," in V. Clark and S. Johnson, *Kaiso! Writings by and about Katherine Dunham*. Madison: University of Wisconsin Press.

2 Vanoye Aikens currently lives in Los Angeles, in a tall modern apartment block on the edge of Koreatown, surrounded by paintings and books and photos of friends and colleagues. There's a picture of Eartha, much later in life, cooking in his kitchen; several of Miss Dunham; another of Josephine Baker. Aikens is still a remarkably handsome man, though on the cusp of ninety years old, reluctant as he is to admit it, and one bedeviled by the dancer's classic complaint, a bad back. He describes his own introduction to the Dunham Company, just after leaving the navy:

> It came about by accident. I was not a dancer to speak of, I was certainly not trained: all my training came from Katherine Dunham. I had taken a Greyhound bus from Boston, Mass., to New York and when I arrived I ran into my friend Lenwood Morris, and he had just started working with Miss Dunham, and I said to Len, "I've always liked dancing," and he said, "Why don't you try out?" So I did. And she took me on, untrained. Actually if you'd had too much of the classic training it wasn't a help, you had to start again from the beginning. I guess I was the right type as I ended up as Miss Dunham's dance partner. I always said we were folk dancers, but we did everything possible. We were all-around dancers.

3 This and all following quotes from Vanoye Aikens come from an interview conducted by the author in Los Angeles during September 2011.

Chapter 6

1 It is possible that Eartha simply cribbed this anecdote from Katherine Dunham: the two stories are suspiciously similar.

2 Quoted in Shaw, A. (1960) *Belafonte: An Unauthorized Biography*. New York: Chilton.

3 Wald, E. (2002). *Josh White: Society Blues*. New York: Routledge.

4 Ibid.

5 This and all following quotes from Gloria Mitchell Thornburgh come from an interview conducted by the author in 2012.

6 You have to love the Runyonesque tone of *Billboard* reviews in the forties and fifties, a world where dancers are always terps and female singers always thrushes.

7 *Billboard*, October 6, 1945.

8 This quote appears in any number of civil rights histories. Its neatness and lack of exact attribution do raise the question of whether it was confected by a civil rights propagandist rather than being the words of an actual soldier: never mind, the sentiment is true enough.

9 The "Babalu" in question is a Santería deity, Babalu Aye. The song, with its furious conga-driven beat and call-and-response sections, was a great favorite across the Latin world, and no doubt in Spanish Harlem too, particularly in the version by Miguelito Valdés. Around the same time as Eartha was performing her version in the clubs it became the signature song of the Cuban-American bandleader and actor Desi Arnaz (and would appear repeatedly in Arnaz's classic—and ground breaking—fifties TV show, *I Love Lucy*).

Chapter 7

1 As Hurok's client and friend Isaac Stern put it, "Hurok knows six languages—and all of them are Yiddish."

2 Aschenbrenner, J. (2002). *Katherine Dunham*. Chicago: University of Illinois Press.

3 Meanwhile Dunham's personal status was further boosted by the publication of her first book, *Journey to Accompong*, an account of her time studying the Maroon people of Jamaica, runaway slaves who had established their own more African way of life up in the remote hills of the island's interior. It attracted a supremely sniffy review from Dunham's great rival in the glamorous anthropologist stakes, Zora Neale Hurston, in the *Herald Tribune*. "After all," Hurston notes, "thirty days in a locality is not much in research and hardly affords time enough for the fieldworker to scratch the surface. Therefore it is to the tremendous credit of the author that she has achieved such an entertaining book."

4 Quoted in Gavin, J. *Eartha-Quake*, liner notes, Bear Family (1994).

Chapter 8

1 A role that was sadly also his last, as he died of cancer shortly afterward.

2 His 1958 *Tamango*, for instance, starred the great Dorothy Dandridge. However, that, like most of Berry's work after *Casbah*, was made in France. Berry was an early victim of the Hollywood blacklist. In 1950 he made a documentary in support of the Hollywood Ten and, for his pains, got himself named as a communist by fellow film director Edward Dmytryk. Disgusted by what was going on, he moved to France and worked there for the next twenty-five years before returning to the United States to make *Claudine*, starring another notable black actress, Diahann Carroll, in 1974.

Chapter 9

1 Now in her early eighties, and amicably divorced from her husband of fifty years, the singer, actor, and activist Harry Belafonte, Julie lives in a grand apartment overlooking the Hudson River, surrounded by artwork from around the world and photos of herself and Harry with an assortment of the great names of the past century, from Martin Luther King to Nelson Mandela.

2 This relationship continued on and off for some years until Marlon introduced her to Harry Belafonte. This is how Belafonte remembers that first meeting with Julie, on a Hollywood film set in 1954:

> I got a call from Marlon Brando that changed my life. I was spending my days on the Twentieth Century Fox set of *Carmen Jones* . . . Marlon was on another Fox set, playing Napoleon Bonaparte in *Desire*, against a backdrop of extravagant ballrooms. "You gotta do me a favor," Marlon said. "This girl I've been dating just got here from Italy, but I can't break away until dinner. Take her to lunch at the commissary and then we'll all hook up later."
>
> Sure, I told Marlon, I was happy to help out . . . I was on a sound stage . . . when the choreographer slid a tall rolling door aside. I saw a slim figure in silhouette, backlit by the sun so she appeared to glow. When we approached each other, I saw she had a perfect dancer's body, with a dancer's poise, bobbed dark hair, shoe-button eyes, and a dazzling smile, almost too big for her face. I had a vague but pleasing memory of Julie Robinson as that Katherine Dunham dancer who'd performed at the New School several years before. She was even more gorgeous than I remembered. "Julie Robinson," she said. "How nice of you to volunteer for foster care."
>
> Over lunch at the Fox commissary, Julie sorted out a number of misperceptions for me . . . I assumed she was black, or if not that, Hispanic. Weren't all the Dunham dancers black? Julie's skin tone was more olive than café au lait, but anyone in the West Indies would have pegged her as a mixed-blood beauty with black roots. With that same skin tone, though, as I would come to see, Julie looked Italian in Italy, Russian in Russia, and Cuban in Cuba. In fact, she was the Katherine Dunham troupe's one white dancer.

Sixty years later, Julie still recalls being amazed when Katherine Dunham allowed her to join the company proper, but makes light of any difficulties she herself might have felt as the odd one out. On the contrary, she remembers it was a happy time. Also, as she points out, the school, if not the company, had soon attracted other white students after she joined.

And it was where she'd first met Marlon Brando, when he took a class she was teaching at the school.

However, while Julie was a valued member of the Dunham School, she hadn't yet appeared in any of the Dunham Company's stage shows, perhaps because Miss D. was nervous about presenting an integrated show in the United States. It was only with the European trip that Julie was finally getting her chance to appear on stage with the rest of the company. Naturally she was thrilled at the prospect.

3 This and all following quotes from Julie Robinson Belafonte come from an interview conducted by the author in New York during September 2011.

4 This and all following quotes from Kenny Gordon come from an interview conducted by the author in London during July 2011.

5 Jackson, S. (1947). *An Indiscreet Guide to Soho*. London: Muse Arts.

6 *The Times*. June 4, 1948.

7 *Observer*, September 12, 1948.

8 Ibid.

9 Atkins, C., Malone, J. (2001). *Class Act: The Jazz Life of Choreographer Cholly Atkins*. New York: Columbia University Press.

Chapter 10

1 *Billboard*, Jan 29, 1949.

2 Also said to have inspired the classic Porter tune "Miss Otis Regrets."

3 Davis, M., Troupe, Q. (1990). *Miles: The Autobiography*. New York: Simon & Schuster.

4 As quoted in Summers, B. (2001). *Black and Beautiful*. New York: Amistad.

5 Porfirio Rubirosa was a diplomat from the Dominican Republic and a gossip column staple of his time thanks to his relationships with two of the world's richest women—Barbara Hutton and Doris Duke. Almost all mentions of his name tend to come with innuendo around the rumored size of his penis. The American gossip magazine *Confidential* once ran a front-page splash on Rubirosa with the caption asking the question, "Is the World's Greatest Lover a Negro?"

Chapter 11

1 Frances Taylor later married Miles Davis.

2 Eartha appears to have been unbecomingly jealous of her fellow dancer Othella Strozier's marriage to a Swiss named Peter Wydler. Indeed, in *Thursday's Child* she goes to great lengths to persuade the reader that Wydler really preferred her. In fact Strozier and Wydler are still married and Othella still performs live in Europe under her stage name of Othella Dallas. Perhaps unsurprisingly she declined to be interviewed for this book.

3 Katherine Dunham Papers, 1919–1968. University Archives, Southern Illinois University Special Collections Research Center, Carbondale, Ill.
4 Beckford, R. (1979). *Katherine Dunham: A Biography*. New York: Marcel Dekker.
5 Hewett, I., *Daily Telegraph*, November 15, 2010.

Chapter 12

1 Now in her eighties, Ms. Ross still appears every week in New York's Metropolitan Room, and is as distinctive an artist as ever. She's one of the last survivors of a generation of great cabaret singers, of whom Eartha was perhaps the most prominent. Sitting in the foyer of the Metropolitan, just before showtime, she was glamorous and vibrant, and still sporting her trademark short red hair. She recalled what happened with her and Orson Welles:

> I had met Orson Welles before. I had seen him in New York in *Around the World in Eighty Days*, which was fantastic and then (in Paris) he told me he wanted me to be in this play. So we had a rehearsal, only it wasn't really a rehearsal, it was a casting call. We read over a few pages. Orson then said, "Right let's have a few drinks," and then we had a few more, and he told some stories. I didn't know what was going on!

Nevertheless, as far as Annie could tell, it was now understood that she was in the play. So she was less than pleased to discover that Orson had replaced her with Eartha at the last minute.

2 This and all following quotes from Annie Ross come from an interview conducted by the author in New York during September 2011.
3 Mac Liammóir, M. (1961). *Each Actor on His Ass*. London: Routledge & Kegan Paul.
4 There's an Ellington composition called "Orson" that may have its genesis as something written for *Time Runs*.
5 Mac Liammóir, *Each Actor on His Ass*.
6 *Harp Magazine*, March 6, 2006. (From an interview with Eartha conducted by the singer Nellie McKay.)
7 Mac Liammóir, *Each Actor on His Ass*.
8 Ibid.
9 Placed in a very difficult situation, Josh dealt with it by an unhappy compromise involving a statement rejecting many of his former friends. In the short term it allowed him to keep on working, but it alienated him from his natural supporters on the left and his career in the United States soon went into decline. His reputation as an artist has never entirely recovered from this, though Elijah Wald's fine biography does a great job of attempting to right that particular wrong.

Chapter 13

1 *Daily Mirror*, January 6, 1951.

2 *Saturday Evening News*, February 20, 1955.

3 A garbled source suggests Eartha may have been having an affair with one of the brothers.

4 He had started working for the BBC in the thirties and had soon become what we'd now call a DJ but which was known then as "a compiler of gramophone recordings" for the radio. Before long he had his own show, *Radio Rhythm Club*, playing mostly jazz. When the war intervened he spent three years in the RAF, flying missions as a wireless operator. Having survived that, he started an armed forces radio station in Ceylon, before returning to the BBC. Later on he would work on everything from the *Goon Show* to his enormously popular creation, *Journey into Space*. He had a great passion for American music, and in the early fifties, made a series of radio programs about American history that used jazz, folk, and blues to bring that history to life. When Josh White arrived in the UK in 1950, Chilton felt he had found the ideal collaborator.

At the time of this interview Charles Chilton was still living in London and acting as an occasional walking-tour guide around his native city, despite the fact that he was ninety-four years old. He remembered Josh White with great fondness and told me that he still had one of Josh's old guitars. The folklorist Alan Lomax had "borrowed" it for a while, and Chilton had had a hell of a time getting it back. Sadly Charles Chilton died, age ninety-five, just before this book went to press.

5 This and all following quotes from Charles Chilton come from an interview conducted by the author in London during November 2011.

6 I spoke to the woman in question, who denied any close relationship with Eartha at all. "Why," she said, "we never even went to a movie together," in a rebuttal that was more poignant than convincing. Still, no need to include her name.

Chapter 14

1 Apart from her daughter, Kitt Shapiro, who managed Eartha in her last years.

2 *Variety*, December 19, 1951.

3 *Billboard*, December 29, 1951.

4 This and all following quotes from Virginia Wicks come from an interview conducted by the author in Los Angeles during September 2011.

5 Sillman, L. (1959). *Here Lies*. New York: Citadel.

6 Ibid.

7 Eliot himself was tickled by this as his friend and publisher Robert Giroux remembered:

Soon after the musical *New Faces* opened on Broadway, I told Eliot that the hit song, Eartha Kitt's rendition of "Monotonous," contained the line, "T. S. Eliot writes pomes to me." He immediately took out his card, inscribed it to Miss Kitt, and asked me to have the florist send her roses. I happily did so, and the only indication that the flowers reached her was an item in a newspaper column to the effect that "Eartha Kitt claims that T. S. Eliot sent her a bouquet"—a line Eliot enjoyed almost as much as the one in her song. (Robert Giroux, "A Personal Memoir," in Tate (ed.) (1966), *T. S. Eliot: The Man and His Work*. New York: Delacorte.)

Chapter 15

1 Sillman, L. (1959). *Here Lies*. New York: Citadel.
2 Sillman, L. (1959). *Here Lies*. New York: Citadel.
3 Ibid.
4 This and all following quotes from Mel Brooks come from an interview conducted by the author in Los Angeles during September 2011.
5 On which note it receives a telling mention in Bob Dylan's *Chronicles*, Vol. 1 as he describes his time in New Orleans in the nineties making an album and pondering his future: "The radio was on as usual. A singer was singing that life was monotonous, life is a drag. It was Eartha Kitt. I thought to myself, 'That's the truth, Eartha. That's plenty good. I'm friends with ya. Go ahead and sing.'"
6 Sillman, *Here Lies*.
7 There's an interesting letter written by an aristocratic white civil rights supporter from South Carolina called Elizabeth Waring to a prominent black civil rights activist, also from South Carolina, called Ruby Cornwell. In the letter Mrs. Waring talks of going to see Eartha in *New Faces* and being snubbed after she sent the star a note explaining that she was from South Carolina, and asking if she might come to see her backstage. Eartha had clearly kept her name in order to let her fellow South Carolinians know that she had made it, but she was damned if she was going to let them get close to her, no matter how well-meaning they might be.

Chapter 16

1 A great Negrophile, author of the 1927 *succès de scandale* novel *Nigger Heaven*, which had done much to spark the interwar Harlem vogue, and the photographer who had snapped every black artist and entertainer of note since the twenties.
2 And something Eartha too tended to do any time she wanted out of an engagement.
3 Part of the lyrics to a popular Bazooka bubble gum jingle which appropriated a Gershwin tune.

4 Gavin, J. (1994). From the liner notes to the definitive collection of 1950s Eartha Kitt recordings *Eartha-Quake* on the excellent Bear Family reissue label.

5 Born in Chicago, he had made his name in the music business in the twenties, writing cowboy songs for the likes of Roy Rogers and the Sons of the Pioneers. When his brother Jack set up the American arm of Decca records, Dave joined as an A&R man and spent much of the thirties touring the South finding talent such as Milton Brown and Ernest Tubb for what was then known as the hillbilly division, as well as working with Bix Beiderbecke. Later on he launched the careers of the Ink Spots and the Andrews Sisters. He left Decca following his brother's death in 1949 and was at RCA for what would turn out to be a relatively brief stay.

6 This song which Eartha would return to repeatedly over the years—once in an English version as "Paint Me Black Angels"—originally appears in the 1948 Mexican film of the same name. In the film a white father sings it to his mixed-race daughter in a touching attempt to give her pride in her color.

7 A part-Swahili number written by a Harlem contemporary of Eartha's, the black actor and later film-maker William Greaves.

8 From the 1946 Broadway musical, *Lute Song*, set in China.

9 This was the period in which various forms of long-playing record were just coming into common use and there was an array of rival formats. In the case of *RCA Presents . . .* it was available in a small box containing two four-track 45 rpm EPs, or as one ten-inch microgroove album playing at 33 rpm.

10 The coverage in *Jet* shows a selection of grinning black and white celebrities. Poignantly, the magazine is at pains to point out the instances in which black and white people are holding hands. This was a world in which a radiantly elegant Lena Horne still risked Southern fury for holding hands with a group of disabled white Marines.

11 Some readers may be aware of a 2008 play by Bonnie Greer called *Marilyn and Ella* which is based on the notion that the Mocambo was a segregated club until 1955 when MM persuaded the Mocambo to book Ella Fitzgerald. This is clearly nonsense. Charlie Morrison, the owner, had long been booking black entertainers. He may well have been wary, however, of booking an out-and-out jazz singer like Ella.

12 "Fire in Ice." *Collier's*, 133, (June 11, 1954): 92–94.

13 Ibid.

Chapter 17

1 A cover version by Madonna was a clear tip of the hat from one material girl to another.

2 *Jet*, December 1953.

3 Quoted in *Gonna Do Great Things: The Life of Sammy Davis Jr.* by Gary Fishgall.

4 Finstad, S. (2011) *Natasha: The Biography of Natalie Wood*, New York and London: Random House.
5 *Jet*, January 1954.
6 "Fire in Ice," *Collier's*, 133 (June 11, 1954): pp. 92–94.
7 Ibid.
8 Ibid.

Chapter 18

1 Sillman, L. (1959). *Here Lies*. New York: Citadel.
2 This and all following quotes from Terry Carter come from an interview conducted by the author in January 2012.

Chapter 19

1 By late 1954 *Confidential* was a creepily powerful new American institution. It was obsessed with homosexuality and interracial sex. Any Hollywood star who engaged in either of these activities—and there were plenty to choose from—was immediately in the firing line, as were any remaining communists. *Confidential's* founding editor, Robert Harrison, had established a network of informants—private detectives, bell boys, et al.—around LA, and his magazine was an immediate hit, soon selling four million copies of each issue. And each copy would be read by any number of others too embarrassed to buy it themselves. (As Humphrey Bogart commented, "Everybody reads it, but they say the cook brought it into the house.")
2 *Confidential*, November 1954.
3 *New York Times*, December 2, 1954.
4 *Brooklyn Eagle*, December 3, 1954.
5 The song was written by Rose Marie McCoy and Charlie Singleton, two young black songwriters who had recently written a hit for Big Maybelle. They would go on to write a song called "Trying to Get to You" for black vocal group the Eagles, which would be covered—extremely faithfully—by Elvis on his debut album: a piece of luck that brought Rose McCoy a Cadillac and a house in New Jersey, where she still lives. A subsequent fascinating career in R&B songwriting included an unlikely role as vocalist with Albert Ayler in the troubled jazz genius's last band.
6 *Sarasota Herald-Tribune*, January 22, 1955.
7 In later years Eartha would talk about her Einstein visit and cast it in a very different light. In a 1969 interview with a Montreal paper she declared that Einstein had saved her from suicide. She had been on the point of drowning herself off a Californian beach, when a voice inside her head asked if there wasn't anyone she wanted to meet before she died. And the name Einstein had popped into her head. She had got out of the ocean and arranged to meet the great man. And in this version Einstein was wearing not a sloppy joe sweater but a Mickey Mouse T-shirt and told her that it

was wonderful that she was in show business as she brought joy to millions of people. It's a clear example of the way that over time Eartha's own version of her life became inextricably muddled up with her dreams and her terrors. (Einstein in a Mickey Mouse T-shirt!)

8 An African-American political scientist, Bunche won the Nobel Peace Prize in 1950 for his role in negotiating the armistices that ended the 1948 Arab-Israeli War.

9 *London Evening Standard*, February 7, 1955.

Chapter 20

1 This quote from John Gilmore comes from an interview conducted by the author in Los Angeles in September 2011.

2 The godfather was noted jazz critic Leonard Feather.

3 Pigs' intestines, chopped and boiled then, usually, fried. Notoriously foul-smelling before cooking. A thoroughly down-home taste.

4 *Pittsburgh Courier*, July 21, 1955.

5 *Evening Standard*, May 17, 1955.

Chapter 21

1 Unlikely as it sounds, this was quite possibly true. Sarah Churchill was an actress and alcoholic who was then living in the States with her second husband and had met Eartha in LA. She was evidently a disorganized person—her telegram to tell her father of her marriage arrived after the press had already reported the fact—so sending her Christmas presents over late, and via Eartha Kitt, was fairly typical behavior.

2 *Evening Standard*, December 31, 1955.

3 *NME*, January 5, 1956.

4 *Daily Sketch*, January 5, 1956.

5 Ironically enough, though, at the same time RCA was negotiating for a new British label to release its product in the UK. Decca won the contract ahead of the previous distributor, EMI. In Britain this was reported as "Decca Grabs Eartha Kitt"—as opposed, say, to "Decca Grabs Elvis Presley"!

6 *Daily Mirror*, April 24, 1956.

7 That's the name of a stage lighting color, so I've just discovered.

8 *Observer*, May 6, 1956.

9 *News Chronicle*, May 21, 1956.

10 This is an ever-changing figure in Eartha Kitt interviews: those who knew her well doubt she spoke many of them—beyond French and Spanish—to any great degree. Rather she had a good ear which allowed her to sing in any number of different languages.

11 *News Chronicle*, June 28, 1956.

12 Bourne, S. (2005). *Elisabeth Welch: Soft Lights and Sweet Music*. London: Scarecrow Press.

13 There are some classy, if predictable, choices: Ella Fitzgerald, Frank Sina-
   tra singing "A Foggy Day" and Judy Garland with "You Made Me Love
   You." There are a couple of classical pieces that go beyond the obvious:
   Felix Mendelssohn's Symphony No. 3 in A minor and Ottorino Respighi's
   "Fountains of Rome," one of the Italian composer's so-called "musical
   picture postcards." There's a nod to her café society days with Burl Ives
   performing "The Woman and the Chivalrous Shark," though sadly no
   Josh White, and there's some jazz piano with Erroll Garner's "I Cover the
   Waterfront." The one real oddity is her opening tune "Oba Grelegbuwa" by
   Irewolede Denge—a pioneering slice of prewar Nigerian high-life music,
   which suggests that Eartha must also have been exploring London's African night life scene.
14 Also launching books at the event were a campaigning lawyer named
   Pauli Murray and the boxer Henry Armstrong.
15 Gilbert Millstein, *New York Times*, October 14, 1956.

Chapter 22
1 *Ellensburg Daily Record*, October 22, 1956.
2 *People* magazine, October 25, 1999.
3 He wasn't any such thing when Eartha was a child, but he was already a
  famous campaigner for Indian independence.
4 By that time the Mountbattens' marriage existed in little more than name.
  Edwina had had a series of affairs, beginning very early on in their relationship and so, eventually, did her husband. Her most controversial affair
  was with the West Indian bandleader Leslie "Hutch" Hutchinson; this
  lasted for over twenty years, and among the gifts she gave him were a gold
  bracelet with her name engraved on it, a gold cigarette case and, remarkably, a jeweled penis sheath from Cartier.

Chapter 23
1 Well-known African-American journalist, noted for his atypical antiso-
  cialist line. His autobiography was entitled *Black and Conservative*.
2 Hughes, L. *The Chicago Defender*, April 27, 1957.
3 Perhaps inspired by Eddie Bracken, who was a lifelong advocate of the
  charms of the suburban American circuit of "summer stock" theater.
4 Alias, D. (2003). Retrieved from www.digitalinterviews.com.

Chapter 24
1 Ironically the one prominent black entertainer to criticize Armstrong for
  his stance was Sammy Davis, Jr., the man who had once accused Eartha of
  being insufficiently devoted to her race.
2 Sannella, R. (2005). *My Nine Lives*. Lincoln, Neb.: iUniverse.

3 Yordan was the most unorthodox of screenwriters, however. He was essentially an ideas man, who also acted as the front for many of the blacklisted screenwriters of the fifties, so the debate still rages as to how many of his scripts he actually wrote.

4 Ultimately it was the actors themselves who refigured the play. One of them, Ruby Dee, saw the play transmute during rehearsals: "I remember watching [director] Harry Gribble and some of the actors during rehearsal as they improvised on the script—making up dialogue on the spot, throwing out scenes, and creating new ones. There was much writing, rewriting, then hopping up onstage to try it all out."

5 Crowther, *New York Times*, January 15, 1959.

6 Albright, B. (2008). *Wild Beyond Belief*. Jefferson, N.C.: McFarland.

7 Leachman would later win an Oscar for her role in *The Last Picture Show*, but was then best known for her role in the *Lassie* TV series.

8 Katherine Dunham Papers, 1919–1968, University Archives, Southern Illinois University Special Collections Research Center, Carbondale, Ill.

9 Ibid.

10 It was a sorry fact that the Dunham Company had never received the public subsidy of which it was richly deserving, and always had to struggle along in the private sector.

Chapter 25

1 Today Bob Dix lives in Chatsworth, where the Los Angeles sprawl meets the Santa Susana Mountains, the neighborhood where Roy Rogers and Errol Flynn once had their horse ranches. He's a very fit eighty-something, finally settled and happy after a turbulent life, and now married to the charming Mary Ellen, whom he's known since childhood, when she was just his best friend Bill McDonald's kid sister. Bob's a regular participant at movie fairs where he's something of a draw, thanks to the run of outlandish exploitation features he appeared in during the late sixties, films such as *Satan's Sadists* and *Blood of Dracula's Castle*. More casual moviegoers are likely to remember him for his cameo at the beginning of a James Bond film, *Live and Let Die* (he's the CIA guy watching a New Orleans funeral and asking who the dead guy is, only to discover that it's about to be him).

2 This and all following quotes from Bob Dix come from an interview conducted by the author in Los Angeles during September 2011.

3 *Daily Mirror*, November 4, 1958.

4 *Sunday Graphic*, November 9, 1958.

5 Albright, B. (2008). *Wild Beyond Belief*. Jefferson, N.C.: McFarland.

6 *Jet*, March 1959.

7 Ibid.

8 Ibid.

9 Power himself had died of a heart attack shortly before his and Deborah's son was born in January 1959. Arthur had stepped in to console the young widow, but consolation had quickly turned to something else and Deborah soon became pregnant again. Arthur, who had avoided marriage for years, and not only to Eartha, was finally obliged to do the decent thing. He married Deborah in Las Vegas at the end of September. He would divorce her three years later on the grounds that he didn't want to be "tied down." Which does rather suggest that Eartha's subsequent idealization of Loew as the one that got away might be somewhat misplaced.

10 Wikipedia entry for Revson.

Chapter 26

1 *Evening Standard*, May 12, 1960.
2 This and all following quotes from Mary Ellen Dix come from an interview conducted by the author in Los Angeles during September 2011.
3 Yes, shrapnel really does that.
4 The magazine was owned by her uncle. Marjorie remained close friends with Eartha until she (Eartha) died.
5 This and all following quotes from Christine Wicks come from an interview conducted by the author in Los Angeles during September 2011.
6 This and all following quotes from Nancy Carlin come from an interview conducted by the author in Thousand Oaks during September 2011.
7 *Daily Mirror*, August 31, 1960.
8 *Sunday People*, September 4, 1960.
9 *Daily Mail*, August 14, 1961.
10 *Jet*, January 18, 1962.

Chapter 27

1 *Daily Mirror*, February 9, 1962.
2 According to Eartha's long-time publicist Alan Eichler, Bill's bedroom was a virtual dungeon reachable only via a spiral staircase that led down from Eartha's bedroom.
3 This is a bit disingenuous as by this stage Bill's job was essentially managing Eartha.
4 *News and Courier*, January 13, 1963.
5 *Jet*, May 30, 1960.
6 *Evening Standard*, May 15, 1963.
7 *Daily Express*, September 2, 1963.
8 *Evening News*, January 13, 1964.
9 *Jet*, March 19, 1964.

Chapter 28

1 So too did Juliette Gréco, of all the people you wouldn't think of casting in *Uncle Tom's Cabin*.

2 In the film, however, the fact that Chuck and Betty were married is conveniently glossed over, they are portrayed simply as coworkers.

3 In fact Katherine Dunham had repeatedly asked Eartha to invest in her Haitian property which she hoped to turn into some sort of hotel. Eartha clearly preferred to have a Caribbean hideaway of her own.

4 *Playboy*, May 1969.

5 The daughter in question, Wanda Lee Evans, would later become Eartha's understudy in a Broadway show.

6 The play was subsequently filmed with the lead female part, previously always played by a black woman, going to Barbra Streisand.

7 Which was nice of her as a few years earlier *Sports Illustrated* quoted him as listing her as a typical Negro sell-out.

> Jackie Gleason's trying to show me why I shouldn't be a Muslim. He said, "Champ, why don't you think about it?" He's not the onliest one. All the big whiteys are trying. They want me to be their nigger. The whites made all the big niggers rich. Like, you take all the big Negroes, Lena Horne, Eartha Kitt, Diahann Carroll, Chubby Checker, Sammy Davis. Take those big niggers, Floyd Patterson and Sonny Liston. The whites make 'em rich, and in return they brainwash the little Negroes walking around. Liston lives in a white neighborhood, Patterson lives in a white neighborhood. Liston carried a little white boy right on his lap, promoting a little white boy. I carried a little colored. I can live in the Fontainebleau, anywhere I want, but I live here in a slum with my people. I could have taken money from the whites, but it would brainwash all the black children. (*Sports Illustrated*, May 2, 1966).

8 Even more oddly I came across the following undated anecdote in an essay by Bruce Friedman about Ali's first great rival, Sonny Liston: "The only person to outstare him was Eartha Kitt in the Cork Club in Houston. They put on some staring contest, like two death rays going at each other, anyone steps in the middle gets zapped. They were both rough cut, out of the same package. They didn't shake hands and wind up buddies, either."

Chapter 29

1 Kitt, E. (2002, October 15). Archive of American Television.

Chapter 30

1 Associated Press wire report. January 11, 1968.

2 Ibid.
3 *Jet*, February 8, 1968.
4 Brown, Helen Gurley. (1962). *Sex and the Single Girl: The Unmarried Woman's Guide to Men*. New York: Bernard Geis Associates.
5 Carpenter, L. (1969, April 4). Oral History Interview II, LBJ Library. (J. B. Frantz, interviewer).

Chapter 31

1 Haskell had recently arranged both "Bridge Over Troubled Water" and "Ode to Billie Joe."
2 This and all following quotes from Denny Diante come from a telephone interview conducted by the author in March 2012.
3 Roberta Flack, a young singer from DC who had something of Eartha's versatility, and a much more direct link to the new black radicalism, had revived it the year before.

Epilogue

1 The marriage itself, however, didn't last. Kitt is now married for a second time and is devoting herself to preserving her mother's legacy. She has a fine website at www.earthakitt.com.
2 In 1996—nominated for Best Traditional Pop Vocal.
3 *Jet*, January 29, 2007.
4 Taken from the DVD *Eartha Kitt Live at the Cheltenham Jazz Festival* (SFE 2008).
5 *Dispatch*, October 22, 1956.

BIBLIOGRAPHY

Albright, B. *Wild Beyond Belief*. Jefferson: McFarland (2008).

Atkins, C. & Malone, J. *Class Act: The Jazz Life of Choreographer Cholly Atkins*. New York: Columbia University Press. (2001).

Avary, M. L. *Dixie after the War*. New York: Doubleday (1906).

Beckford, R. *Katherine Dunham: A Biography*. New York: Marcel Dekker (1979).

Bourne, S. *Elisabeth Welch: Soft Lights and Sweet Music*. London: Scarecrow Press (2005).

Bricktop *Bricktop* New York: Atheneum (1983).

Buckle, R. (ed.) *Katherine Dunham, Her Dancers, Singers, Musicians*. London: Ballet Publications (1949).

Caflisch, E. *Die Othella Dallas Story*. Bern: Benteli (1981).

Clare, A. *In the Psychiatrist's Chair*. London: Heinemann (1992).

Clark, V. & Johnson, S. *Kaiso! Writings by and about Katherine Dunham*. Madison, Wisc.: University of Wisconsin Press (2005).

Davis, M. & Troupe, Q. *Miles: The Autobiography*. New York: Simon & Schuster (1990).

Fales-Hill, S. *Always Wear Joy*. New York: HarperCollins (2003).

Fitz-Simon, C. *The Boys*. London: Nick Hern Books (1994).

Gavin, J. *Intimate Nights: The Golden Age of New York Cabaret*. New York: Grove (1991).

——, *Eartha-Quake,* liner notes. Bear Family (1994).

——, *Stormy Weather: The Life of Lena Horne*. New York: Simon & Schuster (2009).

Hajdu, D. *Lush Life*. London: Granta (1997).

Hughes, L. & Meltzer, M. *Black Magic*. New York: Bonanza Books (1967).

Jackson, S. *An Indiscreet Guide to Soho*. London: Muse Arts (1947).

Kitt, E. *Thursday's Child*. New York: Duel, Pearce & Sloane (1956).

——, *Alone with Me*. Chicago, Ill.: Regnery (1976).

——, *I'm Still Here*. London: Sidgwick & Jackson (1989).

——, *Rejuvenate!* New York: Scribners (2001).

Leaming, B. *Orson Welles*. New York: Viking (1985).

Levy, S. *The Last Playboy*. London: Fourth Estate (2005).

Liammóir, M. M. *Each Actor on His Ass*. London: Routledge & Kegan Paul (1961).

Marouani, E. *Pêcheur d'étoiles*. Paris: Robert Laffont (1989).

Marquis, D. *archy & mehitabel*. New York: Doubleday (1927).

Sannella, R. *My Nine Lives*. Lincoln, Neb: iUniverse (2005).

Schoener, A. (ed.) *Harlem on My Mind*. New York: The New Press (2007).

Sillman, L. *Here Lies*. New York: Citadel (1959).

South Carolina Writers' Project. *South Carolina: A Guide to the Palmetto State*. New York: Oxford University Press (1941).

Wald, E. *Josh White: Society Blues*. New York: Routledge (2002).

Zec, D. *Some Enchanted Egos*. London: Allison & Busby (1972).

INDEX